# CODE WARS

# CODE WARS

How 'Ultra' and 'Magic'
led to Allied Victory

JOHN JACKSON

Pen & Sword
**MILITARY**

First published in Great Britain in 2011 by
Pen & Sword Military
An imprint of
Pen & Sword Books Ltd
47 Church Street
Barnsley
South Yorkshire
S70 2AS

ISBN 978 1 84884 510 7

A CIP catalogue record for this book is
available from the British Library

̣et in Ehrhardt
C MEDIA LTD

bound in England
by CPI

̣td incorporates the imprints of
d Family History, Pen & Sword Maritime,
rd Discovery, Wharncliffe Local History,
̣ncliffe Transport, Pen & Sword Select,
Pen & Sword Military Classics, Leo Cooper, The Praetorian Press,
Remember When, Seaforth Publishing and Frontline Publishing

*For a complete list of Pen & Sword titles please contact*
PEN & SWORD BOOKS LIMITED
47 Church Street, Barnsley, South Yorkshire, S70 2AS, England
E-mail: enquiries@pen-and-sword.co.uk
Website: www.pen-and-sword.co.uk

# Contents

# Foreword

For some thirty years historians wrote about the Second World War in total ignorance that Britain and its allies, particularly the United States, had been reading the most secret signals of Hitler, the German armed forces, security services and railways, as well as those of Italy and Japan. The breaking of the secret messages of the Enigma cipher machine, the intelligence from which was codenamed Ultra, and of the Lorenz SZ 40/42 – the German High Command top-secret teleprinter-enciphered traffic – enabled a rich vein of high-grade intelligence to be read by the codebreakers at Bletchley Park, which has led to many events of the war to be reassessed. It has been said that Bletchley Park probably shortened the war by as much as two years. This book gives snapshots of the part played by codebreakers in some of the key events of the war. Although purists will point out that Bletchley Park was mostly engaged in breaking ciphers and not codes, the title of this book reflects the fact that those engaged in this highly secret work were known as codebreakers. For a fuller understanding of how codebreaking affected these events, the reader is referred to the bibliography.

I wish to thank a number of my volunteer colleagues at Bletchley Park for their help in some of the chapters – Frank Carter, John Gallehawk, John Harper and Tony Sale – and Kelsey Griffin of the Bletchley Park Trust. However, any errors are entirely mine.

JOHN JACKSON

## Chapter 1

# Secrets of the Polish Forest

Deep in the woods outside Warsaw a group of worried men from three different countries came together in the utmost secrecy in what, unknown to them at the time, was to have incalculable consequences for the Second World War, which was just six weeks away. It was July 1939 at Pyry, in the Kabackie Woods near Warsaw, where the Polish General Staff's Cipher Bureau – codenamed 'Wicher' (Gale) – had called a meeting with their British and French counterparts to share a sensational secret with them. The information was so sensitive that its identity was not to be made public until thirty years after the Second World War had ended. Without that meeting in the forest, the war that was about to engulf Europe and much of the rest of the world could well have lasted much longer than it did. It was in the 1930s, even before Hitler came to power, that the Polish Cipher Bureau realised that the best people to break codes were not necessarily the military, but mathematicians, and the decision to recruit from academia is behind the story of their breaking of Enigma, the cipher machine used by the German armed forces. In their choice of three such mathematicians in particular, the Poles, unknowingly at the time, played a large part in the eventual downfall of Nazi Germany.

The growing Nazi threat and the Soviet regime in Russia were potential life-threatening problems for the Poles, who only re-emerged as a nation in November 1918 as the Armistice was signed following the end of the 'war to end all wars', having previously been carved up by those two countries and Austria in the late eighteenth century. The subsequent treaty gave Poland a corridor that linked it to the Baltic – its only route to the sea – with the port of Danzig, with its large German population, a free city under international control. What enraged the Germans was that the corridor cut off eastern Prussia from the rest of Germany, and Prussia had traditionally been the home of German militarism. So, German antagonism to Poland long pre-dated Hitler coming to power. Squeezed between Germany and the Soviet Union, the Polish position was unenviable. The Poles kept a close eye on both their powerful neighbours through their codebreaking operations. They had been deciphering Soviet codes since 1919 and broke the German Army hand cipher in the 1920s. On the diplomatic front, Poland signed a political and military treaty with France, giving the Poles a considerably increased (but as it subsequently turned out mistaken) sense of security. Then they signed a non-aggression pact in 1934 with the new Nazi government in Germany, revoked by Hitler in a rage in April 1939 after Britain and France guaranteed to back Poland in the event of a German invasion.

It was to Poznan University that Poland's Cipher Bureau turned for recruitment in January 1929, when the Polish General Staff held a cryptographic course for outstanding mathematicians at the Institute of Mathematics. This led to the recruitment to the Cipher Bureau's German branch (BS4) of three young mathematicians, Jerzy Rozycki, Henryk Zygalski and Marian Rejewski, who were to become legendary within the closed world of codebreakers.

In November 1931 the French Secret Service was unexpectedly brought into the Enigma picture in a bizarre twist that would eventually lead back to the Poles. The story that was to unfold would have severely tested the most imaginative pen of Hollywood scriptwriters. An official from the German Cipher Office of the Defence Ministry in Berlin, Hans Thilo Schmidt, had been trying to make contact with the French Secret Service. Schmidt had financial problems, a wife and two children and was a womaniser who needed money to finance his lavish lifestyle. Schmidt met the head of the French intelligence section D – the Service de Renseignements – Captain (later General) Gustave Bertrand.[i] At this meeting, the forty-three-year-old Schmidt booked into the Grand Hotel in Verviers, just inside Belgium and bordering Germany. He not only knew the Enigma secrets, but also had a highly placed brother in the military, Rudolf, who later became a General in the German Army. Schmidt, who was given the codename Asché by the French, later brought to his handlers a veritable treasure trove of secrets, including the manuals for operating Enigma. In all, Schmidt produced more than 300 highly classified documents.

But back in Paris the codebreakers were less than impressed and said the information showed how to encipher a message, but would not enable them to break the Enigma machines. The French decided to offer the secrets to British intelligence, but Britain reasoned that because of the small quantity of intercepts and the fact that the Germans were using low power on medium frequencies, breaking Enigma would be extremely difficult and interception from Britain would be hard. However, the French had previously had dealings with the Poles. Would they look at the documents? Yes, came the reply from Warsaw. Having examined the documents, the Poles asked the French if they could obtain the current Enigma settings. Schmidt obliged, and these vital documents helped to open up the Enigma secrets, the Asché information being provided to Rejewski between December 1931 and September 1932. It included the monthly key lists for December 1931 and May, September and October 1932. The Poles received the first documents on 7 December 1931 and these were passed on to the Poles until August 1938.

But Schmidt's treachery was nearly discovered when the Abwehr – German military intelligence – intercepted a message sent to Paris in November 1937 by André François-Poncet, the French Ambassador in Berlin. The ambassador, using a diplomatic cipher that the Germans had broken, revealed information provided by Schmidt about a secret top-level meeting in Berlin. The Abwehr began a manhunt for the traitor in their midst, but miraculously the secret of the breaking of Enigma remained safe. It was the first of what were to become several scares that the secret of having broken Enigma might be revealed.

Schmidt's role was eventually revealed to the Germans during the war by Rodolphe Lemoine, his French Secret Service handler (codename Rex), whom he had first met at the initial meeting at Verviers. Lemoine was known to the German security services, for he had been arrested by the Gestapo in Cologne in March 1938, but released. German-born, Lemoine, then called Stallmann, became a naturalised French citizen in 1900, having taken on his French wife's maiden name as his surname. As a result of the Cologne incident, he was warned off by his superiors not to go near Schmidt again in case he had been compromised. When the Germans occupied Paris in 1940 they found documents in police headquarters that a member of the German Cipher Office had written about a German code. Lemoine's name was mentioned. By this time Lemoine had moved to a hotel in Marseilles in what was now part of unoccupied Vichy France, near to the Spanish border, to enable an escape. He had even been about to board a British minesweeper, but in a rage following a row with one of the ship's officers, refused to go on board. In February 1943 the Abwehr arrested him, and the following month he revealed everything about Schmidt and the Enigma manuals. The Germans also found incriminating documents on an abandoned train pointing to a traitor in the German Cipher Office. Schmidt, who was now working for the German Air Ministry's Forschungsamt, a research section that involved telephone-tapping, was arrested by the Gestapo on 1 April 1943, and in September was found dead in the prison, apparently having committed suicide. But even with Schmidt in their hands, the Germans had still refused to believe that Enigma had been compromised.

The Poles obtained a commercial Enigma at the end of 1932 when it was purchased by engineer Antoni Palluth, of the Cipher Bureau, and co-founder and co-owner of the AVA radio manufacturing company. In February 1933 AVA built a replica commercial Enigma and a prototype constructed to the specifications of Rejewski and his two companions. The company did other work for the Polish General Staff, including making short-wave radio transmitters, and eventually became its main supplier and construction plant. Some of the construction details of the machine were already known, as an Enigma had previously been sent to Poland by the German authorities in error and examined while in transit at a Warsaw Post Office by Palluth and another engineer, Ludomir Danilewicz. Rejewski, in particular, showed special talent, and was asked by Major Maksymilian Ciezki, head of the Bureau's German section, if he would take on a job so secret, he could not even tell his two companions. Rejewski agreed, and Ciezki handed him the files on Enigma. Rejewski got to grips with Enigma in his spare time, and in one of the greatest cryptography feats in the history of codebreaking mastered the intricacies of what the Germans believed was an unbreakable system. He tackled the problem by using pure mathematics and discovered the internal wiring of the wheels and that of the non-rotating reflector. In a book published in 2005 by the city council of Bydgoszcz, where he was born, it states:

> Rejewski tabulated the results of his observations of the encrypted reports in the form of permutated equations. Although the number of unknowns excluded in practical terms the possibility of solving the equations, the application of this method represented a breakthrough in cryptography on a global scale.[ii]

The task of the Polish codebreakers had been greatly complicated by the changes the Germans were bringing to the machine, not least by changing the keys every three months, then monthly and later daily. A major mistake, spotted by Rejewski in 1932, was that the message setting – the position of the three rotors or wheels on the Enigma when the first six letters in the message were enciphered – was enciphered twice and placed at the beginning of the message. This broke a golden rule of codebreaking – that nothing should be sent twice unless it was a dire emergency, as it provides the opportunity to pick up a pattern in the code. The operator enciphered each message using a different start position which he selected – a trigram. This was doubly-enciphered using a disguised six-letter 'indicator' with the wheels set to a common 'ground setting' or Grundstellung (usually known as the 'Grund'), used for a particular day by all operators on that particular network. For example, that day's Grund might be GLX. The operator would first turn his three wheels to this position, then choose a message setting, say VGD, which he would encipher twice, i.e. VGDVGD, which might give him SKRLJB. The operator would then return his wheels to the message setting – VGD – and encipher the message. At the other end, the recipient – or recipients – would reverse the process to recover the message setting and decipher the text. The object of the double encipherment was to remove any possible errors as to the message setting, but it proved a weakness of the system, exploited by Rejewski. He deduced that, for example, the doubly-enciphered SKRLJB meant that the first and fourth letters – SL, the second and fifth letters – KJ, and the third and sixth letters – RB – were related. It was the exploitation of this weakness which gave Rejewski his way into the Enigma machine.

Rejewski was able to work out the electrical connections of the three rotors in December 1932. As a result of his breakthrough, the Poles began reading German Army Enigma messages in January 1933, the month Hitler came to power, but there were too few Navy and Luftwaffe messages to make regular breaking possible. To find the daily settings needed the receipt of between sixty and eighty messages. The indicator system on German Naval Enigma changed on 1 May 1937, making the Polish breaking methods inapplicable to naval keys. By January 1938 the Poles were reading about seventy-five per cent of the encrypted messages received. On 15 September 1938 – two weeks before British Prime Minister Neville Chamberlain went to see Hitler in

Munich – the Germans altered the set-up from a prescribed initial position to go before the message setting, to allowing operators to choose their own initial position, sent in clear, followed by the double encipherment of the message setting. To overcome these difficulties, in November 1938 the Poles devised an electro-mechanical machine comprising six Enigmas called the 'bomba', the colloquial meaning of the word being 'splendid' or 'sensational'. Bomba was also the name of a popular ice-cream dessert in Warsaw. The Bomba components, which had been produced at the AVA plant, were brought to the German section of the Cipher Bureau, BS4, in November 1938 and assembled by technicians sworn to secrecy.

At the July 1939 meeting near Warsaw the British and French codebreakers were told the Polish secrets, which came as a surprise to Bletchley Park. The Polish contribution probably saved Britain ten months to a year in working on Enigma. Without the Polish success it would probably not have been possible to get started until May 1940, when Enigma machines were captured in Norway, which also supplied a full set of Army and Air Force wheels. In addition, the Poles devised a perforated card method named after its inventor, Henryk Zygalski. The system was known by the German name 'Netzverfahren' or 'Netz' – 'net procedure'. On 15 December 1938, the Germans increased the number of wheels from three to five, from which three had to be selected as per the monthly settings sheet, which provided the key for each day of the month. This meant that the number of wheel orders had increased from six to sixty, and would require a tenfold increase in the number of perforated 'Zygalski' sheets. These were painstakingly cut using a razor blade. They comprised twenty-six perforated sheets for each of the six possible ways in which the three wheels could be placed in the machine, each sheet relating to the ring settings of the left-hand wheel – the slowest of the three. This 26 x 26 matrix represented the 676 possible starting positions for the middle and left-hand wheels. The sheets were punched with holes to indicate where 'females' could occur. Females were where the same letter appeared in positions one and four, or two and five or three and six, e.g. **L** RG **L** VD, **KD** X **BDZ** or FCP ZWP. But the increase in the number of rotor wheels to five would mean a bomba having to link sixty rather than six bombas, a tenfold increase and a task beyond them given their limited resources. However, the SD – the Nazi security service Sicherheitsdienst – continued to use the old system with the two new wheels until 1 July

1939, enabling Rejewski to find the wiring on the new fourth and fifth wheels in January 1939. The Germans increased the number of plugboard settings on New Year's Day 1939 from five to eight to seven to ten, decreasing the bomba's effectiveness.

Rozycki developed the 'clock' method to try and find which rotor was at the right-hand side of the Enigma machine for a particular day, this being the wheel that moved one step each time the keyboard was depressed. Another device that did not need to know the plugboard connections was the card catalogue, constructed using the cyclometer – which took over a year to compile – and which comprised two sets of Enigma wheels, and was used to discover the length and number of cycles of permutations that could be generated by the machine. Each of the 17,576 possible positions were tested for each possible sequence of wheels – there were six possible positions at the time, as only three wheels were being used – so the catalogue comprised 6 x 17,576 = 105,456 entries. By this means the daily keys at this stage could be found in around twenty minutes. However, this was only valid when the indicators were enciphered twice.

Bletchley Park developed their own perforated sheet system known as the 'Jeffreys sheets', after John Jeffreys, but was a different catalogue to that produced by Zygalski, being a catalogue of the effect of any two wheels and the reflector. However, Bletchley Park also made Zygalski sheets. In December 1939 Alan Turing delivered the Jeffreys sheets to the Poles in France, enabling them to make the first wartime break of Enigma on 17 January 1940 – three days before Bletchley Park.

As the storm clouds of war gathered, the Poles had made gigantic strides in breaking Enigma, but if Poland was invaded and occupied, all that information would be lost. The rumblings of war grew louder as the months passed. In July the Poles decided that they had gone as far as their limited resources would allow them in tackling Enigma, and they took the momentous decision to share all their information about the machine with the French and British secret services. A meeting was arranged on 9–10 January 1939 by the French in Paris to include themselves, the Poles and Britain. At this meeting the Polish position was only to reveal what they knew if it was clear Britain and France had also made progress. However, as neither country had done so, the Poles gave very little away. The next venue, the Polish Cipher Bureau site at Pyry in July 1939, was completely different – this time the Poles revealed everything as the Germans massed on their borders, when

Britain and France were shown the replicas of Enigma and the bombes made by AVA and Zygalski's sheets. In addition, they received all the necessary instructions and explanations regarding the method of reading German ciphers, and were given the most important conclusions from the card-index record, the basic database of every deciphering outpost which would help further in the struggle to crack Enigma messages.

The British trio at the meeting were a Cambridge professor of classics, Dilly Knox, one of the all-time greats in cryptography, and a veteran of the legendary First World War codebreaking organisation known as Admiralty Room 40 OB (Old Building), Alastair Denniston, head of the Government Code & Cypher School – both of whom had been at the January meeting – and Commander Humphrey Sandwith, head of the intercept and direction-finding stations. They were joined by Gustave Bertrand and Captain Henri Braquenié, a French cryptanalyst. From the Polish side were Lieutenant Colonel Gwido Langer, head of the Cipher Bureau, and Major Maksymilian Ciezki, who ran its German section. The British and French were dumbfounded when the Poles not only revealed that they had broken Enigma but had two reproduction models of the machine to give them. Knox had one key question for the Poles.

What had been puzzling Bletchley Park about Enigma was how the wirings inside the entry disc in the machine were set up. In the commercial Enigma, the order was that of the twenty-six letters of the alphabet to be found on a standard German typewriter keyboard: QWERTZUIOASDFGHJKPYXCVBNML. In this way Q was wired to the first contact, W to the second etcetera through the circle of the twenty-six letters of the alphabet on the contact on the entry ring. Dramatically, the Poles told Knox that the wiring sequence was ABCDEFG and so on! So A was wired to the first contact, B to the second – in its simplest form. Knox could not believe it – a straightforward A–Z wiring. The brains of Bletchley Park had not discovered this, although they had considered the idea but rejected the possibility without testing it! And how stupid of the Germans!

On 1 September 1939 the Nazis attacked Poland, the Poles having foreknowledge as they had identified eighty-ninety per cent of the German army units on their borders, thanks largely to reading Enigma decrypts, forcing the Polish codebreakers to flee to Brest Litovsk on the Polish–Russian border ahead of the invading Germans, along with their

Enigma replicas and the secrets of how they had broken the messages. Over several months they were to face considerable hazards. They fled to Romania, crossing the border on 17 September – the day the Russians invaded eastern Poland – a journey that was long and difficult, and they had to destroy their valuable cargo in their flight. When they arrived in the Romanian capital Bucharest they headed for the Polish Embassy, where they were given permission to contact the British or the French. They went to the British Embassy, but feared there might be a delay obtaining clearance to travel to England, so they went to the French Embassy instead. Here they were quickly given all the documents they needed to get to Paris. Travelling via Yugoslavia and Italy to France, on 20 October they found themselves at Château de Vignolles at Gretz-Armainvilliers, about twenty-five miles south-east of the French capital – codenamed PC (Poste de Commandement) Bruno, operating under the codename 'Ekipa K'. The first wartime Enigma message was broken here on 17 January 1940 – the key of 28 October the previous year. They had beaten Bletchley Park to the first wartime break by three days! But on 1 May 1940 the Germans changed the indicator system – now the three-letter message setting would only be enciphered once, putting an end of the Netz system.

Meanwhile, Langer and Cieski were stuck in a Romanian refugee camp, but they, too, eventually made it to France. When the Germans invaded France in May 1940 the Polish team was moved from Gretz-Armainvilliers to Paris, and as the Germans advanced on the French capital, the Poles took flight again, this time to Algeria, where they remained for three months. They returned to the south of France to the Château des Fouzes near Uzès (codenamed Cadix), in the unoccupied Vichy zone, resuming clandestine operations in October 1940, although not being involved in breaking Enigma keys. The château had been organised by Bertrand, now known as 'Monsieur Barsac'. Rejewski was 'Pierre Renaud', a lycée professor from Nantes, Zygalski was 'Renée Sergent', Langer was 'Charles Lange' and Antoni Palluth was 'Jean Lenoir'. In early 1941, the Cadix unit set up a branch office at the Château Kouba on the outskirts of Algiers, codename 'PO1 Kouba', headed by Cieski. However, the Germans could occupy Vichy at any time, and its intelligence service was allowed to operate there, so their safety was far from guaranteed. Indeed, on 6 November 1940, a German direction-finding truck stopped outside their château, but did not enter. On 11 November 1942, the Germans occupied Vichy, and the following day entered the château, so they had a lucky escape. A number of abortive attempts to get the Poles out of France also came to nothing. They were in Toulouse in January 1943, and then went to Perpignan the same month in preparation for entering nearby neutral Spain. On 29 January, Rejewski and Zygalski made it to Spain, but not before their guide had robbed them at gunpoint, and they later spent an uncomfortable time in prison, being released on 4 May 1943, and going to Madrid, which they left on 21 July, then to Portugal. From here they boarded HMS *Scottish* to Gibraltar before being flown to Hendon Airport in England on the night of 2–3 August.

The third member of the Poznan University trio, Rozycki, was among 222 passengers who drowned on the passenger ship *Lamoricière* on 9 January 1942 when returning to the Cadix station after working at the Algiers branch. The ship sank in unclear circumstances near the Balearic Islands. In March 1943, Langer and Cieski were betrayed by their guards and were captured in the Pyrenees attempting to cross into Spain, ending up in an SS concentration camp. It was one of the miracles of the Second World War that the Germans never realized that the secrets of the Enigma machine had been broken – but they came close on more than one occasion. In March 1944, a German technical commission interrogated Langer and Cieski and they took a gamble and admitted that they had broken the machine, but that it had been the old commercial version, but that the improved military version with the plugboard had proved too tough for them. And as the Germans were always confident that the Enigma *was* unbreakable, they heard what they wanted to hear and were convinced by the story given to them by the two Poles. Had they not been convinced, the outcome for signals intelligence gathering by the Bletchley Park codebreakers could have been catastrophic, particularly as the interrogation was within three months of the planned invasion of Normandy. The two Poles had outwitted the Germans. They were both liberated by the Americans at the end of the war. Antoni Palluth was also captured and sent to a concentration camp and was killed during an Allied air raid. Bertrand was also eventually captured – in Paris on 5 January 1944 – and he pretended to agree to work for the Germans. He was allowed to return to Vichy with his wife, Mary, but went into hiding. Then, on 2 June – four days before D-Day – he and his wife were flown clandestinely to England. Bertrand retired from French intelligence in 1950 and later became mayor of Théoule-sur-Mer in southern France. In 1973 he

nty-four, and was buried with military honours in Warsaw. In
jewski, Zygalski and Rosycki were posthumously awarded the
Cross of the Order of Polonia Restituta, and in July 2005
ksi's daughter Janina Sylwestrzak received the British 1939–1945
Medal from Britain. In 1983 a Polish postage stamp was issued to
the fiftieth anniversary of the breaking of the military Enigma.
re is a memorial to the trio at Bletchley Park. Rejewski has a street
school named after him in his home town of Bydgoszcz. In 2005 a
tcard was issued to commemorate the centenary of his birth, and in
07, a bronze monument was erected in front of Poznan Castle to the
rio.

Zygalski remained in Britain after the war, and lectured in
mathematics at Battersea Technical College and the University of
Surrey. He died at Liss in Hampshire on 30 August 1978 and is buried
in London. Shortly before his death he was honoured by the Polish
University in Exile with an honorary doctorate for his work on Enigma.

The outcome of the war, not least its duration, might have looked
very different but for the brilliance of the Polish codebreakers, and their
crucial decision to reveal all to Britain and France in the Pyry forest.
Now the vital part they played in the Enigma story has been fully
publicly acknowledged, and their long overdue and rightful place in the
history of this epic story of wartime codebreaking well established. In
addition to their tremendous contribution to breaking Enigma, the
heroism of the Polish codebreakers is another reason why their efforts
are today recognized with such acclaim and gratitude. There is a section
dedicated to the Polish codebreakers on public display at Bletchley
Park, a memorial to their contribution to breaking Enigma, and
Bletchley Park also holds an annual events day devoted to the Poles.

published one of the earliest rev.
*Enigma ou la Plus Grande Énigme de* ι.
*Greatest Enigma of the War of 1939–19*η
to the silence of Polish and French codeι.
his official four-volume *History of British In.*
*War*, Harry Hinsley, who worked at Bletchle.

> thanks to the discretion of the Polish and F1
> the loyalty of those among them who were i.
> Germans, no hint ever reached the enemy's eι
> success against the Enigma to which they l.
> contributed.[iii]

In England, Rejewski and Zygalski worked together maii.
SD hand ciphers, but were never sent to Bletchley Park.
based at a Polish Army facility at Felden, near Boxmoor on th.
of Hemel Hempstead, Hertfordshire. All, however, was not sm.
and light with their British hosts. Rejewski wrote to Bletchley Par.
October 1944, requesting the return of the Enigma machine that
been given to them at Pyry in July 1939. He also wanted Britain to sh.
the experience they had gained in the field of German ciphers in th.
past five years. Finally, he wrote that an attempt should be made to
persuade Britain to supply their intercept material, as the Polish
possibilities were very limited.

There was, apparently, no British reply to these requests. On 21
November 1946, Rejewski returned to Poland to rejoin his wife Irena,
their son Andrzej – born in 1936 – and daughter Janina, born three
years later. Tragically, in the summer of 1947, after five days illness,
Andrzej died from polio, aged eleven years. After that, Rejewski refused
to be parted from his family and turned down academic appointments,
as this would have meant him leaving them behind. Instead, he took
mundane jobs such as director of the sales department at Polish Cables,
then as a director of the State Surveying Company. From 1951–1954 he
was employed at the Association of Timber and Varied Manufactures
Co-Operatives. From 1954 until he retired on a disability pension in
February 1967, he was working at a Provincial Association of Labour
Co-Operative. During this period he had come under the scrutiny of
the secret police, but they had no idea of his wartime Enigma
involvement. In 1978 he was awarded the Officer's Cross of the Order
of Polonia Restituta. He died of a heart attack on 13 February 1980,

*Chapter 2*

# Death from the Depths

As an island, Britain has historically relied on much of its vital supplies from overseas. That was why trade had always followed the flag, why the Royal Navy had reigned supreme on the high seas for centuries, and its merchant shipping tonnage was vast. But as the Germans showed in the First World War, the use of a new form of warfare – the submarine – could put Britain's vital imports in jeopardy. The Second World War battle between the Royal Navy and its protection of merchant shipping against the combined forces of Germany's U-boats – which accounted for seventy per cent of Allied shipping losses in terms of the Atlantic – the surface ships and the Luftwaffe was to prove the deadliest arena of the conflict and to last the entire six years of the war. As Churchill was to put it, nothing scared him more during the entire war than the U-boat menace.

The Battle of Britain having been won against the Luftwaffe in the skies above Britain in the summer of 1940, the German Air Force intensified its attacks on Britain's seaborne supply line from North America. The intercept station at Cheadle in Cheshire had been keeping a wary eye on a new Luftwaffe unit, I KG40, which had been equipped with Focke Wulf 200 aircraft – the famous Condor – for long-distance attacks on Atlantic merchantmen and was operating out of Bordeaux, inflicting serious losses. Ominously, co-operation between I KG40 and U-boats was intensifying. In addition, I KG40 made weather flights between Bordeaux and Stavanger in Norway. The Condor could fly from their French base right round the British Isles, refuel in Stavanger and return to Bordeaux the next day, destroying merchant ships en route and alerting U-boats to convoys. Britain's problem was that more ships were being sunk than could be built to replace them, while damaged shipping exceeded the ability to effect repairs, congesting the ports, which were under air attack. The situation was grim.

Churchill wrote after the war that 'this mortal danger to our life-lines gnawed at my bowels'. It was he who introduced the phrase 'Battle of the Atlantic' following the famous 'Battle of Britain' slogan. It meant the war at sea around Britain's coasts was to have the highest priority. Hitler had made a speech on 30 January 1941 threatening death and destruction with the U-boats. His threat was to see the launch of the 'wolfpacks' – U-boats operating together to attack a convoy en masse. On 6 March 1941 Churchill issued his Directive, which said: 'In view of various German statements, we must assume that the Battle of the Atlantic has begun.' A key decision was to establish a Western Approaches Command based in Liverpool to co-ordinate and oversee the defence of the convoys. Germany's surface fleet was also being used for raids in the north Atlantic, including the battlecruisers *Scharnhorst* and *Gneisenau* and the cruiser *Hipper*. However, the German navy had entered the war totally unprepared – Grand Admiral Raeder, the Germany navy supremo, had warned Hitler that he needed until 1944 to be ready. U-boat commander Admiral Doenitz also said he needed more time to build a substantial fleet of U-boats.

Frustratingly at this time, while Bletchley Park had broken Luftwaffe keys, they were not reading naval Enigma traffic, although naval W/T and traffic analysis was proving useful. The brilliant Cambridge University mathematician Alan Turing headed up the naval section at Bletchley Park to break in to Enigma, and he started on his own before a team was built up in Hut 8. Then in the spring of 1941 came the big breakthrough – Bletchley Park found its way into naval Enigma at long last. In March that year a second big breakthrough occurred – the United States Congress passed the Lend-Lease Bill which enabled merchant ships to be sent to Britain. In addition, the Americans provided facilities for British warships and the merchant fleet to be repaired in US docks. President Roosevelt also established an air base on Greenland – the Germans had weather stations on the east coast of Greenland opposite Iceland – and then on Iceland. Then Roosevelt decided to extend America's security zone and patrol areas to a line covering all North Atlantic waters of twenty-six degrees west, a vast expanse of water that included all British territory in or near the US, Greenland, the Azores and Iceland. Then in September 1941 the Americans for the first time gave direct protection to the Halifax (Nova Scotia) convoys. Inevitably there was a price to be paid for this help, and America suffered its first casualty at the end of October 1941 when the destroyer *Reuben James* was torpedoed and sunk. For a neutral country, these measures by the US President and Congress were only a wafer-thin jump away from open war with Germany. However, despite pleas from Grand Admiral Raeder, Hitler would not allow the U-boats more latitude, fearing that the US would be dragged into the war as a result.

Bletchley Park had by now received an unpleasant piece of news – the naval Enigma machine could now be set up using three out of eight wheels as against three out of five for Army and Luftwaffe messages, thus considerably complicating the task for the codebreakers. However, Bletchley Park had discovered that the German navy used just two Enigma keys – Home (Heimisch) and Foreign (Ausserheimisch) – but only used the latter when operating in distant waters. The Foreign key was never broken. Information was provided from various 'pinches' when Enigma naval keys and codebooks were captured in specially organised raids, and by the end of June 1941 Bletchley Park had six bombes used for codebreaking, of which one was permanently available for naval decryption. In addition, from spring 1941 the codebreakers were reading the dockyards and fairways hand cipher (Werft), and this proved an invaluable source of information, as did the German navy's meteorological cipher.

In May 1941 Germany's surface raiding fleet had suffered a severe setback with the sinking of the battleship *Bismarck*. Although codebreaking played only a minor role in this huge morale booster to a besieged Britain, Enigma decrypts were instrumental in enabling the tankers and supply ships for the battleship to be sunk. But Bletchley Park did produce one vital piece of information regarding *Bismarck* that gave a strong pointer to western France as her destination. This came about as a result of tracking German W/T traffic, when it was discovered that the battleship's normal W/T frequency control station of Wilhelmshaven had been switched to Paris. Then a colossal security blunder by the Germans confirmed *Bismarck* was heading for France, when the Luftwaffe Chief of Staff, General Hans Janosschek, who was in Athens planning for the forthcoming invasion of Crete, made enquiries about the ship's whereabouts because he had a relative on board, the answer to which, decrypted at Bletchley Park, revealed her ultimate destination. June 1941 saw a major advance by the codebreakers when, for the first time, naval Enigma began to be decrypted currently. The importance of this breakthrough was that the Home Waters key was common to both the surface fleet and the U-boats in the Atlantic. Apart from a few days in the second half of 1941, Bletchley Park was to read the Home Waters traffic to the end of the war with a maximum delay of seventy-two hours and often after only a few hours. Harry Hinsley, who worked at Bletchley Park in the naval intelligence section, explained that a feature of the naval Enigma machine was that while its outer settings changed daily, its inner settings changed only every other day:

> It was more difficult to break the inner than the outer setting, and the breaking of the outer setting normally followed within an hour or two of the beginning of the second day's traffic.[iv]

One of the earliest successes of reading the Home Waters traffic was to successfully track the pocket battleship *Lützow*, enabling the RAF to cripple her with a direct hit with a torpedo. There was also success against the German auxiliary raiders, although the damage they inflicted on merchant shipping was substantially less than that of the U-boats and Luftwaffe. But the greatest advantage in being able to read naval Enigma was that convoys could now be re-routed around the U-boat wolfpacks.

By now U-boats were moved to the Mediterranean and – on Hitler's personal orders – also to Norwegian waters because of his fear of a British invasion, and by New Year 1942 there were virtually no U-boats in the Atlantic except around Gibraltar and the Azores. Meanwhile the B-Dienst, the German equivalent of Naval Section at Bletchley Park, had broken Navy Ciphers No 2 and No 3, the latter used for Anglo-US-Canadian communications for the Atlantic convoys. This failure of the U-boats to find convoys had led the Germans to suspect their security, but never did they believe that Enigma was compromised, although such a possibility was examined.

However, they decided it was time to tighten up security and, on 1 February 1942 – one of the blackest days in Bletchley Park's history – the naval Enigma added a fourth rotor position for U-boats operating in the Atlantic and the Mediterranean. There was a double blow, however, in that as the fourth rotor came into effect the success of the B-Dienst in breaking Navy Cipher No 3 came about. At the very moment when Bletchley Park went blind, the German navy was seeing much more clearly. However, this may have turned out to be a blessing in disguise, as the introduction of the fourth wheel by the Kriegsmarine for the Atlantic Enigma also coincided with the German decision to concentrate the U-boat offensive against the American coasts. But for this, the improvement in their performance against convoys might have led U-boat Command to conclude that its earlier difficulties had been because the three-wheel Enigma was insecure.

The importance of the B-Dienst codebreakers has been acknowledged by Patrick Beesly, who worked in the Admiralty's Operational Intelligence Centre from 1940 to 1945:

> from 1940 up to the middle of 1943 the contribution made by the B-Dienst to the success of Dönitz in the Battle of the Atlantic must have been equal to at least an additional fifty U-boats.[v]

For the hard-pressed U-boat crews, the second 'happy period' was about to begin, not least because they were also operating off the eastern coast of the US from early in 1943 and the pickings were easy. The four-wheel Enigma blackout was to last until mid-December 1942, and it was not until August 1943 that Shark – the Bletchley Park name for the four-wheel system, called Triton by the Germans – was being read daily and it continued to do so until the end of the war. Fortunately, both the surface fleet and the U-boats operating against the Arctic convoys from Norway, as well as those in the Baltic, continued to use the Home Waters key. Despite this, Britain was left with red faces after the battlecruisers *Scharnhorst* and *Gneisenau* successfully raced up the English Channel from Brest in February 1942 along with the heavy cruiser *Prinz Eugen*, codenamed *Operation Cerberus* by the Germans. They reached Germany, although both battlecruisers were damaged by hitting mines, *Scharnhorst* being out of action for three months.

Enigma decrypts were also helping in the battle against the German blockade runners delivering vital stores to Germany, as well as the auxiliary ships and the E-boats that carried out raids on Britain's coast. By now the threat to Britain had eased as German resources were switched to the war against Russia. Enigma decrypts were also now being used effectively to enable Britain to move from the defensive to the offensive, particularly to launch attacks on enemy shipping. In addition, Bletchley Park was able to produce figures on ships sunk or damaged from minelaying, which showed this was much more effective than direct attacks on shipping. But with Bletchley Park now blind on the whereabouts of the U-boats, sinkings of merchant vessels increased and in November 1942 reached what was to be the highest monthly total achieved throughout the war – 721,700 tons. Doenitz was back on top

again – at least temporarily – because in December came the great news
that Bletchley Park had broken into the four-rotor Enigma and the naval
codebreakers were back in business. But that relief was tempered by the
fact that Doenitz now had almost 230 operational U-boats at his
disposal, with about double that number in commission. The next five
months to May 1943 was to see the final showdown with the U-boats in
which Enigma was to play a crucial role. The American naval
cryptanalysts were now working with Bletchley Park on Shark decrypts,
but although the key had been broken, unfortunately in the first few
months of 1943 there were often delays in being able to read messages.
One particular problem was that of decoding the means by which U-
boat geographical dispositions were disguised in Shark. In mid-June
1941 the U-Boat Command had taken steps to tighten up on the
enciphering of U-boat positions because they were concerned at the
increasing difficulty in finding convoys. Then, to tighten security
further, in August 1941 messages were sent to U-boats by the names of
their commanders, not their boat number. A further security measure
took place in November that year to the 'address book' system, and
while Bletchley Park eventually overcame these problems,
unfortunately the Shark blackout began shortly afterwards.

It was an error by a German naval wireless operator who used the
four-wheel Enigma prematurely in error, then repeated the message in
the three-wheel machine, that led to codebreakers working out the
wiring of the fourth wheel. What seemed clear was that whereas the
three-wheel bombes were all right for three-wheel Enigma, there would
need to be a four-wheel version for breaking Shark. At this time there
had been a considerable increase in both Luftwaffe and German Army
keys, taking up much bombe time, with the need for more three-wheel
bombes the priority. However, it was with three-wheel bombes that
Bletchley Park had broken into Shark in December 1942, and the four-
wheel variety did not come on stream until June 1943. By a good piece
of luck, just as Shark came on stream, so the B-Dienst, which had been
reading Naval Cipher No 3 – covering the convoys – was changed and
the Germans went blind. But by February 1943 the German navy's
codebreakers were back into the cipher, again putting the convoys under
increased threat.

The capture of secret signals material from U559, sunk near Port
Said on 30 October 1942, provided a major breakthrough into Shark.
Among documents captured from U559 was the short signal weather

code book. Operators used three wheels, with the fourth set at neutral. Bletchley Park was able to break the message, which left them with having to find the set position of the fourth wheel, because it did not move or turn over which proved not too difficult. Then, on 10 March 1943, this code book was changed, which immediately sent alarm bells ringing, but brilliantly the codebreakers recovered and they took only nine days to get back into business. However, the short signal book continued to be used for operational matters. In May 1943, Doenitz gave up the struggle in the north Atlantic and withdrew his U-boats. Two months later, in July, an alternative fourth wheel, known as Gamma, came into operational use in addition to the original single fourth wheel, called Beta. Again, Bletchley Park was fortunate in that the switch between Beta and Gamma occurred only monthly. This, in addition to the continuing bad security habit of transmitting a message in both three-wheel and four-wheel Enigmas, provided a big help to the codebreakers. By August the number of British high-speed bombes had been increased with the addition of their American counterparts, greatly assisting in the breaking of Shark. By the end of 1943 the US navy had taken over all responsibility for breaking Shark settings. Also in August, Bletchley Park had broken the Enigma key they called Sunfish, used by the blockade runners.

The outcome of the Battle of the Atlantic was largely decided on the intelligence being gathered by both sides, in which, eventually, the British codebreakers were to prevail. But it was a close-run thing. One of the biggest coups for Bletchley Park was that through reading the Officer-only (Offizier) ciphers in the Shark key, they discovered that the Germans were reading the Allied convoy key. However, in June 1943 the Admiralty replaced the Navy No 3 convoy cipher and the B-Dienst did not recover from that setback. This had followed a sustained period of German success due to the B-Dienst, with far more U-boats operational, resulting, in March 1943, in the biggest convoy losses of the war when U-boats found both HX229 and SC122, and twenty-one ships were sunk from both convoys, but only one U-boat went down.

However, other factors were turning in favour of the Allies. Since the successful landings in Tunisia – Operation Torch – ships were being redeployed in the Atlantic, as were warships from the Arctic, while more aircraft were available and the weather – the worst for many years – was beginning to improve. At the same time defensive measures were improving, not least that HF/DF – High Frequency Direction Finding

(Huff-Duff) – was now on board many escort vessels, able to detect U-boats at sea. In addition, more accurate 10 cm radar had been introduced on both ships and aircraft. The highly effective forward-firing depth charges, known as Hedgehogs, had been deployed, and the notorious air gap south of Greenland and north of the Azores, where air support for convoys had been missing, was now being met by a new aircraft – the American Liberator. The U-boats were becoming extremely vulnerable, and sinkings began to increase.

However, the Germans, too, were obtaining better attack weapons, with the magnetic torpedo pistol and the torpedo that zig-zagged to its target, known as the FaT, coming into operation. The FaT or Federapparat (spring apparatus) torpedo made an immediate course change when fired, then travelled in a straight line, then entered a 'ladder' phase, which could start left or right and was set before launch. But as soon as it came into operation, the British had devised a countermeasure called Foxer that created a noise that led to premature explosion of the FaT. There were two types of torpedo pistol: one which fired the detonators on hitting the target, and the other was detonated as the torpedo passed through a ship's magnetic field.

One growing concern of the U-boat crews was the increasing threat from air attack and the much improved warship security surrounding convoys, although at the beginning of May the Operational Intelligence Centre of the Admiralty estimated U-boat strength at a record 128. The failure of the U-boats to inflict heavy losses on the merchant fleet was frustrating Doenitz, particularly as the B-Dienst was able to point the raiders at the convoys with considerable accuracy, thus frustrating Allied re-routeing. All this frustration – and the accuracy of the B-Dienst intelligence – was being read in the Shark key. How much longer would Doenitz allow such losses to continue for such small reward? The answer would not be long in coming. U-boats sighted convoy SC130 on 18 May, but lost five boats with no merchant shipping losses. Then, on 22 May, a wolfpack of twenty-two U-boats headed for convoy HX239 but lost another three boats with again no merchant shipping losses. To lose eight boats without sinking anything was too heavy a price to pay. Doenitz, in announcing the withdrawal from the Atlantic, blamed his U-boat failure largely on Allied location devices, and most of the U-boats were transferred to safer waters south-west of the Azores, which, however, were occupied by the Allies in October 1943.

The US navy was by now having considerable success against the

German supply U-boats – known as the 'milk cows' – that refuelled operational U-boats, which led to boats being forced to return to base early. In addition, the RAF was now fitted with VHF radar, and as a countermeasure the Germans were able to use a French-produced VHF receiver for U-boats known as the Metox, which was introduced in August 1942. The battle was now taking place on the U-boats' doorstep, in Biscay, as they left their bomb-proof pens in south-west France. Getting out on patrol and returning from operations was now a steadily mounting hazard, many being forced to return to port shortly after departure.

With plans to return to the north Atlantic in September, the U-boats had been re-equipped with an improved system on Metox, known as the Wanze, which automatically scanned radar frequencies. There was also a new acoustic torpedo, the Zaunkönig (Wren), known to the Allies as the Gnat – the German Naval Acoustic Torpedo – brought into service in August 1943 as an anti-escort vessel weapon. In November 1943 the U-boats abandoned the transatlantic routes. Furthermore, the much-vaunted wolfpack system was coming to an end, and the last such attack by U-boats in the war came in February 1944 when twenty boats failed to find twelve large convoys that had left the Western Approaches during the previous four weeks, lost eleven boats and only managed to sink one merchant vessel, one escort and shoot down two aircraft. Through Enigma the Admiralty knew that the number of U-boats based on Atlantic ports – 110 to 115 – was the lowest since July 1942. There was one major disaster avoided when U385 fired three torpedoes at the *Queen Mary* without success while on her journey from the US to England with nearly 12,000 American servicemen on board. Despite these setbacks, Doenitz was producing new, more modern types of U-boat which could stay submerged for longer. A new device, the schnorchel, was being put on older boats to enable them to recharge batteries while just under the water instead of having to surface, enabling them to travel at periscope depth using their diesel engines. However, using the schnorchel, although it made detection harder, reduced the manoeuvrability of the U-boats. By the beginning of November 1942 the U-boats were exploiting their ability to stay submerged. They usually submerged when they left their bases and only surfaced again, up to eight weeks later, when returning home. As Captain Roskill commented in his official *War At Sea*, as destroyers of merchant shipping, the surfaced U-boats of the 1941 wolfpacks were immeasurably superior to the submerged 'Schnorkellers' of 1944, creeping unseen around Britain's coasts. He added:

> and, even if the latter caused us much irritation and wasted effort, they never came near to becoming a serious threat to our Atlantic life-line – as the former certainly did.[vi]

The new type of boats were the brainchild of Professor Hellmuth Walter, the submarine construction expert of the German navy, whose designs were known as 'Walter boats' and were smaller, causing concern at the Admiralty. It was thanks to Bletchley Park's Japanese diplomatic decrypts of messages, sent from Berlin by Vice-Admiral Abe, head of the Japanese Naval Mission, to Tokyo, that full details of the U-boat construction programme became available.

The Normandy invasion led, by September 1944, to the evacuation of the U-boat pens in south-west France, with many boats heading for Norway. There was now also a concerted effort to attack shipping off the south-west coast of Ireland and in the English Channel. The schnorchel was enabling U-boats to submerge for long periods, resulting in the number of sinkings of boats decreasing. Indeed, sightings of U-boats were becoming scarce. Enigma decrypts revealed that U-boats were remaining submerged for up to seventy days in some cases. Moreover, the Germans now had a new search receiver (Samos) that could intercept the Allies' centimetric radar, and the new Type XXI and Type XXIII U-boats might be operational in the autumn, when a renewed attack on Atlantic convoys was feared by the Admiralty. The decrypt of a Doenitz briefing to Atlantic U-boat crews in October 1944 led to the belief that a major offensive would be underway by the end of the year, which could have a serious effect on the land war in Western Europe. However, it was discovered through Japanese diplomatic decrypts that construction had been delayed because of air attacks. The fact that the German navy – particularly the U-boats – fought right up to the surrender is underlined by the sinkings of merchant ships in the first four months of 1945, when 398,000 tons went down, 263,000 tons of which was attributed to U-boats, higher than any quarter for 1944. In a last-ditch effort, the wolfpack system was resumed, but the *Seewolf* pack of six U-boats, sent to the Azores region, were eventually all sunk.

In 1944 decrypts had revealed a new system of off-frequency high-speed communication called Kurier (known to the Allies as Squash) and a new key for individual U-boats in the English Channel (Sonderschlüssel). Kurier was based on special communications apparatus and had been revealed in June 1944 following the capture of U505, which was towed in to Bermuda. Trials of Kurier took place in August and November 1944, but never went operational. By February 1945 special keys were carrying practically all U-boat operational traffic, and on 1 April 1945 a new setting procedure was introduced in the Baltic which was planned to be extended to the main western key on 1 May. Fortunately, the war ended before this could be put into operation – a relief for Bletchley Park in the final days of the conflict.

However, Bletchley Park was still kept busy on naval Enigma right up to the surrender. Indeed, the highest number of decrypts in the entire war was 19,902 in the week 11–17 March 1945, the month the underwater fleet reached its peak of 463 boats. Between November 1944 and February 1945, however, the Allies gradually lost the ability to decrypt the most important part of U-boat traffic. Indeed, from the beginning of April 1945, when it first encountered problems in breaking the main Baltic key, Bletchley Park was aware that it would inevitably lose its long-held grip on naval Enigma if hostilities lasted much longer.

It has been said of military intelligence that it does not win wars, but is indispensable helping to win them. It was the growth and improved technology of air power that forced submarines to normally operate fully submerged. Maritime air power, backed by Ultra, also devastated the U-boat fleet when it attempted to renew the offensive with improved torpedoes in late summer. Churchill, who was well aware of the valuable contribution Ultra had made in the struggle against the U-boats, was never in doubt of the importance of winning the Battle of the Atlantic. He confessed that the Battle of the Atlantic was the dominating factor all through the war. Everything happening elsewhere ultimately depended on its outcome, and amid all other cares 'we viewed its changing fortunes day by day with hope or apprehension'.

As Wellington observed after Waterloo, it had been a close-run thing. So, too, had the outcome of the Battle of the Atlantic been in the balance for so long during the war. Bletchley Park's role in that success is now shown to have been crucial.

# Chapter 3

# Churchill and Coventry

Londoners were in open revolt. An angry mob had stormed Buckingham Palace and so the time was ripe for the largest air attack yet on Britain. Such, according to a captured Luftwaffe pilot, was the view of Hermann Goering, supreme commander of the German Air Force. Unknown to the pilot, his comments to a fellow prisoner had been secretly listened to by British intelligence officers. And this pilot, speaking three days after he was shot down on 9 November 1940, was inadvertently to play a central role in what was to ultimately lead to one of the most hotly debated episodes of the Second World War: what advance intelligence (if any) did wartime Prime Minister Winston Churchill have of the massive German air raid on Coventry on the night of 14–15 November 1940? The 'Churchill knew' theory is that Ultra – the intelligence derived from the decrypted messages from the German Enigma cipher machine – warned of the Coventry raid in advance, but that he took the decision, agonising as it was, not to alert the city that the attack was coming, in order to retain Britain's greatest wartime secret: that the innermost secrets of the 'invincible' Enigma cipher machine was known to the British. Churchill was reputed to have said on one occasion that it would be better to lose a battle than lose the secret information coming from Enigma. Would ensuring the Enigma secret be worth leaving a city to the fate of German bombers? To have to take such a terrible decision underlines the absolute loneliness of the supreme commander in wartime. But what really happened?

The captured pilot had set British intelligence alight with further comments to his fellow prisoner-of-war that Goering was to bring out the entire German Air Force in a single mass attack aimed at destroying workmen's dwellings, as the 'London revolt' was believed by Goering to have originated among the working class. The attack, the pilot confided to his colleague, would take place between 15 and 20 November during the full moon, and the target would be Coventry or Birmingham. This coincided with information uncovered by the Bletchley Park codebreakers that the Luftwaffe planned a mass air raid codenamed 'Moonlight Sonata' – the popular name for Beethoven's Piano Sonata No 14 – thus hinting that it would coincide with the full moon period. It also confirmed the view of Air Ministry Intelligence the previous month that the Luftwaffe would concentrate on night raids using around 600 bombers. However, Bletchley Park had different information – that the target was either London or the Home Counties, and would be in retaliation for a recent RAF bombing of Munich. This confusion as to the actual target was to frustrate Bletchley Park and the RAF over the next few crucial days and into the final hours leading up to the actual raid.

It was during the summer of 1940 that 'The Few' of the RAF had fought their gallant and successful Battle of Britain against the Luftwaffe, which had attempted to destroy Britain's air defences as a prelude to the invasion of England. Goering's boast to Hitler about the invincibility of the Luftwaffe, and that the RAF was on its last legs, had left him in a rage when the Luftwaffe failed to break the back of the RAF. Factories producing vital parts for the aircraft industry were based in the midlands around Coventry and Birmingham, so Goering, out for revenge, provided his answer: bomb the civilians in the cities, particularly London. The next phase of the air war over England – the Blitz – was about to begin. It was to become one of many great blunders committed by the Germans. In this case, switching the attack from airfields to civilian populations bought valuable time for the RAF and enabled it to regain its strength, while bombing cities had the exactly opposite desired effect – rather than forcing a capitulation by Britain, the nation's resolve was strengthened.

To understand the events leading to the Coventry raid it is necessary to recount how the German planes were guided to their targets by radio-directed navigational beams. After the Germans had overrun Western Europe, the Luftwaffe had set up a string of thirty-eight beacons and eleven broadcasting stations stretching from Norway to Bordeaux, plus those within Germany itself. The beacon transmissions comprised a call-sign followed by a twenty-second continuous note, which provided the aircraft with a bearing to the beacon's target. Initially the call-signs and frequencies were changed at midnight, and this information was passed by the intercepting units to RAF Commands. Countermeasures included what was known as 'meaconing' – the masking of the German beacons by re-radiating the original beacon signal with the same characteristics (so that pilots could not detect it), but a different radiation point. This sent the pilots off course, and they dropped their bomb loads (hopefully) harmlessly over open ground. By the end of August 1940 there were fifteen beacons on five sites.

The first information about German technical developments involving aircraft range-finding had come in November 1939 in a document, known as the Oslo Report, one of the most remarkable 'cloak-and-dagger' incidents of the Second World War. A document was mysteriously received by Captain (later Rear Admiral) Hector Boyes, the British naval attaché in Oslo, offering to provide information on German technical secrets. But the anonymous writer said he would only supply the information if Britain gave a positive indication that it was interested, and to signify this they should alter the opening words of the BBC's German news broadcasts with 'Hallo, hier ist London ...' This opening phrase was duly broadcast, and subsequently a package was sent to the attaché comprising a box and a seven-page memorandum. Professor RV Jones, head of Air Scientific intelligence, was subsequently given the package and memorandum in London. The box contained an electronic triggering device for use with anti-aircraft shells, and the highly technical notes included information on a whole range of top-secret technical developments, including an aircraft range-finding device for friendly aircraft. The Service ministries dismissed the report, believing it to be a German 'plant', but Professor Jones was convinced the information was genuine – as indeed it was. But the Oslo Report did not give any name for this new range-finding device. It was, in fact, a radio-beam system known as 'Knickebein' or crooked leg, which had the big advantage of being able to be used at night as well as by day. Then the Germans deployed a more sophisticated system called X-Gerät or X-Apparatus. Information about Knickebein first came to light from a crashed Heinkel 111 in March 1940, and two months later a diary entry in another downed Heinkel 111 also referred to 'Knickebein'. What intrigued the technical experts was that Knickebein did not involve special apparatus in the cockpit, but utilised the blind-landing radio receiver in the aircraft's cockpit. Bletchley Park's first Enigma decrypt mentioning Knickebein was on 9 June, and as a result of these developments, in October 1940 the RAF formed a special unit, 80 Wing, based at Radlett in Hertfordshire, to counter the threat.

The Knickebein beams were codenamed 'Headache' and the countermeasures 'Aspirin' and its transmissions were intercepted by the Y station at Kingsdown on the Kent coast, with the countermeasures themselves being devised by the Telecommunications Research Establishment (TRE) at Swanage in Dorset. Churchill was sufficiently concerned to instruct Air Marshal Joubert to investigate Knickebein, and on 14 June another captured pilot revealed that it was a system involving two intersecting beams for dropping bombs on a target with accuracy. The pilot also alerted Intelligence to the fact that Goering was to adopt new tactics of large-scale night raids preceded by pathfinders lighting up the target with flares and incendiaries. Then, on the night of 21–22 June, the RAF found a narrow beam 400–500 yards wide, and discovered a second beam that synchronised and intersected the first, although the identity of the transmitter was not discovered until September.

Early that month the more sophisticated X-Gerät radio beam navigation system was mentioned for the first time in an Enigma decrypt, and revealed its high degree of accuracy – its beam was no wider than 20 yards at 200 miles. Enigma was to provide vital information about the X-Gerät, involving operational messages giving beam settings, bearings and references to numbered targets. Crucially, X-Gerät was identified with one Luftwaffe unit, KG (Kampfgruppe) 100, which flew Heinkel 111s and whose headquarters were at Vannes in Brittany. Six transmitters were found to be linked to the X-Gerät system with the codenames of the German rivers Weser, Spree, Elbe, Rhein, Oder and Isar. Two of these transmitters were on the Hague peninsular north-west of Cherbourg, three were near Calais and one was near Brest. The British authorities dubbed them the 'Rivers Group' and codenamed the rivers after the Nazi leaders Hitler, Himmler, Goering, Hess, Ley and Ribbentrop. The aircraft flew along a beam (known as the Director Beam, and transmitted from Cherbourg), which was laid directly over the target, and instead of one cross-beam there were three, situated in the Calais area, with a distance of 15 km between the first two and 5 km between the second and third as the aircraft approached the target. The pilot would listen for the Director Beam signal, while the bomb aimer listened for the cross-beams signal. At the first cross-beam the bomb-aimer started a mechanical computer involving a stop clock, while at the second he heard the main signal which stopped the clock after the mechanical computer had been fed the correct height from his altimeter. After this the mechanical computer calculated the point at which the bombs would be released automatically – a big advance on Knickebein. There was also a reserve Director Beam in case of emergency. The Director Beam was transmitted by 'Weser' and the reserve by nearby 'Spree'. To be successful against the system, it was necessary to knock out three beams, preferably the Director, its reserve and one cross-beam.

In addition, KG100 could bomb two different places the same night. The first operational use of X-Gerät was against coastal targets in mid-August, and it was not until November 1940 that jammers could be brought into action against the system. Unfortunately – and this was to have an effect on the night of the Coventry raid – the jammers were incorrectly set at 1,500 cycles per second when they should have been set at 2,000 cycles per second. Scientists at the TRE had devised a jamming system for both Knickebein and X-Gerät, codenamed 'Domino'. But unless the countermeasure signal was transmitted on exactly the correct modulation frequency, the enemy controller would notice the difference. To strengthen the countermeasures, a second Domino site was set up on Beacon Hill near Salisbury, and then a third site was established at Honiton in Devon to handle enemy attacks on western areas such as Bristol.

In September 1940 Bletchley Park made a major breakthrough when they broke a Luftwaffe Enigma key, which they codenamed 'Brown', used between the signals experimental regiment that was developing the X-Gerät system, and KG100. Information from the decrypts included radio frequencies and the location of ground transmitters, vital information in tracking the bombers. In developing counter-measures it was found possible to locate, in advance, where the beams intersected – i.e. the target – often in the afternoon for that night's bombing raid. But Brown was just a code link for X-Gerät stations, so its operational information was not necessarily up-to-date. The code died out in May 1941, but meantime was read by Bletchley Park almost every day. Night attacks began in August, and on 24 August stray bombs fell on London, but the blitz on the capital began on 7 September with the first night raid on the city. From then until 13 November London was bombed every night but one with an average of 160 aircraft. During October, KG100 began its pathfinder strategy of dropping flares and incendiaries ahead of the main bombing force.

On the night of 5–6 November, during a raid on Birmingham, a Heinkel 111 of KG 100, carrying the top secret X-Gerät, developed compass failure, was 'meaconed' by the jammers, ran out of fuel and crash-landed on the beach at Bridport in Dorset. There then occurred one of those bizarre incidents that, quite innocently, can have a major impact in a war. The aircraft was guarded by two soldiers, who had been told by their officer not to let anyone touch it – 'not even an Admiral'. Unfortunately, the tide started to come in, washing over the Heinkel. A group of sailors from a local Royal Navy detachment offered to help the soldiers move the aircraft to higher ground, but true to their orders, they refused to allow it to be moved. Consequently the Heinkel was submerged in water and sand, and by the time the boffins had dismantled the secret apparatus it took them several days to clean it out and investigate its workings. Professor RV Jones, Britain's wartime head of scientific Intelligence, lamented:

> The failure to save the aircraft intact may have contributed to the disaster eight days later at Coventry.[vii]

An Enigma message of 9 November revealed orders for KG100 to make ready for attacks on three targets, numbered fifty-one, fifty-two and fifty-three. The beam settings were also given, and Professor Jones worked out that fifty-one was Wolverhampton, fifty-two was Birmingham and fifty-three was Coventry. What was unusual about this message was that never before had targets been sent out more than a few hours prior to an attack. Professor Jones could not, at that stage, say when or in which order the targets would be attacked. A number of questions immediately arose:

- Were all three targets to be attacked in one night?
- Was each target to be attacked on separate nights?
- In what order were the targets to be attacked?
- On what date or dates were they to be attacked?

Then Enigma came into play again when, on 11 November, a signal was read which had been sent two days earlier that referred to 'Moonlight Sonata', and which was guessed to be the codename for a major operation involving KG100 against England. The decrypt revealed that radio signals would be sent out at 1355 each day on a selected frequency, consisting of four-letter groups. The decrypt also referred to Target Areas 1, 2, 3 and 4. The decrypt added that if the raid was called off because of the weather, the code group 'Mond, Mond' – 'Moon, Moon' (another giveaway codename) – would be transmitted three times and the beams would be changed to different targets. To underline the importance of the raid, the operation would be led personally by the Commanding Officer of KG100. But no date was revealed. What did the four target areas signify and where were they? Also in the message was the codeword KORN – German for 'corn'. To what did that refer? Professor Jones originally thought it might be a codename for the appearance of radar screens when jamming was present or when spurious radar reflectors were to be dropped, known by the British as 'Window' and the Americans as 'Chaff'.

The Germans had a bad habit of devising covernames that could actually identify what it was they were trying to hide. Codes for towns usually began with a German word containing the first two letters of the English town, such as Loge (German for a private theatrical box) for London, Bild (picture) for Birmingham, Bruder (brother) for Bristol, and Liebe (love) for Liverpool. However, the Germans spelt Coventry with a 'K', hence KORN. Unfortunately, this connection with Coventry was not made at the time. When sending the decrypt to the Air Ministry, Bletchley Park said only that 'Moonlight Sonata' was assumed to be the codename for a particular operation.

> In a subsequent commentary on the decrypt GC and CS stated that 'there is no evidence that this [the codename KORN] was correctly interpreted as Coventry'.[viii]

In a memorandum to the Directorate of Home Operations, dated 12 November 1940, Air Intelligence gave their view on the four target areas as follows:

(i)   **Target area I**. It is uncertain where this area lies. It is possibly central London. There is, however, a possibility that it is in the Harwich-Ipswich district.

(ii)  **Target area II**. Greater London and within the circle Windsor-St Albans-Epping-Gravesend-Westerham – a little south of Leatherhead-Windsor.

(iii) **Target area III**. The triangle bounded by lines connecting Farnborough Aerodrome-Reading-Maidenhead.

(iv)  **Target area IV**. The district Faversham-Rochester-Sheerness.

The memorandum added that it was not known whether the four targets were all primary target areas or whether they included both primary and secondary targets. These four areas appeared to be too large for bombing targets. Could they be dropping zones for a parachute invasion? This led the Air Ministry to mistakenly believe that the objectives of Moonlight Sonata were somewhere in southern England. In fact, it later transpired that the areas were the alternate targets. A day later had come the revelation by the Luftwaffe prisoner, confirming that a major attack was being planned against Coventry and Birmingham, somewhere between 15 and 20 November – and the full moon fell on the fifteenth. Then on 13 November the Luftwaffe prisoner revealed under interrogation that there would be three separate attacks on three different targets on consecutive nights in 'the industrial district of England'. His evidence was to further confuse the situation, as it conflicted with the interpretation that was being put on the information by Bletchley Park. For example, the RAF top brass believed the attacks would be on all three targets in one night. Moreover, London was still favoured by Air Intelligence as the target.

In the early hours of 14 November, however, the Air Ministry gave out both versions to defence forces that the attack could be in London or the Midlands. Later that morning the Air Ministry sent a note to Churchill, advising him that the target was probably London, but if it was the Midlands, it was hoped to get instructions out in time. That afternoon, Professor Jones recalls, was one of those occasions when the Enigma signals to the X–Gerät stations were not broken in time, and so they were left guessing. Key players in this unfolding drama would be the RAF Y stations at Cheadle in Cheshire and Kingsdown, on the coast between Dover and Deal in Kent. Cheadle could trace the whereabouts, movements and operational strength of Luftwaffe units, and identify the German bomber units soon after an operation started. Kingsdown was also important as sometimes bombers used R/T for keeping formation. Moreover, whereas most of the Luftwaffe HQs and bases were now using landline, KG100 still used W/T. KG100, like many other Luftwaffe units, not only gave advance warning of an impending attack by opening its W/T transmissions half an hour before take-off, but also used W/T in flight.

At around 1300 the beam tunings were intercepted, and by 1500 the beam intersection was shown to be over Coventry, and operational instructions were sent out from the Air Ministry at 1615. At last the target was known. By early evening 80 Wing had asked Professor Jones for help with deciding the frequencies to be used for jamming, and he was given a list of radio frequencies, but he was concerned that they did not match up with figures from the 'Anna' code, the aircraft receiver dial. This receiver used numbers between ten and eighty-five megacycles per second – and was usually a multiple of five – being the frequencies between these two numbers on which the beams were transmitted. Crucially, if the Anna numbers were known in advance, then 80 Wing could be told to which frequencies their jamming transmitters could be set for that night's raid. Professor Jones made a mental correction and telephoned his suggested jamming frequencies to 80 Wing. He recalled that this took no more than five minutes on the telephone, but he was well aware that in taking snap decisions he was probably gambling with hundreds of lives. However, someone had to do it, and he was easily in the best position to do so.

As it turned out, Professor Jones had guessed correctly when he had recalculated the jamming frequencies, as was revealed when the Enigma signals to the beam stations for the Coventry raid were deciphered. When the X-Gerät machine from the Bridport plane was examined, the filters fitted to the receiver allowed the pilot to hear the beam signal, but excluded other noises. But the filter, it was discovered, was tuned to 2,000 cycles per second – roughly a top 'C' on the piano – whereas the jammers were set to 1,500 cycles per second – equivalent to the 'G' below top 'C' – so the filter was able to distinguish between the beam and the jamming even though Professor Jones and his team had correctly forecast the radio frequencies. The night of the raid is vividly remembered by Aileen Clayton, a WAAF intelligence officer, who was the duty officer at the Kingsdown intercept station, listening out for the bombers who would cross the Channel. She recalls:

> Although we heard the German beams being tested earlier in the day, we did not know until two o'clock on the afternoon of the night of the raid that it was to be mounted that night and until three o'clock that the beams were intersecting over Coventry.[ix]

The British response to Moonlight Sonata was codenamed 'Cold Water' and is clear proof that active operations were planned in advance to defend whatever target had been set up under this codename. The countermeasures included attacking bomber airfields in France and the Low Countries used by Luftflotten 2 and 3, and the Cherbourg beam transmission site. The RAF had discovered there was a 'silent zone' immediately above the transmitter site, so they flew along the beam until they reached it, then they dropped their bombs. Jamming would be carried out by 80 Wing, with night fighters and anti-aircraft protection also available. There would also be a heavy bombing raid on a German city, which turned out to be Berlin. The operational orders to implement Cold Water were issued at 0300 on 14 November. As soon as the raid was known to be on, Coastal Command attacked Vannes airfield, the home of KG100, and those at St Leger, Rosendail and Gravelenes as well as the Calais jetty. Bomber Command launched an attack on Berlin, and the airfields of Luftflotten 2 and 3 were attacked at Melun and Chartres. In all, Bomber Command lost ten planes in these various actions, while attacks on the transmitters by special radio bombers put two of these sites out of action. The 'meaconing' radio counter-measures were put into effect, but because the night was so clear, the Luftwaffe did not need radio navigational aids. A total of 121 fighter sorties were sent up during the night, with little effect.

In the Coventry area itself the barrage of fifty-six balloons was increased by another sixteen on the day of the raid, but unfortunately at no time did the attacking force fly below the level of the balloons, so this extra precaution proved ineffective. The city defences were further strengthened with forty high angle anti-aircraft (AA) guns as well as an extra twelve Bofors light AA guns. But, such was the brightness of the night, that the attackers were able to conduct the raid over a wide front. Aileen Clayton recalled that it was obvious that No. 80 Wing's jamming was causing little interference in the reception by the aircraft of the X-Gerät beams.

So what was Churchill's part in all this? That evening Churchill was in his car, speeding out of London towards Ditchley Park, his country retreat just north of Oxford. He opened his red Dispatch Box containing the latest Ultra decrypts that were sent to him regularly to keep abreast with the invaluable intelligence coming out of Bletchley Park. He had also been sent a full appreciation that day of Moonlight Sonata and the Cold Water countermeasures. Showing his bulldog tenacity, Churchill ordered his car to turn round and headed back to London. If the capital was to be attacked – and he had assumed London was to be the target – then he would be there in the thick of it. More than that, he went to the roof of the Air Ministry to get a full view of the expected raid. But no such raid on London occurred. Probably the best-informed person in England that day was Professor Jones, who had a simple answer to the story of the Coventry raid in which Churchill is said to have been presented with the dilemma of evacuating Coventry because of prior knowledge of the raid, or of doing nothing and so preserving the security of Enigma. He commented:

To the best of my knowledge, this is not true ...[x]

Indeed, Professor Jones says he has no recollection of Coventry being mentioned in an Enigma message 'in the way that some accounts have stated', adding that the teleprinter room which brought the messages was immediately across the corridor from his own office. Had any message mentioning Coventry come through, he would have been informed. He has emphasised that, as for any argument as to whether or not Coventry might have been forewarned, he knew nothing of it.

However, there is one totally contradictory story about that day, provided by Group Captain Frederick Winterbotham, of the Secret Intelligence Service, and Churchill's liaison with Bletchley Park. It was Winterbotham's book The *Ultra Secret* that first publicly revealed that the German Enigma machine had been mastered, supplying Ultra intelligence. He claims that the word 'Coventry' was spelled out in an Enigma message. In this he was wrong, although the codename for Coventry – KORN – was revealed, but not understood at the time. Churchill, he said, would have to take a decision. Winterbotham said he had asked Churchill's personal secretary if he would ring him back when the decision had been taken, because if the Prime Minister decided to evacuate Coventry, the press, and indeed everybody, would know there had been pre-knowledge of the raid 'and some counter-measure might be necessary to protect the source which would obviously become suspect'. Moreover, he reasoned, there could be absolute chaos if everyone tried to get out of the city in the few hours available. If, subsequently, the raid was postponed for some reason, such as bad weather, then the whole Ultra secret would have been put at risk for no reason. Further, Winterbotham argued, the RAF had ample time to put counter-measures into operation, which the evidence of both Professor Jones shows to have been an erroneous assumption. However, Winterbotham says that there was time to alert the fire and ambulance services, police and wardens and to be ready to light decoy fires. Winterbotham is wrong about the two days' notice of the raid. Ultra had revealed two days' advance notice of *a* raid, but the target was unknown until 1500 on the day of the attack. Moreover, Winterbotham's version of Churchill's knowledge of events is contradicted by Sir David Hunt, the Prime Minister's private secretary at the time.

Aileen Clayton also recalls that both Kingsdown and Cheadle started hearing the KG100 messages from the pilots. In an attack on the Cherbourg transmitter, two of the Knickebein transmitters were put out of action. She remembers an instruction being given to the X–Gerät station at Cherbourg to switch to another target, but the reply came that it was unserviceable, but was aware that Birmingham and other towns had been given as alternative targets.

There were 509 aircraft on the raid of which 449 reached their target, only one of which was destroyed. The Nazis boasted afterwards that England would be 'Coventryised'. They dropped 56 tons of incendiaries, 394 tons of high explosives and 127 land mines, which killed 554 people, seriously injured 865 and destroyed 50,000 houses as well as the fourteenth-century St Michael's Cathedral. The ancient and historic cathedral has been preserved as a bombed ruin, and today stands proudly as a memorial to the heroism of the people of Coventry following that dreadful night.

# Chapter 4

# 'Pinches' at Sea

Deciphering German naval Enigma was never easy, not least because their operators – particularly on the U-boats – maintained tight security on their transmissions. Their most secret transmissions, sent in the Offizier (Officers-only) cipher, were even more complex. For that and other reasons, the Bletchley Park codebreakers had concentrated on breaking German Air Force ciphers in the early part of the war. Luftwaffe operators were more careless and Bletchley Park had been reading their traffic for some time. In addition, in 1940, naval Enigma had been further complicated in that operators could now choose three wheels out of eight, whereas the Luftwaffe was using three out of five wheels. The four-wheel machines to be used by U-boats with the new cipher known as Shark that were to bedevil Bletchley Park were some distance away. To date, information had been obtained from some captured documents and information received from prisoners-of-war. But this was not sufficient – it was essential to take positive, direct action to obtain vital information. This would entail 'pinches', as they became known, deliberately targeting certain vessels – surface and U-boats – in order to seize their cipher material.

In addition, the capture of U-boats with their Enigma daily setting sheets would also be of vital importance. But the crucial element in 'pinches' and captures was that they would be virtually worthless if the enemy discovered that Enigma material was in the hands of the Allies. They would immediately change the keys, so it was vital that knowledge of captures should not be revealed – boasting about them on radio and in newspapers would be completely counter-productive. To this end, crews involved in such events were sworn to secrecy and the crews of captured U-boats – especially where the crews knew their boat had been taken or had not sunk until after being boarded – had to be kept isolated and not allow information to be sent back to Germany through Red

## TABLE OF ENIGMA 'PINCHES'

| Ship/ U-boat | Type of vessel | When/where boarded | Information recovered |
|---|---|---|---|
| U33 | VIIA | 12.2.40 Clyde Estuary | Three Enigma wheels |
| U49 | VIIB | 15.4.40 Vaagsfjord, Norway | Chart showing U-boat dispositions in North Sea |
| VP2623 | Patrol boat | 26.4.40 Between Germany and Narvik | Looted. Some papers recovered including cipher settings. |
| Krebs | Armed trawler | 4.3.41 Lofoten Islands, Norway | Material to enable reading of traffic for March 1941 |
| München | Weather ship | 7.5.41 North Atlantic | Material enabling traffic for June 1941 to be read. |
| U110 | IXB | 9.5.41 South of Iceland | Offizier settings found; short-signal (Kurzsignale) sighting report code book recovered. |
| Lauenburg | Weather ship | 28.6.41 North Atlantic | Material enabling traffic for July 1941 to be read. |
| U559 | VIIC | 30.10.42 NE of Port Said | Code book taken to help break Shark keys. |
| U505 | IXC | 4.6.44 W of Cape Blanco | Enigma machine captured by Americans. |
| U250 | VIIC | 30.7.44 Gulf of Finland | Enigma machine and codes captured by Russians. |
| U1024 | VIIC/41 | 13.4.45 Irish Sea | Various Enigma material. Zaunkönig acoustic torpedoes found on board. |

Cross letters, although the U-boat men did have a means of sending code this way. This chapter lists the main 'pinches' and captures involving Enigma, but other boats were boarded and may have revealed some information of use to the codebreakers.

### U33 (12 February 1940)

The first British capture of Enigma wheels occurred when U33, which had left Wilhelmshaven commanded by one of the German navy's most experienced officers, Kapitänleutnant Hans-Wilhelm von Dresky, intended to mine the naval base at the Firth of Clyde – a venture that had already failed when attempted by U32 (Kapitänleutnant Hans Jenisch). The minesweeper *Gleaner* (Lieutenant Commander H Price) was on patrol off the southern tip of the Isle of Arran in the outer reaches of the Clyde estuary, and, detecting the U-boat by hydrophone, began dropping depth charges. Von Dresky believed he was being attacked by a destroyer and ordered the crew to abandon ship, distributing Enigma wheels among the officers with orders to ensure they were thrown into the sea. The U-boat surfaced, and *Gleaner* was about to ram when the crew appeared on deck and jumped into the sea as the U33 was scuttled. The U-boat sank, and a rescue operation to save the crew was launched by *Gleaner* (which had itself been damaged during the depth-charging). Along with other ships, seventeen of the forty-two crew, including three officers, survived. It was several days before an attempt was made to try and salvage any contents from the boat, although Enigma wheels were discovered on the bodies of dead sailors found floating on the surface. It has subsequently been questioned why U33 was carrying an Enigma machine, which was banned for security reasons when U-boats were minelaying close inshore. Doenitz knew at once, through his codebreaking organisation the B-Dienst – who had intercepted three signals from *Gleaner* – that U-33 was lost and the minelaying at the Firth of Clyde had failed for the second time.

> The first was an alarm at 0525, reporting U-33 to be on the surface; the second, at 0530, was a notice stating that the U-33 crew was surrendering; and the third, at 0545, was a request for assistance in rescuing the crew.[xi]

Following the loss of U33, naval supremo Grand Admiral Erich Raeder reported to Hitler that such operations were too dangerous and should not be continued.

### U49 (15 April 1940)

The first British expeditionary force to help the Norwegians following Hitler's attack on their country, Convoy NP1, left the Clyde in three liners on 11 April 1940, and the troops were originally to be landed at Narvik. On 14 April two troopships were detached from the convoy with a brigade of troops for Namsos, about 100 miles north of Trondheim, where operations were already being mounted. The remainder arrived at their destination, but before the convoy entered the harbour, U-boats had been detected and the destroyers *Fearless* (Commander K Harkness) and *Brazen* (Lieutenant Commander M Culme-Seymour) went to hunt them. As a result U49 (Kapitänleutnant Curt von Gossler) was sunk near Narvik, with the loss of one crew member, the other forty-one surviving, and documents recovered. These documents revealed that Germany had entered the war with fifty-seven U-boats. Naval Intelligence, with fifty-seven as the starting figure, plus an estimated thirty-eight boats completed between 3 September 1939 – the day war was declared – and July 1940, reached a total of ninety-five boats completed, as against the actual number of seventy-nine.

Jak P Mallmann Showell, a highly respected authority on the U-boat war, has cast doubt on the value of what was found on U49. He says that a sack or kit bag washed ashore was said to contain U-boat clothing with rank badges, and a diary found in one of the pockets was supposed to have been sent to the police in Harstad. He adds:

> It is possible that this sack or kit bag gave rise to the secret papers story, or some documents might have been salvaged but it seems highly likely that whatever fell into Allied hands made only a minor, immediate contribution to the intelligence war.[xii]

What does seem clear is that U49 did not reveal any Enigma information – keys or codebooks – but the broad information about the numbers and disposition of U-boats would, nevertheless, have been of considerable tactical use at the time.

### Patrol Boat *VP 2623* (26 April 1940)

The capture of a converted trawler, the patrol boat (*Vorpostenboot*) *VP 2623* on passage from Germany to Narvik, had been a major breakthrough, giving the codebreakers the golden opportunity in May 1940 to read Enigma naval messages for six days in April. However, a bitter lesson was learned from this capture – the boat had been looted before a detailed search could be carried out, so the Admiralty took urgent steps to see this did not happen again. What Bletchley Park now knew – and it would 'simplify' breaking naval ciphers – was that the German navy, whatever the type of vessel, only used two Enigma keys: Home and Foreign. However, the Foreign key was rarely used, being restricted to operations in far-flung waters, and was never broken.

**Armed Trawler *Krebs* (4 March 1941)**

There was a stroke of luck when the armed trawler *Krebs* was abandoned by its crew shortly before the British raid on the Lofoten Islands off Norway (4 March 1941), enabling the codebreakers to read the traffic for that month. This was followed up by being able to read the traffic for April and much of May. Spare rotors for the cipher machine were discovered, but not the machine or any other material, which had been thrown overboard. But a vital piece of information had now fallen into the laps of the codebreakers – that weather ships, stationed in remote areas of the Atlantic, also carried Enigma machines. The scene was now set for 'pinches' involving the weather ships. These vessels were the main suppliers of weather reports, although U-boats provided daily information and tankers and supply ships would do so when requested. In addition, weather ships also reported sightings of Allied vessels. The weather ships usually remained at sea for at least a month. As well as transmitting in the Home Waters key, they also signalled in the weather cipher (Wetterkurzschlüssel) and some the short signal book, which was extensively used by raiders and supply ships.

**Weather Ship *München* (7 May 1941)**

One of the most important discoveries early in the war was that the Germans were stationing weather ships in two areas – north of Iceland and in mid-Atlantic – and that they carried the naval Enigma. In its report on the German weather-reporting ships, Bletchley Park came to the following conclusions:

> The seizure of one of these ships, if practicable, would:
>
> (1) deprive the enemy of valuable weather reports for a considerable period;
>
> (2) remove a potential source of information concerning our fleet and shipping movements;

(3) offer an opportunity for obtaining ciphers including the Short Signal book (extensively used by German raiders and supply ships) in the case of those ships in mid-Atlantic, as well as

(4) do something to remove German confidence in their ability to sail infested seas.

With this knowledge, the Admiralty decided to seize the initiative and try to capture the weather ships and their Enigma machines and code books. On 7 May 1941, the weather ship *München* was the first victim of a 'pinch' and produced vital information that enabled the codebreakers to read the traffic for June 1941 concurrently.

## U 110 (9 May 1941)

Hardly had the information from *München* been taken off the weather ship when, on 9 May 1941, the Offizier settings and the special short-signal sighting reports, known as the Kurzsignale, were captured. Commanded by Kapitänleutnant Fritz-Julius Lemp, holder of the Ritterkreuz – the Knight's Cross – awarded for sinking 100,000 tons of shipping, U110 was one of the new Type IXB boats. Lemp had achieved notoriety within hours of war being declared when, as commander of U30, he had sunk the passenger liner *Athenia*, 13,850 tons, of the Donaldson line. Bound for Canada, the liner carried 1,103 passengers including women and children and 311 Americans. Fortunately, the death toll was much less than it might have been – 118 dead, including 28 Americans. It was the first U-boat attack of the war, thus opening the Battle of the Atlantic, the longest continuous struggle of the war that was not to end until Germany's surrender in May 1945. Many of the forty-seven crew of U110 had considerable experience, having served with Lemp on the U30, and nineteen U-boats sailed to the North Atlantic in May, and found outbound convoy OB318, comprised of forty ships. U110, sailing from the main German U-boat base at Lorient in south-west France, was on its second patrol. Lemp sank two freighters from the convoy, the 5,000-ton *Esmond* and the 2,600-ton *Bengore Head*. The convoy was guarded for the middle stretch of the voyage by nine warships from the Iceland-based Escort Group 3 – three destroyers, three corvettes and three armed trawlers plus an armed merchant cruiser – led by Commander Joe Baker-Cresswell in his flagship, the destroyer *Bulldog*. Sonar contact had been made on Lemp's boat off the coast of Greenland, and the U-boat fired its first torpedoes just before noon. The corvette *Aubretia* (Lieutenant Commander V Smith) was guarding the flank from which the U-boat attacks were coming. *Aubretia* dropped depth charges despite problems with her Asdic detection gear. Damaged extensively, the boat surfaced and was attacked by *Bulldog*, *Aubretia* and the former US destroyer *Broadway*. Depth charges severely damaged the U-boat, which was flooding aft and slid stern first to 300 feet. Giving the order to surface, before it could be carried out there was a rocking motion, which indicated that the U-boat had surfaced of its own accord. On the bridge, Lemp had the horrifying spectacle of *Bulldog*, *Broadway* and *Aubretia* all firing at him, with *Bulldog* and *Broadway* coming in fast to ram.

Lemp quickly summed up the hopeless situation and gave the order to abandon the boat. As a result there was insufficient time to set the scuttling charges so he gave the order to open the ballast tank vents, which should have ensured that the boat sank quickly, but somehow the vents failed to open. Meanwhile, the crew were seeking to clamber up the conning tower. The Germans were convinced the boat was sinking, but as Baker-Cresswell prepared to ram U110, he noted that, as the crew were jumping overboard, the U-boat did not appear to be going down. Lemp, who was in the water, had also noted the U-boat still afloat. Lemp is said to have shouted to a couple of colleagues to swim back to the boat and was shot by the boarding party. Other reports say he just drowned in the icy water.

Baker-Cresswell took a quick decision to send a boarding party of nine in a whaler to the stricken U-boat, led by Sub-Lieutenant David Balme, who thought the boat could be towed. Baker-Cresswell therefore decided to try and tow her to Iceland, some 400 miles away, and an engineering party went aboard from *Broadway*, which had suffered damage when coming alongside U110. However, it was essential that the Germans who had been taken on board *Aubretia* had no knowledge that the U-boat had been boarded intact. *Aubretia* had also taken the rescued crew of the *Esmond* on board. The boarding party were on the U-boat for several hours, and subsequently the intelligence haul filled two packing cases and included the keys for Heimisch, known at Bletchley Park as Dolphin – the Home Waters code – as well as the much more complicated Offizier (Officers-only) code, the Kurzsignale (short-signal) code and an Enigma machine. This enabled Bletchley Park to read these particular keys for the first time. The towing went well until the following morning, when she suddenly sank by the stern. Lemp and fourteen crew died, but thirty-two were saved.

But the need to keep secret the boarding of U110 was not to end with the boat's sinking. German naval officers who were prisoners-of-war used a code, originating from the First World War, to communicate back to Germany special information in letters via their families. But the British authorities were wise to the code. One officer who survived the U110 sinking, Oberleutnant-zu-See Dietrich Loewe, the First Watch Officer, was suspicious. Loewe's letters with the code were confiscated, and when he went to Canada as a prisoner-of-war, he was deliberately allowed to meet two other crew members, and eventually he was convinced the U-boat had not been boarded. At that point Loewe was repatriated to Germany in an exchange arrangement, which enabled him to report that the U110's secrets had gone to a watery grave. According to Patrick Beesly, who worked in the Admiralty's Operational Intelligence Centre, which received Bletchley Park decrypts direct by teleprinter:

> The tremendous importance of this capture cannot be over-emphasised, for U110's cipher material was valid at least until the end of June and permitted BP to start reading cipher Hydra currently and on a completely up-to-date basis.[xiii]

Hydra was the cipher used by German surface ships in the Baltic and North Sea and for ships operating from or off the occupied territories. As such it was used for minesweepers, as well as anti-submarine and patrol craft in Norway and France. At first it was also used by operational U-boats. So sensitive was the intelligence captured on U110 that the crews of *Bulldog*, *Broadway* and *Aubretia* were sworn to secrecy, and the truth of what happened was not revealed publicly until released by the Admiralty when the official naval historian of the Second World War, Captain Stephen Roskill, published it in a book, *The Secret Capture*.

### Weather Ship *Lauenburg* (28 June 1941)

Following the successes with *München* and U110, the timing of the next 'pinch' from a weather ship, *Lauenburg* (344 tons), was carefully chosen just before the new settings for the following month came into operation. The ship was boarded by a landing party from the destroyer *Tartar* (T Hugh P Wilson), enabling the traffic for July to be read.

*Lauenburg* had left Trondheim on the night of 27–28 May to take over from *Sachsen*, and evidence of the latter's patrol suggested that *Lauenburg* intended to be out until after the end of June.

Patrick Beesly of the Admiralty's Operational Intelligence Centre, which received Enigma decrypts, recalled that while the Enigma machine had been disposed of, ancillary material relating to the settings of the cipher used by the trawlers was secured. Despite the value of the information from *München*, it was not enough, and another operation was planned to catch the second trawler. On 25 June, cruisers and destroyers, again carrying an OIC/Bletchley Park specialist, as had also been the case with the *München*, Lieutenant Allan Bacon RNVR, surprised and captured the *Lauenberg* with documents and cipher material which the Admiralty subsequently described as being of 'inestimable value'. There was, nevertheless, an overriding factor that went in to all of Bletchley Park's thinking – the absolute essential of maintaining the utmost secrecy over the fact that they were reading Enigma messages. To keep capturing vessels would inevitably lead the Germans to the conclusion that their cipher machine was compromised. Therefore, after June 1941, no further deliberate 'pinches' were undertaken. By the end of June, Bletchley Park had six bombes, one of which was permanently available for work on the naval ciphers. As a result, after the first week of August, Bletchley Park was able to decipher all but two days of the Home Waters traffic down to the end of the war, and most of this traffic was read within thirty-six hours.

**U559 (30 October 1942)**
One of the blackest days in the war for Bletchley Park came on 1 February 1942 when the U-boat fleet started using a fourth wheel to the Enigma machine. Bletchley Park – and with it the Admiralty's anti-submarine tracking service of the Operational Intelligence Centre – went blind. This new cipher was known as Triton by the Germans and was codenamed Shark at Bletchley Park. No longer could U-boats be tracked on their way to attack the convoys bringing vital supplies to Britain from the United States and Canada. For nine months Bletchley Park struggled in vain against Shark, and the U-boats were now operating in larger numbers and sinking high levels of tonnage. But fate was to take a dramatic turn in the codebreakers' favour.

On 29 September 1942, U559 (Kapitänleutnant Hans Heidtmann) sailed from Messina in Sicily. A month later, on 30 October, a

Sunderland crew on routine reconnaissance believed they had detected something in the Mediterranean near Port Said, close to the main British naval base at Alexandria. Ships were despatched to the area to continue the search, including the destroyer *Petard*. After prolonged depth-charging and a hunt lasting more than twelve hours, U559 was forced to the surface and the order given to abandon the boat. Seven of the crew lost their lives and thirty-eight survived. Just before 2300 hours the U-boat broke surface and was immediately fired on by *Petard*. However, as in the case of U110, the *Petard* captain, Lieutenant Commander Mark Thornton, thought a boarding party was possible. A whaler was launched, but three of the crew, Lieutenant Antony Fasson, Able Seaman Colin Grazier and canteen assistant Tommy Brown, swam to the U-boat. Fasson and Grazier began collecting items and handing them up to Brown when the boat began to sink. He warned the two men, but they continued the search. Eventually they, too, realised the danger, but water poured down the open hatch before they could escape, and they both went down with the boat. Fasson and Grazier were awarded a posthumous George Cross each and Brown received the George Medal – the Victoria Cross could not be awarded as their efforts had not been under fire. But Fasson and Grazier had not died in vain. The haul of Enigma information was incredible and enabled Bletchley Park to break into Shark after nine months in the dark, decrypting settings with some regularity from 13 December 1942 until early March 1943. Shark was also invaluable in tracking down blockade-runners heading for Biscay from the Far East.

## U505 (4 June 1944)

The capture, by the United States Navy, of U505 (Oberleutnant Harald Lange) did not yield a great deal of extra information for the codebreakers when a boarding party from the destroyer *Pillsbury* boarded her near Cape Blanco off the west coast of Africa two days before the D-Day landings in Normandy. A hunter-killer group comprising the aircraft carrier *Guadalcanal* and five destroyers had sailed from the US naval base at Norfolk, Virginia to hunt for U-boats south of the Canary Islands, where they were known to refuel. On the morning of 4 June, the destroyer *Chatelain* made a sonar contact, believed to be a submarine. The US hunter-killer group began to hunt U505, and were aided by aircraft from *Guadalcanal* that had spotted the submarine at periscope depth and it was forced to the surface. After its capture it was taken to the US. One crew member died and fifty-nine survived.

A boarding party recovered an Enigma machine and code books. But here lay the dilemma: on the eve of D-Day, if the Germans discovered that one of their U-boats had been captured, they would automatically assume code books and an Enigma machine could have been found and might change U-boat security. It was imperative that the capture of U505 should remain secret. Special precautions were taken to avoid German suspicions that her ciphers had been compromised. The boat's crew were kept in strict isolation, but one of her officers managed to pass a message back to Germany that her signal and cipher equipment had been captured. This led U-Boat Command to conclude that this was why, in the summer of 1944, Allied forces had 'contrived to turn up at pre-arranged rendezvous times with the same punctuality as the U-boat themselves'.

However, this had little influence on the Kriegsmarine's programme for improved cipher security, which was well advanced by the time it was received. Instead of heading for Dakar and Casablanca, where German agents were known to be active, the decision was taken to take the U-boat on the long voyage to Bermuda, where they arrived at Port Royal on 19 June, seven days after the destroyer *Jenks* had safely handed the Enigma material in at the same destination. For the Americans, it turned out to be quite an event – the first foreign war vessel to be captured by the US navy since 1815. The U505 eventually ended up as an exhibit at the Chicago Museum of Science and Industry. The secret intelligence hoard included the Atlantic and Indian Ocean U-boat cipher for June 1944, the current grid chart cipher, the reserve short weather cipher and bigram tables and the current short weather cipher. Documents also referred to a short signal procedure called Kurier (codenamed Squash by the Allies), which indicated that U-boats might be changing to a new means of sending short signals. Kurier used special communication apparatus and a sufficient number of transmissions were obtained by mid-December 1944 to enable the codebreakers to take counter-measures. However, Kurier never became operational.

## U250 (30 July 1944)

The sinking and raising of this U-boat from the Gulf of Finland in the Baltic Sea was carried out by the Russians in a remarkable operation, after it had been attacked by two Soviet motor patrol boats, suffering direct hits. Half a dozen of the crew, who were in the central control room, including its commander, Kapitänleutnant Werner-Karl Schmidt, were able to get to safety, but forty-six perished. Obtaining no worthwhile information from the Germans, the Russians decided to try and recover the U-boat under the guns of the Finnish batteries – Finland being an ally of Germany. In addition, the German navy had both depth-charged the U-boat and placed mines around it. The boat was upright and the Russians managed to get hawsers underneath and lift it to the surface, successfully bringing it to the naval base at Kronstadt. Despite the damage to the boat, an Enigma machine and code books were found along with vital information about the acoustic torpedo known as the Zaunkönig. The Admiralty was keen to inspect these torpedoes, but naval experts sent to Kronstadt were refused permission by the Soviet authorities to see them close-up.

### U1024 (13 April 1945)

The last U-boat to be captured that was to reveal Enigma information was U1024, in an incident that occurred as the conflict drew to a close. U1024 (Kapitänleutnant Hans-Joachim Gutteck) left for its only wartime operation from its Norwegian base in March 1945, heading for the Irish Sea. Forced to surface after being depth-charged south of the Isle of Man, the U-boat was fired on by the frigate *Loch Glendhu* (Lieutenant Commander E Knapton), but the crew were in no position to fight back. Eight crew lost their lives and thirty-seven survived. An attempt to tow the boat to port failed and she sank while underway. A boarding party from the frigate *Loch More* (Lieutenant Commander R Cambridge) retrieved Enigma secrets, but with the war approaching its end, this haul was of little operational use to Bletchley Park.

# Chapter 5

# Let Battle Commence

W hen the war began, Bletchley Park had to organise from scratch, and its eventual development would be on a scale never before known – surpassing by far the outstanding First World War codebreaking operation of the Admiralty's Room 40 Old Building successes. However, several Room 40 veterans were to play major roles at Bletchley Park, including director Alastair Denniston, the eccentric Greek scholar Dilly Knox and sometime thespian Frank Birch among them. This 'blank sheet of paper' approach led to Bletchley Park setting up a unique organisation to sift the enciphered Enigma messages, break their secret contents and disguise their origin before feeding the information to those senior military commanders in the field who had been 'indoctrinated' (i.e. were in the know) into the Ultra secret. Bletchley Park's Hut 3 was given the task of handling intelligence involving the German Army, Air Force and Mediterranean naval traffic. A smoothly run system was essential, and one of Hut 3's great successes was the high level of inter-Service co-operation at a time when all three armed Services had separate ministries – there was no overall Ministry of Defence. The path of intelligence work does not always run smoothly, and relations between Hut 3 and its codebreaking partner, Hut 6, could be difficult, so a liaison officer was appointed in Hut 3 to handle priority issues between the two huts.

The primitive conditions in Hut 3 were described by Ralph Bennett, a Cambridge historian who went to Bletchley Park in 1941. He says it was a ramshackle wooden building and its atmosphere was nauseating by night when the blackout trapped the fumes from the leaky coke-burning stoves. Peter Calvocoressi, who worked in Hut 3's German Air Section, talks of rooms running off a pokey, longitudinal corridor. Something like chaos reigned in the winter of 1941–1942 under a regime of divided control, but a complete reorganisation in the spring of 1942 restored welcome order. Intelligence was first handled in the central 'Watch' room where the Watch and advisers from the three Services worked round the clock. These three Sections checked and directed the work of the advisers, and took from them any overflow, maintained card indexes and other records, procured information from other sources and – crucially – co-ordinated liaison with government ministries and military Commands. Behind this trio was a general intelligence Section, divided into specialist sub-Sections. These looked at the longer-term and more complex issues, with the results being fed back to the more current Sections. Good communications with government departments was essential and meant factual reporting of German signals in translation, plus any notes.

For military Commands, the direct service of signals from Hut 3 to them had two crucial factors. Firstly, satisfactory signals demanded constant and skilled reference to German originals. Secondly, instead of going first to ministries, it was time-saving to signal intelligence direct to Commands as soon as Hut 3 had the information. Under the most favourable conditions, the time of origin of the English signal was often only four to four and a half hours later than the time of the original German signal, and could be less. There was an additional one and a half to one and three-quarter hours for encoding, transmission, decoding and delivery of the Hut 3 signal to intelligence staffs. The decrypted messages went through fifteen major processes in those six hours, an average of twenty-four minutes for each process. One great friend of Hut 3 was the Luftwaffe liaison officer with the German Army, the Fliegerverbindungsoffizier or Flivo, based at Army HQ, who was usually extremely careless when re-enciphering in a Luftwaffe key (which Bletchley Park was reading) an Army key (which Bletchley Park was probably not reading), thus allowing a break into the Army key.

Hut 3 was effectively the sole responsible authority for transmitting its intelligence to Commands, and its first great operational test came with the German invasion of Norway in April 1940. Here, the ciphers broken were almost exclusively German Air Force. Indeed, so successful was Hut 3 at disguising their source, that ministries were reluctant to take its intelligence seriously. In a revolutionary innovation, the sifting and sorting of messages was carried out by Hut 3 on the spot, thus making it the judge not only of the intelligence value of messages, but also of the urgency of a message. These fell into four categories and became known as Piles 1, 2 and 3 and Quatsch – the last being the name given to the 'nonsense' pile. Procedure was also radically altered at this time, which was maintained for the remainder of the war. This is how the system worked:

1. Breaking of the key for a particular day by Hut 6.
2. Passed in batches to Hut 3, with the most urgent messages deciphered first.
3. Skimming for urgent intelligence by the No1 of the Watch, who read decodes unemended and decided quickly into which pile they should go. While there was material in Pile 1, nobody touched Pile 2, etc.
4. At the end of his turn of duty, the No 1 collected and edited all that his Watch had turned out. The chits were then passed, both those teleprinted and those not, to typists.
5. Only after decodes had been dealt with or rejected as containing no intelligence were they passed to the German Book Room typists.
6. Finally, the German Books were again looked at to ensure nothing had been missed to enable compilation of a full card index.

The Norwegian campaign saw the beginning of the long-term intelligence that was one of Hut 3's outstanding achievements. The Germans also introduced the key in Norway known as Yellow at Bletchley Park, which was quickly broken, sometimes in under an hour. The traffic was considerable, but underlined the point that where the enemy has overwhelming force, intelligence is not much use.

The invasion of France on 10 May 1940 saw the introduction of the Luftwaffe machine key known at Bletchley Park as 'Red'. This key was broken ten days later and remained Hut 3's chief standby for the rest of the war. It was the principle single source of Ultra intelligence for German Air matters, and because of the close liaison between the Luftwaffe and the Army and Navy, for those Services as well. The war so far had been 'one key' campaigns – 'Yellow' in Norway and 'Red' in France. But soon after the Battle of France the splitting and multiplying of keys took place and were to become characteristic of the later years of the war. This multiplication of keys began with 'Brown' – the Luftwaffe key for special navigational beam units in the late summer of 1940 connected with the night raids on London and other industrial centres.

A major task of Hut 3 came after the breaking of 'Fish' – non-Morse wireless teleprinter German High Command traffic – which provided more work, but did not present problems fundamentally different from Enigma. Detail was everything. No scrap of information was too small. For example, even aircraft markings or a works number in a decrypt were recorded, enabling a picture to be built up of German aircraft production, type by type. It could also be very depressing work. About forty per cent of all decrypts were useless as intelligence, and a few more German linguists in Hut 3 would have eradicated much of this problem. This language issue raised another important problem late in the war: the need to keep an eye on the Russians. It was believed that there was no more than one Russian scholar for every fifty German scholars, because Russian was a very difficult language.

Hut 3 was divided into a number of Sections. The Military Section began in February 1940 as a one-man band with an officer who was expert in both the German Army and military intelligence, and eventually grew to a fifty-strong outfit. Unlike Air Section, which was seen by Air Ministry as its most important source, Military Section did not establish its reputation with the War Office until the North African campaign. In early summer 1942, German Army keys began to be broken regularly, and military intelligence in Ultra was no longer principally acquired through Air Force sources, and the scope of military advisers increased considerably. From now on, military intelligence was to disclose how the enemy was thinking, and to produce a regular flow of appreciations at strategic level. In the North African campaign, for example, every German formation and unit was known and placed, and the enemy could not bring in reinforcements without Bletchley Park knowing about it. After El Alamein, Ultra was most valuable in the planning periods between battles rather than during the actual fighting.

As the scope of Ultra increased, the military advisers found themselves dealing with wider issues such as V-weapons and political matters. They also needed to be briefed on German military intelligence, the general strategic picture, and on Allied intentions and Order of Battle so as to be able to judge the importance and urgency of decrypts. In September 1943, an adviser was appointed to handle SS Ultra traffic. He was also responsible for liaison with Bletchley Park's German Police Section.

One key area of liaison was between military Section and Traffic Analysis (TA), also known as Sixta, formerly No 6 Intelligence School.

A key essential of TA was to present intelligence with evidence rather than definite conclusions. TA had to be in the know on the general intelligence picture as it often produced intelligence independent of decodes. Another important role was that of the military adviser, who had to signal what the Germans said, and not what they thought the Germans meant to say. The military adviser had to convey in his signal to what extent the emender – whose job it was to handle errors and corruptions in the message – had needed to reconstruct the German. Keeping up to date was a major problem for military advisers, and when they came on shift it could take them at least an hour to read through the two bundles of teleprints and signals handled by the previous shift.

Indexing was one of the great achievements of Bletchley Park, and was a major function of Hut 3 – its output was priceless. It was primarily a record of military information from Ultra sources. Later it was supplemented by information from other Bletchley Park Sections, and by non-Ultra sources such as prisoner-of-war reports. During the greater part of its existence the index was understaffed because, while trying to recruit and train staff, an enormous amount of material was constantly coming in. The crucial point was reached in the North African campaign when detailed information was coming in on transport and supply, the British Order of Battle from German intercept sources and reports from British HQ in the field. It was not possible to increase staff at this time because they were working in a room 30ft x 10ft, which also contained the battle maps. As such, the scope of the index was being adjusted to the capacity of the available staff. Mistakes, often very simple typing errors, could not be avoided, but had to be spotted. One classic was when a message giving the German Army HQ in North Africa as at Cape Bon and not Bizerta, where they were expected to make their last stand. Thankfully, the error was discovered by an eagle-eyed member of the Index.

Knowledge of enemy supplies was also crucial. A visit by Bletchley Park to Mediterranean Commands in November 1943 revealed the great importance attached by military commanders to enemy supplies, and a specialist Section to handle this information was formed in Hut 3 early in 1944. Intelligence supplied about traffic on railways was crucial and fell into two sections. Firstly, items of primary Order of Battle interest, usually in loading timetables. Here, Hut 3 broke the consignment number and the location code systems. Secondly, information came through railway day returns, outlining details of air raid damage to bridges and tracks, and estimates of repair times. The most valuable information on supplies, however, came from the Chief Quartermaster's supply returns, and anything up to an hour was required to service and signal a single document.

Deception was also crucial. Deceiving the enemy as to Allied intentions was being carried out by a highly secret group known as 'A' Force. The discovery of the importance of this shadowy group by Bletchley Park was probably the most striking example of the value of liaison visits to Commands by Hut 3 when they went to the Mediterranean in November 1943. Quite by accident they discovered the existence of 'A' Force when they met the officer in charge of this unit. 'A' Force was almost entirely dependent on Ultra for discovering German reactions, but had no idea of the wider areas in which Bletchley Park could help. For example, success in tactical deception depended largely on knowing in advance enemy appreciation of the Allied Order of Battle, and this came to Bletchley Park from the German intercept service.

Air Section also played a vital role in Hut 3. The most important task of advisers was signals to Command. The fundamentals of signal drafting were threefold: selection, clarity and brevity – in that order. Provision of comments by advisers was also of great importance, providing information to enable Commands and ministries to complete the picture. All comment was preceded by the word 'Comment' and bracketed off from the rest. Another key job of advisers was routeing – who should receive the message. In the closing stages of the war there were up to forty-nine possible recipients of a message. Overseas visits were important, and during the Ardennes offensive in December 1944, an air adviser was sent out to help the American IX Tactical Air Command.

Every detail of the text, however small, had to be indexed and cross-indexed. After three years there were 2,300 cards for one Luftwaffe Command alone. There were also two special indexes for locations and strengths, and from D-Day the number of indexers fluctuated between thirty-five and forty-five. Hut 3 obtained a complete picture of the organisation of the German Air Ministry and GAF ground organisations. One breakthrough involved German fighter pilot training, obtained when a string of figures were decoded which, after tabulation, turned out to be strength returns, providing very accurate figures of pilot numbers.

Hut 3 also dealt with the German Navy in the Mediterranean. Hut

3's Naval Section began with a two-man band just before the naval Mediterranean key known as Light Blue began providing information on sea transportation of German forces in Libya. Then the Italian naval key was broken, and such was the volume of traffic that a direct service was provided to Alexandria. Later the German submarine key Turtle was broken, but not as regularly as the other naval keys, but it did yield good quality intelligence. At its peak, Naval Section had fifteen staff, and significantly, seven of these were indexers. The backbone of the naval index was the ship cards, detailing every scrap of information about a vessel. In August 1942, the naval Mediterranean key known as Porpoise became available, and until the collapse of Italy in 1943, enabled information to come from several sources – the Italian and German navies, the Luftwaffe and the German Army, and so, before El Alamein until Italy's collapse, the enemy supply situation could be followed in considerable detail.

Early in 1944 a new problem arose for Naval Section – the formation of the German Small Battle Units – the Kommando der Kleinkampfverbaende or KdK, originally operated by German military intelligence, the Abwehr, but later taken over by the navy. They carried out sabotage and other undercover work, very similar to the British Special Boat Squadron, and were active right to the end of the war, and even then they were conducting a dozen operations at the same time for sabotage and landing of agents. The KdK introduced a cipher known as Bonito to communicate with its subordinate units and this, too, was quickly broken. Then they introduced another key – Bounce – used among its subordinate units, which involved liaison between the special Hut 3 naval unit monitoring the KdK and that looking at Abwehr traffic, as this was the only way a full understanding could be made of the KdK messages.

One key area for indexers was hydrographic intelligence – gathering information on enemy mining operations, swept ways and routes. Discovering the cover names for these operations was a major task. As the Allies progressed in the Mediterranean, Naval Section was reading new keys – Bloater for the Adriatic and Catfish for the Aegean. Much later another cipher, Trumpeter, a High Command key in the south-eastern area, was broken fairly regularly.

One crucial development of Hut 3 occurred in March 1942 with the appointment of duty officers to provide a co-ordinating authority to take a broader perspective. Nothing could be teleprinted to Service ministries or signalled to Commands in the field without their approval. The decision in March 1941 to institute sending signals to Commands overseas led to new techniques of selecting messages for signalling, or wording signals clearly and of assessing their priorities. This revolutionary change of sending signals direct overseas began after Rommel landed in Tripoli in March 1942, when Hut 3 was empowered to send signals direct to General Archibald Wavell, Commander-in-Chief, Middle East, in Cairo. However, not everything went smoothly. There was frustration among duty officers, for example, when they thought General Montgomery was making unnecessarily slow progress against Rommel in North Africa, despite Ultra telling him of the German commander's dire situation. There was similar criticism of the American General George Patton over the Anzio landings. On the other hand, among the best use of Ultra by generals was after Normandy when the Germans were trapped at Falaise. This brought out the best in Eisenhower, Patton and other generals in their handling of Ultra.

It was also essential to ensure that intelligence from Hut 3 was delivered accurately and promptly to Ultra recipients, and this went through a special signals Section. Interestingly, at the beginning of the war, preparations were also made for this Section to provide a wireless telegraphy (W/T) service to Home, Scottish and Northern Ireland Commands in the event of a German invasion. A teleprinter circuit was installed between Hut 3 and GHQ Home Forces but was, thankfully, never used.

The breaking of the Luftwaffe cipher known as Brown – which handled navigational systems – led to the formation of a teleprinter circuit from Hut 3 to 80 Wing RAF at Radlett in Hertfordshire, to provide Fighter Command with advance information on nightly Luftwaffe bombing targets. In March 1941, Hut 3 again signalled abroad to BAF Greece, the British Military Attaché in Belgrade, General Freyberg on Crete and to Cairo. This eventually led to the setting up of the Special Liaison Units (SLU) and Special Communications Units (SCU), which provided each Command with its own W/T and cipher units in the field, solely to handle Ultra traffic.

At times the enemy had to be fooled with dummy traffic. For instance, when it became clear the enemy would evacuate Tunisia, and the volume of high-grade German traffic would fall as a consequence, it was necessary to pass enough dummy traffic to keep up Hut 3's normal level, and it had to seem real. Again, in February 1945, dummy traffic became necessary to avoid the enemy realising the type of traffic being carried.

As to the British Typex cipher machines, one operator could handle a daily average of 1,500 groups on the machine or 1,000 groups on one-time pads. Handling included deciphering, typing, registering, checking and delivery. Staff numbers varied from three or four officers at a small pad-station handling 4,000 groups a day, to five officers and sixteen sergeants at a big Typex station handling over 30,000 groups a day. The SLU staff was diverse, and could comprise Royal Navy, Army, RAF, US Army, US Air Force, WRENS, ATS, WAAF, WAC and civilians. However, as it was physically impossible and undesirable to have SLU units on board ship, the Navy retained its own Ultra service to all naval units.

Another crucial part of the Hut 3 intelligence team was the German Book Room (or GBR), which conducted the typing of the emended German decodes. At the beginning, in the summer of 1940, the daily commitment averaged about 300 teile or parts of messages, each averaging 200–250 letters, with a staff of six, and by the beginning of 1942 there was fourteen staff. To this was later added the Fish non-Morse traffic, as well as Mediterranean naval intelligence, then the daily emending of aircraft movements. By the start of the North African campaign, the number of staff had increased to twenty, while the invasion of Italy and the handling of SS traffic led to further staff increases. Fish messages were a particular problem, as they were often very much longer than those involving Enigma, and could be divided into as many as twenty separate messages or paragraphs. The German Book Room also had a system for aircraft markings and movements as well as aircraft works numbers and aircraft engine works numbers. Interestingly, this type of work was thought to be best suited to twenty to thirty year olds with good typing and eyesight, sound German and a university background. It was thought the strain of this specialised typing for long hours was not suited to older people. A lot of overtime and even double shifts was involved.

On 1 September 1942, a special liaison Section was formed in Hut 3. Its role was liaison with cryptography and traffic analysis, working in close collaboration with the Service intelligence Sections, inter-Service and special investigations, detailed knowledge of the needs of Hut 3, representing intelligence, and timely knowledge of Allied intentions. In preparation for D-Day, a meeting of Hut 6 and Sixta was convened by

Liaison Section, and a reserve of fifty-six full-time and thirty-nine part-time wireless sets intercepting Enigma was established. At the end of 1944, the number of sets intercepting Enigma overseas was 130 compared with 500 in the UK. After D-Day, the output of decrypts was at a level of 2,000 teile a day and this amount of traffic continued until the end of 1944.

Hut 3 found that there was five or six times as much traffic available for study of Luftwaffe keys as Army keys. Between D-Day and March 1945 the bombe time needed to produce a given volume of decoded traffic was eight times as high for the Army as for the Air Force. The non-Morse Fish traffic was largely non-operational, with practically no tactical information. The bulk of the Fish traffic was routine reports on supplies, strength returns, tank returns and traffic situation reports. Producing Fish decodes was much slower than for Enigma, and only a small proportion of Fish reached Hut 3 within forty-eight hours of currency. In July 1944, about thirty distinct keys were broken daily. On Fish traffic, in early 1944 the intake was about 50 pages a day, each containing 720 letters – about three times as long as Enigma teile. This rose to ninety pages daily in summer 1944, to 120 pages that autumn, 200 in spring 1945, with 240 pages in March. On a letter-for-letter basis the total intake of Hut 3 during the war was Enigma eighty-six per cent, Fish eleven per cent and Nile (Mediterranean naval Enigma keys) and Nuts (all other naval Enigma keys) three per cent. In the first four months of 1945, when Enigma was relatively at its lowest, these proportions were Enigma 66 per cent, Fish 27.5 per cent and Nuts/Nile 6.5 per cent. The teleprinter call signs found at the head of Fish signals were indexed and finally totalled 3,600 cards, some with over 50 entries.

Yet another Hut 3 Section covered general intelligence and the first Enigma decodes for this Section were received huddled round a small, bleak wooden room with nothing but a table and three chairs on a snowy January morning in 1940. The Section's role was to serve the rest of Hut 3 by extracting from texts the last possible grain of meaning, and to service ministries and Commands. The original idea of this Section was that Bletchley Park had no business to do intelligence but merely break, decode and translate. It was even held in some quarters that far from producing intelligence, Bletchley Park should not even receive it. This attitude was overcome by producing intelligence that proved itself. They were often helped by the Germans, who were notorious for providing easy to work out cover names. For example, German cover names for English cities and towns obligingly began with the same letters, such as Bild for Birmingham and Liebe for Liverpool, Loge for London. The one they missed was the bombing raid on Coventry – the German code was Korn – as they spelt Coventry with a K. Another give-away was the parachute attack on Crete, which was codenamed Merkur (Mercurius), after the winged God Mercury. Another gift for Hut 3 was a Luftwaffe list of 72,000 five-letter groups based on the Rudolf Mosse codebook that had been published by the American Chamber of Commerce in Berlin before the war.

Each arm of the German forces had its own intercept service, and the study of Luftwaffe interception was closely studied by Hut 3 and was tied up with another cipher, Mustard. It was never broken in its entirety, although it gave a frightening picture of the insecurity of Russian Army and Air Force signals. Another security worry was the Americans. For example, an impressive list of leading US military personnel could be obtained by a subscription to *Stars and Stripes* magazine, while the US *Geographical Magazine* re-published a complete set of American divisional insignia!

Reference has been made to the extensive index. General Intelligence Section had to provide standard translations for all German Army and Air Force technical terms and a special Section was formed in October 1942, and by the end of the war, there were some 10,000 abbreviations and more than 16,000 equivalents. Indeed, no member of the German armed forces was acquainted with even a fraction of this huge vocabulary! This Section also looked after field post offices and railways dealing with transport organisation.

One of the most notable liaisons in Hut 3's history was between the Section led by Frederick Norman, Professor of German at King's College, London and Professor RV Jones, Assistant Director of Intelligence (Science), which led to vital information being provided about Hitler's secret weapons – the V1 or 'doodlebug' pilotless plane and the V2 rocket. This co-operation went right back to the autumn of 1939.

Not only had Hut 3 been successful in integrating the three Services with civilian personnel, but one of the great triumphs of Bletchley Park was how the Americans were successfully integrated into the system. The function of Hut 3's American unit was to see that Ultra was properly disseminated to the various US HQs authorised to receive it.

The Hut 3 US Section – known as 3US – grew out of a visit by American intelligence officers in April 1943. There were difficult and protracted negotiations on what part G2 – as American intelligence was known – and Arlington Hall, HQ of the US Army Signal Intelligence Service, should play with Ultra. Bletchley Park wanted to maintain a monopoly, while the Americans wanted to set up a separate establishment in Washington. There was suspicion on both sides. In May 1943 an arrangement was signed known as BRUSA – the British-United States Agreement – that provided for a complete interchange between the two countries. In August 1943, the first Ultra material was signalled to Washington. At its peak, 3US comprised sixty-eight people, of which nineteen were in Special Liaison Units in the field (which only handled Ultra traffic), twenty-four as specialists at Commands, three in London and twelve advisers in Hut 3. The remaining ten Americans were the 3US Section.

The Official History of Hut 3, looking at the first talks between Bletchley Park and the Americans, described the two sides as eyeing each other like two mongrels that had just met. The lack of confidence on both sides delayed the setting up of 3US. But relations within Bletchley Park were excellent. Lieutenant Colonel Telford Taylor, who headed the US Section, and later became a prosecutor at the Nuremburg War Crimes Trials, recorded the warmth and patience of Hut 3 personnel. It was this wartime co-operation between Bletchley Park and US signals intelligence that led to the close relationship between the two countries in this important field of information-gathering during the cold war and beyond to the present day co-operation between GCHQ and America's National Security Agency.

# Chapter 6

# Dead on Time

A New Zealand hero of the First World War, Lieutenant General Bernard Freyberg VC, who had recently been appointed commander of Allied forces on Crete, was having his breakfast when the drone of aircraft could be heard overhead. Freyberg looked at his watch and commented to an aide 'They're dead on time' as German parachutists descended from the sky on 20 May 1941. But the rumblings of the defeat on Crete were to continue long after the battle was over. Ultra – the codename given to Bletchley Park's codebreaking intelligence – was to play a central role. There were to be two Inter-Service Courts of Inquiry, in which Ultra played no part as those who sat on the Inquiry had no knowledge of it, and Freyberg could not reveal what he knew. Histories critical of Freyberg would be written before the Ultra secret was declassified, and even after it became public knowledge.

Rarely had a commander had such advance warning of an invasion than that provided to Freyberg by Ultra. It was during the Greek campaign that Ultra was sent to commanders in the field for the first time. With Greece overrun, Churchill wanted Crete defended at all costs. Allied forces had occupied Crete when the Italians invaded Greece on 28 October 1940. Though the Italians were initially repulsed, subsequent German intervention drove 57,000 Allied troops from the mainland. The Royal Navy evacuated many of them, while around 35,000 went to Crete to bolster its garrison, bringing the total for 'Creforce', as it was known, to 42,000. Freyberg wanted to evacuate 10,000 from Crete because they had no weapons. British plans were to use Crete as a base to attack the vital German-held oilfields at Ploesti in Romania, but defending the island was extremely difficult, given its topography. In the event, the Germans were to considerably underestimate Allied strength.

Crete had considerable strategic value, not least that the Royal Navy could refuel its ships at Suda Bay, providing added protection to battered and besieged Malta. But the Germans had complete air superiority in the region. Moreover, the Italian fortress on the Greek island of Rhodes and its ample airfields were only 100 miles away. Indeed, an Allied invasion of Rhodes had been contemplated. Churchill had wanted Suda Bay fortified, referring to it as a 'second Scapa' – a reference to the Home Fleet base at Scapa Flow in the Orkneys. But while the Allies held Greece, sending troops and planes to the island was not an option. However, planning for the defence of the island had been severely hampered by having six commanders in as many months. The infrastructure was poor, with only one road that ran along the length of the northern coast of the island and included the airfields of Maleme, Rethymno and Heraklion as well as Suda Bay. Churchill wrote his epic history of the Second World War before the secret of Ultra was revealed, but he hints at it over Crete when he commented:

> At no moment in the war was our Intelligence so truly and precisely informed ... In the last week of April we obtained from trustworthy sources good information about the next German stroke.[xiv]

It was on 25 March that Ultra revealed German plans for airborne operations when Fliegerkorps XI was preparing to take possession of Ju-52 transport planes for towing gliders, having been ordered to move up to six Gruppen of these planes to Plovdiv in Bulgaria. Five days later Ultra revealed the presence of a detachment linked to General Süssmann, who was associated with Fliegerdivision VI, part of Fliegerkorps XI, which had carried out airborne operations in Holland. Other units were also arriving, including one involved with night glider towing. But there was no clue at this point as to the target. By mid-April, the Bletchley Park link to Cairo had been extended to Crete, and warnings were given on this line that airborne operations were being planned from Bulgaria. Churchill decided that the Enigma material should continue to go to Crete, and General Freyberg, who took command on 30 April, received it from Bletchley Park as information supplied by an SIS agent in Athens.

While it was known through Ultra that the Germans planned to mount an invasion, the actual destination was not discovered until 26

April, when railway Enigma revealed large-scale movement from Germany to the Balkans. The same day Hitler issued his Merkur (Mercury) Directive – the codename for the invasion of Crete. A pro-German coup in Iraq by Rashid Ali led to British troops arriving at Basra on 18 April. Fighting broke out on 2 May and Rashid Ali appealed to Germany for air support. But the British High Command thought the German target could still be switched to Syria or Cyprus as a stepping stone to Iraq. The military chiefs even believed that references to Crete in the decrypts might be a cover for an attack on Syria or Cyprus. In London on 28 April the Joint Intelligence Committee made an assessment that a simultaneous airborne and seaborne attack was imminent. They believed that the enemy could muster 315 long-range bombers, 60 twin-engine fighters, 240 dive-bombers and 270 single-engine fighters. The Germans might drop 3,000–4,000 paratroopers in the first landing and two or three sorties a day from Greece and three or four from Rhodes, plus fighter escort. Heavy bombing would be involved and there would be plenty of troops and ships to launch a seaborne invasion. Crete had been warned of a possible airborne attack as early as 18 April, and had a permanent garrison of three infantry battalions, two heavy anti-aircraft (AA) batteries, three light AA batteries and coastal defence artillery. In addition, many of the troops evacuated from Greece were exhausted and only lightly armed – where they had weapons at all. At Churchill's suggestion, General Freyberg was appointed to command the island. The two had known each other since the First World War, and Freyberg, at Churchill's request, had even shown him twenty-seven separate scars in the 1920s from his military encounters. Freyberg had the courage and nerve that Churchill wanted for the grim defence of the island that lay ahead.

And grim indeed was the reality as Freyberg advised his immediate superior, General Sir Archibald Wavell, Commander-in-Chief, Middle East, with the comment that the forces at his disposal were 'totally inadequate' for the task ahead. Increased air and naval forces were essential, and following the evacuation from Greece, there was no artillery available. There was very little transport and equipment and ammunition was in short supply. Land forces alone, Freyberg pointed out, were not enough. So concerned was he that, as commander of the New Zealand division, he felt obliged to inform his own government of the situation, not least that on the island he only had six Hurricane fighters and seventeen obsolete aircraft. He urged the New Zealand government to bring pressure on Churchill to supply him with the wherewithal to defend the island or to prepare for evacuation. Wavell had argued that to defend the island effectively at least three brigade groups were required and a considerable number of AA units, but that its current composition was three British regular battalions, six New Zealand battalions, one Australian battalion and two composite battalions made up of those evacuated from Greece between 24 and 29 April, which were weak in numbers and equipment, and the Greek troops, who were mainly untrained and unarmed.

Churchill told the New Zealand Prime Minister, Peter Fraser, that the problem of reinforcing the island was caused by the physical difficulties of getting aircraft and their servicing personnel to Crete. Freyberg was, despite his problems, taking on a positive note as he told Churchill. He was not anxious about an airborne attack, had made his dispositions and felt he could adequately cope with the troops he had at his disposal. However, the sting in the tail for Churchill was Freyberg's comment that a combination of a seaborne and airborne attack would be different. The combination of Luftwaffe control of the air, and that all supplies had to be sent to the north of the island, led to less than 3,000 tons of supplies being landed in the first three weeks of May against 27,000 tons, with the rest turning back with a loss of a further 3,000 tons. General Freyberg had sixteen heavy AA guns (3.7 in mobile), thirty-six light AA Bofors guns, twenty-four AA searchlights, nine infantry tanks and sixteen light tanks. They were reinforced by around 2,000 men from the Mobile Naval Defence Organisation, which included one heavy and one light AA battery. However, such was the German superiority in the air, that the decision was taken on 19 May – the day before the invasion – to evacuate the remaining aircraft to Egypt. The defending forces needed all the help they could get, and Ultra was there, invisible but alert, and was about to be tested for the first time under actual battle conditions. Ralph Bennett, who worked in Hut 3 at Bletchley Park, has observed that it was the German assault on Crete which saw the first serious test of Ultra under operational conditions.

> In fact, it was probably only Ultra's warning which enabled the defenders to come so near success and to inflict such heavy casualties on the German airborne troops ...[xv]

On 2 May, the first two waves of Fliegerkorps XI left Hanover. Military history was about to be made because never before had there been a mass airborne landing by an invading force, comprising Fliegerkorps XI made up of Fliegerdivision VII and the Mountain Division V with Mountain Division VI in reserve. A significant pointer for British Intelligence was that Fliegerkorps XI had controlled the 1940 air landings in the Low Countries. In all, more than 22,000 troops would be involved, of which over 8,000 would come by parachute and glider and nearly 14,000 by troop carrier. These were elite forces, many of them recruited from the Hitler Youth movement, anxious to prove their worth to Führer and Fatherland. They were about to jump into the unknown for an operation the Germans had codenamed Operation Merkur – Mercury – the winged God (the Germans had a bad habit of using codenames that hinted at the kind of operation being planned) following Directive 28 from Hitler on 25 April, while the allies had codenamed Crete 'Colorado' and the German invasion 'Scorcher'.

In a wry comment to a query from Churchill about sending reinforcements to Crete, General Wavell replied that he had done his best to equip Colorado 'against beetle pest'. And Churchill, never one to understate a situation, had told Freyberg that success in repelling the German invasion would affect the whole world situation. The Prime Minister was later to refer to the German invasion as 'ruthless and reckless' and who were prepared to take heavy casualties in order to capture the island.

While Churchill, the top brass in Cairo and London, and Freyberg on Crete had been keeping each other informed, Bletchley Park had also been alert. Ultra intelligence from Bletchley Park was sent to Cairo with the prefix OL – Orange Leonard – at that time, before the three-figure number of the message. OL was also used as the prefix for those Ultra messages with four numbers (numbered in the 2000 series) subsequently passed on to Crete. They were originally received on Crete by Group Captain Beamish, Air Officer Commanding on the island, then to Freyberg when he was appointed to command all troops on the island. An early message (OL 2155, dated 1 May 1941) revealed that to assist the Luftwaffe to carry out planned operations, there would be no mining of Suda Bay or destruction of airfields on the island. This message could, therefore, be interpreted as forewarning of either an airborne landing or invasion from the sea – or even both. In the early hours of 3 May, OL 2157 advised that air transport units would not be ready for a large-scale attack before 6 May at the earliest, but that other preparations appeared to be complete. The following day OL 2165 reported that the staff of Fliegerdivision VII had moved to Salonika and would arrive at Athens on 8 May.

Plans for the capture of Crete had been drawn up by General Kurt Student, commander of Fliegerkorps XI, which comprised parachute and glider troops, and it was originally planned to land on the island on 17 May. Ultra had detected the movement of troops and, significantly, Ju-52 transport aircraft to Romania and southern Bulgaria for Fliegerkorps XI. But this could mean the possibility of attacking almost any target, as was news of the planned move of the 22nd Air Landing Division to Skopje in Yugoslavia. Other pointers towards a possible invasion of Crete were that General Wilhelm Süssmann, commander of the parachute division, had expressed interest in a reconnaissance of an unspecified area on 17 April, and that Fliegerkorps XI planned to assemble about 180 Ju-52s in Bulgaria on 21 April. However, information came to the Allies between 25 and 27 April of reports of air reconnaissance of Crete by Fliegerkorps VIII and XI and General Süssmann. Petrol stocks were also being made available for Fliegerkorps XI, and the planned move of the 22nd Air Landing Division and Fliegerdivision VII to Athens. Moreover, fifty-one Ju-52s had arrived in Bulgaria and Fliegerkorps VIII had taken receipt of photographs and maps of Crete.

Just before midnight on 6 May, Ultra (OL 2167) gave the first details of the planned invasion of Crete. This revealed that the preparations for the invasion would probably be completed by 17 May. Fliegerdivision VII plus Corps troops of Fliegerdivision XI would seize Maleme, Candia (Heraklion) and Rethymno. Dive bombers and fighters would move to Maleme and Candia. The next air landing would be the rest of Fliegerkorps XI including HQ and subordinated army units, followed by flak units, further troops and supplies. Third Mountain Regiment from Twelfth Army, armoured units, motorcyclists and anti-tank units were also detailed for Fliegerkorps XI. Admiral Schuster (Admiral South-East) would provide protection with Italian torpedo boat flotillas, minesweepers and possibly U-boats. Sea transport would be by German and Italian vessels. The invasion, said the Ultra decrypt, was to be preceded by a sharp attack on RAF military camps and anti-aircraft positions. The following day OL 2168 informed that the flak units, further troops and supplies mentioned in OL 2167 were to proceed to the island by sea. The same day (7 May) OL 2169 advised that the island of Melos was to be occupied that day with a view to preparing an airfield.

Just under an hour later OL 2170 produced a detailed assessment of how the attack would be likely to develop. On Day One, on the eve of the invasion, there would be a sharp bombing attack on RAF and military objectives. Day One would also see paratroopers dropped and the arrival of some operational aircraft. The first or second day would see arrival of air landing troops with equipment including guns, motorcycles and possibly AFVs – armoured fighting vehicles. Seaborne forces and supplies would arrive on Day Two after arrival of air landing detachments. The Ultra message said that there were about 450 troop-carrying aircraft in the area, which could be increased to 600 if required. The first day could see as many as 12,000 men landed in two sorties, with 4,000 on the second day and 400 tons of equipment. If an air landing operation took place on the first day, then parachutist effort would be reduced by half. Attacks could be expected by long-range bombers and twin-engined fighters based in Bulgaria and at Salonika, Athens and possibly Rhodes. The bombers might manage 105 sorties and the fighters 100 sorties in a day, using ninety Ju-80s and sixty Me 109s respectively. The airborne attack would probably start from Athens. These details, the Ultra message emphasised, were the maximum envisaged, as the assessment excluded any effect of Allied action or lack of facilities in the Athens area.

Six days later the full plan for the invasion was sent to Freyberg in OL 2/302. It is worth setting out this message in full to show the detail of information which Bletchley Park was able to impart to Freyberg, via Cairo, timed at 1745 on 13 May:

The following summarises intentions against Crete from operation orders issued.

Para 1. The island of Crete will be captured by the 11th Air Corps and the 7th Air Division and the operation will be under the control of the 11th Air Corps.

Para 2. All preparations, including the assembly of transport aircraft, fighter aircraft, and dive bombing aircraft, as well as of troops to be carried both by air and sea transport, will be completed on 17th May.

Para 3. Transport of seaborne troops will be in cooperation with Admiral South-East, who will ensure the protection of German and Italian transport vessels (about twelve ships) by Italian light naval forces. These troops will come under the orders of the 11th Air Corps immediately on their landing on Crete.

Para 4. A sharp attack by bomber and heavy fighter units to deal with the Allied air forces on the ground as well as with their anti-aircraft defences and military camps, will precede the operation.

Para 5. The following operations will be carried out as from day one. The 7th Air Division will make a parachute landing and seize Maleme, Candia, and Retimo [Rethymno]. Secondly, dive bombers and fighters (about 100 aircraft of each type) will move by air to Maleme and Candia. Thirdly, air landing of 11th Air Corps, including corps headquarters and elements of the Army placed under its command probably including the 22nd Division. Fourthly, arrival of the seaborne contingent consisting of anti-aircraft batteries as well as of more troops and supplies.

Para 6. In addition the 12th Army will allot three Mountain Regiments as instructed. Further elements consisting of motor-cyclists, armoured units, anti-tank units, anti-aircraft units will also be allotted.

Para 7. Depending on the intelligence which is now awaited, also as the result of air reconnaissance, the aerodrome at Kastelli [Pediados] south east of Candia and the district west and south west of Canea will be specially dealt with, in which case separate instructions will be included in detailed operation orders.

Para 8. Transport aircraft, of which a sufficient number – about 600 – will be allotted for this operation, will be assembled on aerodromes in the Athens area. The first sortie will probably carry parachute troops only. Further sorties will be concerned with the transport of the air landing contingent, equipment and supplies, and will probably include aircraft towing gliders.

Para 9. With a view to providing fighter protection for the operations, the possibility of establishing a fighter base on Skarpanto [Scarpanto – an island south of Rhodes] will be examined.

Para 10. The Quartermaster General's branch will ensure that adequate fuel supplies for the whole operation are available in the Athens area in good time, and an Italian tanker will be arriving at the Piraeus before May 17th. This tanker will probably also be available to transport fuel supplies to Crete. In assembling supplies and equipment for invading force it will be borne in mind that it will consist of some thirty to thirty-five thousand men, of which some 12,000 will be the parachute landing contingent, and 10,000 will be transported by sea. The strength of the long-range bomber and heavy fighter force which will prepare the invasion by attacking before day one will be of approximately 150 long-range bombers and 100 heavy fighters.

Para 11. Orders have been issued that Suda Bay is not to be mined, nor will Cretan aerodromes be destroyed, so as not to interfere with the operations intended.

Para 12. Plottings prepared from air photographs of Crete on one over ten thousand scale will be issued to units participating in this operation.

Ultra kept the information flowing to Freyberg. On 16 May he was warned of an expected attack on the airfield at Heraklion, with the Luftwaffe transferring to the island of Scarpanto about twenty Ju-87 aircraft to close the Kaso strait that ran between Crete and Scarpanto. Bletchley Park also warned the same day that the invasion of Crete was likely the following day – 17 May – but a forty-eight-hour postponement was likely. A later message said the nineteenth was the earliest date for an attack. Then, in the early hours of 19 May, Freyberg was advised that a conference of officers commanding Luftwaffe units would take place at Eleusis aerodrome regarding the forthcoming invasion. On 6 May Ultra revealed that the Germans estimated that they would probably complete preparations by 17 May. Decrypted messages listed the exact stages of the plan, beginning with the landing of paratroops through to the transfer of dive-bombers and fighters to Cretan bases, to the sea transport of troops and equipment. The Germans had selected for their airborne attack areas which corresponded closely to those to which the defenders were already giving prominence. Enigma information gave the defenders added confidence and the time to concentrate all their forces at these points, and the value of the intelligence was all the greater because the acute shortage of shipping, equipment and troops throughout the Middle East had prevented Britain from giving much attention to Crete's defences.

To date, there had only been two parachute operations of significance by the Germans – Britain had no paratroops at this stage – the capture of the Belgian fortress of Eben Emael and two bridges over the Albert Canal on 10 May 1940. But they were on a scale nowhere near the size of Operation Merkur. Also, unbeknown to the Germans, their parachutist manual had been captured in May 1940, and the attack on Crete was planned similar to that in Holland. After the war, General Student said that had he known this manual had been captured, his tactics would have been different.

On 20 May the invasion began. At its heart was the German need to capture the airfield at Maleme, but Freyberg had been told to expect both an air and a seaborne invasion. With the Luftwaffe in total control of the skies, the Royal Navy would find it tough engaging the sea landing. As it turned out, once Maleme fell, German reinforcements were able to pour in and turn the tide when the outcome had been in the balance. However, both sides had miscalculated. For Freyberg, the weight of the attack coming from the air, the ferocity of the German onslaught and their willingness to accept high casualties came as a shock – around 100 planes crash-landed in the Maleme area alone – and the level of resistance of the defenders was completely underestimated by the Germans, who had also totally miscalculated on the number of Allied troops on the island. The battle report of Fliegerkorps XI admitted that Allied strength on the island was three times what they had calculated. Their intelligence had been very poor indeed. The Royal Navy was also in action against the seaborne attack, an estimated 4,000 German troops being drowned on the first night. The Navy's role was magnificent, but unfortunately they sustained severe losses of men and ships, but they had done their job – the Germans failed to land any troops ashore until the land battle was over.

During the fighting Churchill kept urging the generals on, but on 27 May General Wavell sent a message to the Prime Minister advising him that Crete was no longer tenable and that troops had to be withdrawn as far as possible. In particular, Wavell explained, it had been impossible to withstand the weight of the enemy air attack which, he added, had been on an unprecedented scale and practically unopposed. The decision to evacuate was taken, the Navy again playing a heroic role to bring the Army out, seeing it as their duty. As Admiral Andrew Cunningham, Commander-in-Chief of the Mediterranean fleet, put it: 'It takes the Navy three years to build a new ship. It will take 300 years to build a new tradition. The evacuation will continue.' The rescue ended on 30 May, by which time 16,500 troops had been brought safely to Egypt, and nearly another thousand rescued later by various commando operations. Most troops left on the island surrendered, but many escaped into the mountains and were looked after, at considerable personal risk, by the islanders, resulting in severe German reprisals. Churchill was so appalled by German brutality against the civilian population that he later proposed that local crimes should be locally judged, and the accused persons sent back for trial on the spot, and this is what eventually happened.

Of the total Allied strength of more than 42,000 there were over 1,700 killed or missing, around 2,225 wounded and more than 12,000 prisoners taken. The Royal Navy had about 2,000 killed and 183 wounded, underlining their crucial role. Three cruisers and six destroyers were sunk, four capital ships, six cruisers and seven destroyers damaged. The Germans had a strength of more than 22,000 of which over 3,500 were killed or missing, with more than 300 air crew dead or missing. For the Germans it had been a pyrrhic victory. They had sustained more losses than in the entire Greek campaign, and such was the shock of the losses sustained that Hitler never again allowed a mass parachute drop during the war. However, the evacuation was not the end of the Ultra story and the island. A special SS security police unit, the Sonderkommando von Kühnsberg, were looking for intelligence material left behind by the Allies. Luftflotte 4, in their report on the battle, concluded that the day of the invasion was known to the British because of an efficient espionage system in Greece. At no time was the security of Enigma ever called into question by the Germans. Indeed, Fliegerkorps XI stated confidently that there had been no breach of security on the German side. But included in the captured documents sent to Berlin for further investigation lay potentially what could have been the greatest German intelligence breakthrough of the war – proof that Enigma had been compromised. This was a handwritten first page of an Ultra signal OL21/428 of 24 May:

---

Telegram From London     ZZZ

No. 797    Desp.  24.5.41
           Rec'd. 24.5.41         648 GMT

May 24th   797

Personal for General Freyberg
OL21/428

According to most reliable source, by midday May 23rd German troops had reached coast near Ag MARINAS and cut off British elements east of MALEMES. Units of centre group then to attack Suda Bay. It was proposed a ... more companies ...

---

The expression 'most reliable source' was Ultra, but probably the Germans considered this phrase to mean a British agent in Athens. The German belief in the long tentacles of the British Secret Service had almost certainly led them into not pursuing any alternatives as to the origin of 'most secret source' including the possible vulnerability of Enigma. Moreover, although the Ultra intelligence Freyberg received was very detailed, it came only from Luftwaffe decrypts. Crucially, Enigma messages referred to seaborne operations, which seriously affected Freyberg's troop deployment, detracting from the defence of the main German objective of the Maleme airfield. Enigma decrypts had proved invaluable in the battle of Crete, and Freyberg was subsequently criticised for his handling of events. Indeed, there were doubts that Freyberg had been 'indoctrinated' into the Ultra secret, but this is dispelled by Freyberg's son Paul, in an autobiography of his father. He makes clear that General Archibald Wavell, Commander in Chief Middle East, told his father about Ultra, but as he had never heard of it the two went to a villa for further talks in private. Wavell told Freyberg what it was, where it came from, and how it would be brought to him. Paul Freyberg adds:

> Wavell then gave Freyberg two specific orders. First he was not to mention the existence of Ultra to anyone else on Crete. Second, he was never to take any action as a result of what he learnt from Ultra *alone*.[xvi]

Freyberg's enforced silence over Enigma meant he could not explain why he had not reinforced Maleme airfield – the key to the invasion – because to have done so might have warned the Germans that their plans were known to the Allies. The rule that operations could not be conducted purely on Ultra information alone was instilled in all who were indoctrinated into its secret, and this strict rule was only relaxed on rare occasions later in the war, and then only on the specific approval of higher authority. No such approval was ever sent to Freyberg.

However, the success of the German invasion rested on their ability to seize the airfields. Consequently, it has been claimed in a biography of Freyberg by his son Paul, that his father wanted Maleme airfield reinforced, but the general was expressly forbidden from doing so for fear that the breaking of Enigma might be compromised. The main charge against Freyberg was that he concentrated more on a possible seaborne landing than a parachute invasion, but he had a particular concern at his ability to retain the island if there was both an airborne and seaborne attack at the same time. Freyberg's performance was also attacked at the time by several of his subordinates. Brigadier James Hargest, commanding 5 Brigade, complained to New Zealand Prime Minister Peter Fraser that he did not 'keep control over the conduct of operation', failed to take his senior officers into his confidence and occasionally left doubts as to his intentions. Brigadier Lindsay Inglis also raised doubts about Freyberg at a subsequent meeting with Churchill in London.

So serious was the loss of Crete that a Court of Inquiry – the Inter-Services Report on Crete – was set up under the chairmanship of Brigadier Guy Salisbury-Jones. Its conclusions became dynamite when it reported on 2 July 1941. Among its findings that sent shock waves through Whitehall and the military establishment was that the major lesson to be learned from the campaign was that to defend such a large island with a relatively small force, lying under permanent domination of enemy fighter aircraft and out of range of the RAF, was impossible. The report was also highly critical of the top brass at GHQ Middle East in Cairo. Wavell was furious and demanded the report's withdrawal. Subsequently, the report was hushed up and a second Court of Inquiry produced a sanitised version. But the elephant in the room of both Inquiries was Ultra. The Inquiry board members on both inquiries were not aware of Ultra's existence and Freyberg could not call it in his defence. All references which might have hinted at Ultra were erased in the second report, along with the criticism of the military hierarchy. However, in 1972, the Public Record Office (now The National Archives) published the original report and the cover-up was exposed. Following the Crete defeat, Churchill sacked Wavell and sent him to India as Commander in Chief. Churchill also made a statement on the loss of the island to the House of Commons on 10 June 1941.

A post-invasion report by the Germans revealed that they acknowledged that the Allied forces on Crete had been well informed through good intelligence, which they attributed to a spy network, adding that the defenders had been expecting most of the attack to come from the sea. After the war, Freyberg became a Lord and Governor General of New Zealand.

# Chapter 7

# Sheer Bloody Murder

Soviet Russia was a problem during the Second World War and the Arctic convoys were no exception. It was in Britain's interests to ensure that the Soviet Union had the means to defeat Hitler, but at the same time it would entail considerable sacrifice of men and material from Britain's own war effort. Churchill described the Russians as 'surly, snarly, grasping' and indifferent to Britain's fate. The armed services ministries had felt it was like flaying off pieces of their skin. However, very large American diversions of vital equipment for Britain were sent to back Soviet resistance. To support this, Churchill instructed Lord Beaverbrook, Minister for Supply, to give the utmost possible aid to the Russians. The Anglo-American Supply Mission, comprising Lord Beaverbrook and the US envoy Averell Harriman, arrived in Moscow on 28 September 1941. They received a frosty reception, and were given no formal entertainment until almost the last night, when they were invited to dinner at the Kremlin. In the protocol setting out the Anglo-American supplies that would be sent to Russia, it was made clear that neither the Americans nor Britain made any promise about the transportation of these supplies across the Arctic routes. Supplies would be made available by Britain and America, but they would help with the delivery. Churchill told Stalin in October 1941 that Britain would run a continuous cycle of convoys, leaving every ten days. The first delivery was due at Archangel on 12 October.

But it was not only Stalin who was becoming a problem – so was US President Franklin Roosevelt, as relations between the White House and Downing Street became strained as the supply of war material piled up in Britain. The Russians were unable to keep their side of the bargain by picking up the supplies in their own ships as they did not have enough vessels, so this formidable task fell on Britain and America. Churchill told his chief staff officer General Ismay that, while he shared Ismay's misgivings about sending a fresh convoy to Russia, nevertheless he felt it was a matter of duty. To fulfil this duty, he agreed to the sailing of Convoy PQ17. This subsequently ill-fated convoy was to prove a source of frustration to Bletchley Park and the Admiralty's own Operational Intelligence Centre, which received Enigma decrypts direct from the codebreaking centre. There was, however, to be one snag: the First Sea Lord, Admiral Sir Dudley Pound.

The first Arctic convoy – codenamed Dervish – had sailed from Iceland on 21 August 1941 bound for Archangel, but consisted of only six merchant ships, which all reached their destination safely. The first of the PQ convoys – named after the first two initials of the Admiralty's convoy planning officer, Commander Philip Quellyn Roberts – left Iceland on 28 September 1941 and comprised eleven ships, arriving a day early at Archangel on 11 October. But it was to prove a tragic theatre of war, as a hundred Allied merchant ships were lost, of which forty-seven were American and thirty-five British, comprising 604,837 gross tonnage, while twenty-one Allied warships were lost between 17 January 1942 and 16 January 1945. For the Germans, the Arctic losses between 24 March 1942 and 29 April 1945 were a battleship (*Tirpitz*), a battlecruiser (*Scharnhorst*), three destroyers and thirty-two U-boats.

By the end of June 1942 ice conditions had improved, and made it possible to route convoys north of Bear Island, which sat about halfway between Iceland and the Soviet port of Murmansk, but the prolonged daylight made them vulnerable to increased enemy action by the German Air Force, U-boats and surface ships. There had been a delay to PQ17 because much of the Home Fleet had been called from Scapa Flow in the Orkneys, where they were based, to help in Operation Harpoon, to reinforce an eastbound convoy to Malta, which had left insufficient destroyers for escorting the Arctic convoys. There had been an ominous forewarning of what might happen to PQ17 in a telephone conversation between Admiral Sir John Tovey, Commander-in-Chief of the Home Fleet at Scapa Flow, and Admiral Sir Dudley Pound, who suggested that in the event of an attack by German heavy surface ships after the convoy had entered the Barents Sea, he had it in mind to order the convoy to scatter. It was this comment that apparently led to Sir John Tovey allegedly remarking that in such an event the result would be 'sheer bloody murder'.

Captain Stephen Roskill, the official Second World War naval historian, wrote that so far the Royal Navy had not had to deal simultaneously with all the enemy's weapons – his heavy ships, light surface forces, aircraft and U-boats. Different convoys had been threatened in the Barents Sea by one, two or even three of these four; but never by all four at once.

> Now, unknown to the Admiralty, the German Naval Staff had just decided to commit the *Tirpitz* to the attempt.[xvii]

But the German admirals were under a distinct disadvantage – unknown to the British naval chiefs – that the capital ships could only sail on the direct orders of Hitler, who was paranoid about Allied aircraft carriers. Hitler was emphatic that the German capital ships should be either out of range of the British aircraft carriers or be taken out by the Luftwaffe before he would allow them to leave their heavily protected berths. Meanwhile, the task of the Royal Navy was to escort the convoy as far as Bear Island, after which it would be left to submarines, unless directly threatened by surface forces, which the cruisers could handle without battleship support.

To help PQ17, a scheme was devised in which a 'dummy' convoy based at Scapa Flow would sail, aimed at deceiving the Germans into believing that an attack on Norway was taking place, playing on the fact that Hitler was particularly concerned that Britain might launch an invasion of Europe through Norway. This 'invasion fleet' comprised five ships of the 1st Minelaying Squadron and four colliers, escorted by the cruisers *Sirius* and *Curacoa* and some destroyers and trawlers. They sailed on 29 June, two days after PQ17 left Iceland, and the battle fleet also sailed the same day, so as to give the impression of being the 'escort' to the dummy convoy. Unfortunately, the Germans did not detect the decoy, and it all came to nothing. In addition, a further bluff by launching a diversionary air raid on southern Norway also failed to interest the Germans.

Then London had a breakthrough involving Captain Henry Denham, the British Naval Attaché in Stockholm, with close links to Swedish Intelligence. He had provided the vital information that led to the sinking of the battleship *Bismarck* in May 1941, and now informed London that Swedish intelligence had intercepted a message sent by what the Germans thought was a secure landline through Sweden to Norway, providing detailed operational orders for an attack on the next Russian-bound convoy. This operation the Germans had codenamed *Rösselsprung* – Knight's Move – with the aim of the total destruction of the next convoy by the use of the battleship *Tirpitz*, the pocket battleships *Hipper* and *Scheer*, and the cruiser *Lützow* working in concert with the Luftwaffe and the U-boats. The Luftwaffe was strongly reinforced in the area, and there was also the U-boat wolfpack *Eisteufel* (*Ice Devil*), stretched out along the expected path of the convoy north-east of Jan Mayen Island. Unfortunately for the Germans, they ran into early trouble when three of the escorting destroyers for *Tirpitz* and *Hipper* ran aground, as did the *Lützow*.

Convoy PQ17 sailed on 27 June 1942 from Iceland and Admiral Sir John Tovey left Scapa Flow two days later. PQ17 comprised thirty-six merchant ships – mainly American – plus the fleet oiler *Gray Ranger*, which was damaged by ice and was replaced by the *Aldersdale*. In addition, the escort included three rescue ships, *Rathlin*, *Zaafaran* and *Zamalek* – the first Russian convoy to include rescue ships – and the CAM (Catapult Armed Merchantman) ship *Empire Tide*. Commodore Jack Dowding, in the merchantman *River Afton*, led the PQ17 merchant ships out of Iceland, but one ship ran aground and another was damaged, so thirty-four continued the fateful journey. On 1 July escort forces fought off the first U-boat attacks. Ominously for the convoy, the U-boats were never to lose contact with PQ17 again over the following days. The westbound QP13, comprising thirty-five merchantmen, had twelve ships leave Archangel on the twenty-sixth and twenty-three ships sail from Murmansk the following day. On 1 July Bletchley Park discovered that the Luftwaffe had found QP13. The original German plan had been to attack with the big surface units where the two convoys passed, anticipating that this would be to the north east of Jan Mayen Island. However, the Germans abandoned the plan. Bletchley Park then warned both convoys of an impending air attack in the evening of 2 July, in which one aircraft was shot down, with no convoy casualties. However, tragedy was to strike QP13 – but not from enemy action. Orders were given to QP13 to split into two sections as it approached northeast Iceland, with sixteen vessels going east of Iceland to Loch Ewe in west Scotland, whilst the remaining nineteen would pass along the north coast to Havalfjord. In poor visibility they mistook a large iceberg for the North Cape of Iceland, and into a minefield laid to prevent German ships from breaking out into the Atlantic to attack shipping. The minesweeper *Niger* (the senior officer's ship) sunk with heavy loss of life, while four merchant ships were sunk and two more seriously damaged.

As PQ17 set sail for Archangel – Murmansk had been put out of action because of bombing – Bletchley Park had been faced with a tough decision about the use of the bombes (electro-magnetic machines used to find Enigma settings). There was a shortage of bombes, and priority had to be decided between PQ17 and the fighting in the western desert, which had become critical after Rommel's Gazala offensive. After consultation with Whitehall, highest priority was given to the Home Waters traffic in view of the threat to PQ17. By now the cruiser force had overtaken the convoy and was on a parallel course, forty miles away, but unseen by the Luftwaffe or the U-boats. Fortunately, the convoy ran into fog that night, which persisted through to the afternoon of 3 July, and this stroke of luck enabled PQ17 to change course for the region past Bear Island into the Barents Sea, again without enemy aircraft spotting them. However, the U-boats were still in touch. Just before midnight on 2 July, the Admiralty signalled to Admiral Tovey that while there were no direct indications of movements of enemy main units, interest in the whereabouts of the Home Fleet and fighter readiness on the Norwegian coast might be significant.

On the morning of 3 July, Bletchley Park advised Admiral Tovey that *Lützow* had been detached and that *Tirpitz* had put to sea, although she was only moving up to Altafiord. Meanwhile, the convoy had altered course northwards and the escort had closed PQ17 to thirty miles northwest of Bear Island. At the same time, Admiral Tovey was between 150 and 200 miles west of Bear Island, where the aircraft carrier *Victorious* could be in a position to defend the merchantmen. Bletchley Park, updating on the movement of the heavy surface ships, reported that the pocket battleship *Scheer* had moved northwards from Narvik, probably accompanied by destroyers, and that while the movement of *Lützow* was uncertain, she was independent of *Scheer*. Bletchley Park also reported that both *Tirpitz* and *Hipper* might have left Trondheim in the early hours of 3 July. Underlining the difficulty in deciphering some messages, Bletchley Park advised that a sequence of signals ciphered on special settings – which would probably not be read – might indicate the commencement of a special operation. In fact, at this time, *Tirpitz* was entering Altafiord. By now German pilots were reporting that both the escort and the convoy were being shadowed. It did not take long for the casualties to begin. On 4 July the Admiralty gave Admiral Hamilton and his cruiser escort flexibility to continue east of 25° east subject to contrary orders from Admiral Tovey, the

Commander in Chief. However, Admiral Tovey ordered Admiral Hamilton to withdraw on reaching longitude twenty-five degrees east unless the Admiralty confirmed that he could not meet *Tirpitz*. That afternoon Hamilton signalled he would stay with the convoy until the enemy surface situation had been clarified, but certainly not later than midday on the fifth. However, during the evening of the fourth he decided to withdraw that night on completion of destroyer refuelling. During this period the *William Hooper* and *Navarino* were sunk.

Among the decrypts and German intentions flashed to the Admiralty was one stating that 'negative evidence indicated that there was no movement of the main surface fleet'. In the Arctic, Enigma settings were changed daily at noon and, as with all naval Enigma, the settings of the second of a pair of days were usually broken within a few hours once the settings of the first day of the pair had been broken. The Enigma traffic for the first of the next pair of days – from 1200 on 3 July to 1200 on 4 July – was broken at 1837 on 4 July. The Enigma decrypts began to reach the Admiralty's Operational Intelligence Centre (OIC) at Whitehall around 1900. Unfortunately, due to an accident, RAF reconnaissance had been interrupted off the North Cape for six hours on 4 July. During this period, OIC twice reported that the GAF had sighted the convoy. In the early hours of 4 July, OIC sent a message to Commander in Chief Home Fleet referring to hourly German naval transmissions since the previous afternoon, and that these messages might indicate the commencement of a special operation by main units.

This surmise of a special operation by main units came from a decrypt of a signal from *Scheer* just before midday on 3 July in which the ship reported she was unable to decipher two recent signals. They were also, not surprisingly, indecipherable to Bletchley Park as well. They may have been indecipherable because they were enciphered in a new four-wheel Enigma key that was coming into use for communication between Flag Officers during fleet operations. Called Barracuda by Bletchley Park and Neptun by the German navy, there was some evidence that this key – rarely used and never broken – was made available to the fleet in time for the intended operation against PQ17. Apart from the two signals received on the morning of 3 July, no indecipherable signals were received at Bletchley Park during that operation. Further intelligence of German activity around the convoy came the following morning, and just after midday on 4 July, Flag Officer commanding the escort, First Cruiser Squadron (CS1), Rear

Admiral Louis Hamilton, was given permission to proceed east of the limit of twenty-five degrees east, or earlier at his discretion, should the situation demand it. There then followed a change of mind when the Commander in Chief qualified the Admiralty's instruction by ordering CS1 to leave the Barents Sea when the convoy was east of the limit of twenty-five degrees east 'should the situation demand it'. At 1800 Admiral Hamilton announced that he intended to withdraw four hours later, but the Admiralty, within an hour after he had signalled his intentions, having found that the Enigma for the period to 1200 on 4 July had been broken, again changed the instructions, and signalled that further information might be available shortly – in other words Ultra decrypts would be to hand. The order to Admiral Hamilton was to remain with the convoy 'pending further instructions'. By the evening of 4 July, the *Official Naval History* paints a positive picture of the convoy, despite losses, stating that the convoy, then about 130 miles north-east of Bear Island, had just come through the heavy air attack remarkably well, and that the convoy discipline and shooting had been admirable and a substantial toll had been taken of the enemy. The *History* adds:

> A feeling of elation prevailed; in the words of Commander Broome, 'My impression on seeing the resolution displayed by the convoy and its escort was that, provided the ammunition lasted, PQ17 could get anywhere.'[xviii]

By now Admiral Sir Dudley Pound was visiting the OIC. It was now known that *Tirpitz* and *Scheer* had arrived at Altafiord, and her destroyer and torpedo boats had been ordered to refuel at once, while two U-boats had been ordered to shadow the convoy. The fateful moments began to tick away as to what decision the First Sea Lord should take about the convoy. Commander (later Sir) Norman Denning of the OIC recollected that he had wanted to add the comment that all the indications suggested that the *Tirpitz* was still in Altafiord, that after some argument the comment was deleted before the signal was sent and that Admiral Pound then asked him why he thought the *Tirpitz* had not yet sailed. Denning replied that he was convinced that in view of her experience while operating against PQ12 the Germans would not allow *Tirpitz* to sail until they had satisfied themselves that she would not be in danger from the Home Fleet, particularly its aircraft carriers.

It was put to Admiral Pound by Commander Denning that a number of other 'negative' indications pointed to *Tirpitz* not having sailed. German planes had detected the escort – the close support cruiser squadron – and reported, wrongly, that it included a battleship. This would indicate a large British force, and therefore it was unlikely that *Tirpitz* would go to sea in such circumstances. Further, there was no evidence that the Germans had detected the Home Fleet, so Denning argued that the enemy might believe the escort to be a major force. Furthermore, no decrypts had come in indicating instructions to U-boats to keep clear of the convoy, and German naval W/T traffic since noon had not shown any of the normal signs associated with the presence of surface ships at sea, and there had been no sightings by British or Russian submarines off the North Cape. Putting all these negatives together were, in Denning's opinion, a good indication that *Tirpitz* had not sailed. Admiral Pound then asked Commander Denning a fateful question: could he assure him that *Tirpitz* was still in Altafiord? Upon the answer to this question there hung the entire future of the convoy. Clearly Denning was not in any position to give such an assurance. But he made the point that he thought his view would be vindicated when Bletchley Park broke the Enigma messages for the twenty-four hours beginning at noon. In the event, the codebreakers broke the Enigma for this period almost immediately, and the decrypts began to reach the OIC at 2000. But it had provided no new positive intelligence bearing on the First Sea Lord's questions by the time the Deputy Director of the OIC, Captain Jock Clayton, had left to attend a staff meeting which the First Sea Lord had called for 2030.

A new decrypt, which Denning remembered showing Jock Clayton as he was leaving, proved that *Tirpitz* had not sailed by noon. But the die was cast, and Jock Clayton returned to the OIC about 2130 to announce that the view was to assume that *Tirpitz* had sailed. Crucially, the view was that, if the German surface ships had sailed as soon as they had refuelled, they could reach the convoy at 0200 the following morning, and therefore the convoy should be scattered. Clearly this did not go down well at the OIC, and so strong was the feeling among the naval intelligence officers that Jock Clayton was persuaded to return to the First Sea Lord to say that the OIC wished to advise the Home Fleet that not only did it believe that *Tirpitz* had not sailed, but that she would not do so until the Germans had located the support ships and their strength. To say the least, that was an unusual – and very brave – step to take, given it was delivered to the highest ranking officer in the Royal Navy. The First Sea Lord was unmoved. There then followed the three signals on the evening of 4 July that eventually sealed the fate of PQ17. Coming as they did in rapid succession – one twelve minutes after the first and the fateful 'scatter' message thirteen minutes after the second – those twenty-five minutes must have caused deep concern with the convoy and its escort, particularly as the messages to Admiral Hamilton escalated in urgency:

**Message No. 1:**
2111 Cruiser force withdraw to westward at high speed.

**Message No. 2:**
2123 Owing to threat of surface ships convoy is to disperse and proceed to Russian ports.

**Message No. 3:**
2136 My 2123 [4][July] Convoy is to scatter.

According to Roskill, the order to scatter came as such a surprise to Commodore Dowding that he asked for it to be repeated. Referring to the 'scatter' order, another authoritative source, the *Official Naval History*, states that the order to scatter was intended merely as a technical amendment of the term 'disperse' (used in the previous signal), which meant that ships would break formation and proceed at convenient speed towards their port of destination, i.e. for some hours they would be in close proximity to each other. The term 'scatter' meant that they would start out on different bearings in accordance with a scheme laid down in the convoy instructions. Out in the Arctic, the impression must have been given to the escorts that because of the quick succession of signals, the German capital ships would soon appear on the horizon. Rear Admiral Hamilton received the Admiralty orders at 2200. At 2215 on 4 July, Commander Broome passed on the fateful signal to scatter to Commodore Dowding, in charge of the merchant fleet. At the same time he and the destroyers steered towards Admiral Hamilton. Only once previously during the Second World War did a convoy receive the order to scatter, when HX84 in November 1941 was about to be attacked by *Scheer*. However, on that occasion, the thirty-seven vessels had the whole of the Atlantic Ocean into which they could disappear and there was no

Luftwaffe to attack them and no U-boats. The only escort ship was the armed merchant cruiser *Jervis Bay*, which honourably and gallantly sacrificed herself in defence of the convoy. *Scheer* sank five of the merchantmen.

The order to scatter PQ17 was given in glaring contradiction to Atlantic Convoy Instructions and the directive of Admiral Sir John Tovey in March that, in the face of heavy enemy ships, convoy escorts should remain in the vicinity to shadow and even to attack the enemy if the opportunity arose. As Sir John Tovey pointed out in his subsequent report, PQ17 had gone more than half its allotted journey with the loss of only three ships, and the decision to scatter he regarded as premature and disastrous. If proof were needed that Denning had been right all along, his opinion was confirmed in the early hours of 5 July when, at 0500, the GAF finally sighted the home fleet. They were 500 miles from the convoy. Bletchley Park was still monitoring the situation, and the scattering of the convoy occurred while there was a total lack of reference in the decrypts to the German surface ships. As time dragged on and the German battle fleet failed to appear, both Admiral Hamilton and Commander Broome were puzzled by what was going on. It was not until the forenoon of 5 July that the situation regarding the enemy surface fleet was made clear to him. The cruiser force was not sighted until 1740 on 5 July, when a Focke Wulf reconnaissance aircraft made contact and gave its position. As a result, Admiral Hamilton decided to break wireless silence and inform Admiral Sir John Tovey of his position, course and speed – and this was the first time that Tovey knew Commander Broome's destroyers were still with the cruisers. Then, at 1700 hours the same day, *Tirpitz*, *Scheer* and eight destroyers were sighted at sea by a Russian submarine, which mistakenly claimed to have hit *Tirpitz* with two torpedoes. About an hour later an aircraft reported eleven strange ships, and the British submarine P54 reported *Tirpitz* and *Hipper* and at least six destroyers and eight aircraft. However, after these sightings, nothing more was heard of the German surface ships for two days. Roskill is scathing in his comments about the 'scatter' decision and wrote that if it was felt that there was a possibility that dispersing the convoys would turn out to be the less perilous action, such a proposal, and the grounds on which it was made, could justifiably have been sent to the responsible officers, for them to carry out or not as they saw fit. He adds:

It is beyond doubt that had this been done the convoy and escort would have been kept together.[xix]

The German decision to sail the capital ships had been taken on 5 July, when Grand Admiral Raeder had finally received permission from Hitler. The big ships were to attack the convoy the next day. However, one hour and fifty minutes later – at 2219 – they were recalled. The U-boats and Luftwaffe were slaughtering the convoy, and there was no reason to put *Tirpitz* and the other major surface ships at unnecessary risk. However, because of the time needed to decrypt the message, the Admiralty was unable to pass on the information until 1317 on 6 July, and confirmation of their return to port was confirmed when the ships were sighted at 1045 the following morning by a PRU (Photo Reconnaissance Unit) Mosquito, flying from Vaenga, near Murmansk. The ships moved to Narvik two days later. Rear-Admiral Hamilton's cruisers, with eight destroyers, made for Seidisfjord at 1230 and the battle fleet turned southward shortly after, all ships reaching harbour on 8 July. There were only eleven survivors out of the thirty-four merchantmen that made the hazardous journey. However, not a single Royal Navy vessel had been lost in the carnage. Except for three ships, the heavy losses occurred after the order to scatter the convoy. As to the role of the big German surface ships, the *GC&CS Naval History* is less than flattering. It states that the part played by the main units in Operation Roesselsprung was generally agreed to have been useless. In a summing up of the reasons for their failure, German Naval War Staff complained that every operation of fleet forces was stifled by Hitler's excessive anxiety to avoid losses and setbacks. No sortie could ever succeed in these conditions, and to achieve results, it was inevitable that risks be accepted, because the German navy was small. The *History* adds that the implications of the main unit sortie against PQ17 were that never again could they be effectively employed, since, if it were deemed inadvisable to use them then, when the danger was so remote, it was certain that no such advantageous situation would again present itself, and therefore their future inactivity was assured.

Their only purpose in remaining in the north appeared then to be the subsidiary task of defence against an invasion attempt.[xx]

That was little consolation to the merchant seamen who lost their lives on the PQ17 convoy. Winston Churchill was mortified at the heavy losses of PQ17. Churchill, who had been First Lord of the Admiralty during the First World War and at the start of the Second World War, felt a special affinity with those at sea – whether Royal Navy or merchantmen. Post-war, he wrote that Admiral Pound would probably not have sent such 'vehement orders' if only British warships had been concerned. But this was the first large joint Anglo-American operation under British command, and Churchill was concerned that two United States cruisers could be destroyed. The wartime Prime Minister reasoned that this may well have disturbed the poise with which Admiral Pound was accustomed to dealing with such decisions. Churchill admitted that so strictly was the secret of these orders being sent on the First Sea Lord's authority guarded by the Admiralty, that it was not until after the war that he learned the facts.

In the immediate aftermath of the PQ17 disaster, Churchill sent a minute to Admiral Pound, stating that he had not been aware that it was Admiral Hamilton who had ordered the destroyers to quit the convoy. Churchill was also unhappy that the inquiry into the conduct of those concerned took a 'considerable time' and assigned no blame to anyone. Churchill asked how this could have been the result of the inquiry in view of the signals made on the orders of the First Sea Lord.

Churchill was, of course, fully aware of the role that Bletchley Park had played in providing vital intelligence for the PQ17 convoy, but he was unable to talk about it in his memoirs. It was still a closely guarded secret. But he made clear his disapproval that the cruiser squadron was withdrawn and that he regarded their withdrawal as a mistake, arguing that all risks should have been taken in defence of the merchant ships. There were also lessons for the German naval staff, who had seen the surface fleet make no impact on the convoy at all. Admiral Northern Waters, in his summing up of the PQ17 operation, suggested a possibility for their alternative employment in the form of operations against the hitherto largely neglected westbound convoys. On 15 July, Churchill ordered the First Sea Lord to suspend the sailing of the next convoy – PQ18 – which did not sail from Loch Ewe until 2 September, when the period of daylight had shortened. PQ18 comprised forty merchantmen accompanied by an aircraft carrier and a strong escort, but following heavy attack from the air, twelve ships were sunk, but the remainder of the convoy – and the escort – arrived safely in Archangel. In all, according to Roskill, the fate of PQ17's cargo was as follows:

|  | Delivered | Lost |
|---|---|---|
| Vehicles | 896 | 3,350 |
| Tanks | 164 | 430 |
| Aircraft | 87 | 210 |
| Other cargo | 57,176 tons | 99,316 tons |

(Source: Roskill, *The War At Sea*, vol II, table 11, p. 143.)

Some ships disabled by the Luftwaffe and abandoned were subsequently sunk by U-boats. German losses were slight. Of the 202 aircraft which attacked the convoy, only 5 were lost. Roskill points out that it was never likely that the *Tirpitz* would be put at risk:

> it is plain that the enemy was never likely to risk the *Tirpitz* in close attack on a convoy protected by an escort which was heavily armed with torpedoes. That ... had always been Admiral Tovey's opinion; but the Admiralty had never accepted it.[xxi]

According to respected sources such as the German naval historian Professor Jürgen Rohwer, the final tally is probably as follows:

| Sinkings | Number | Tonnage |
|---|---|---|
| Luftwaffe | 8 | 40,425 |
| U–Boat | 7 | 41,041 |
| Luftwaffe/U–Boat | 9 | 61,255 |
| **Total** | **24** | **142,721** |

The real tragedy of PQ17 was counted in the human tragedy – the loss of 153 merchant seamen, although 1,500 were saved. In July Churchill wrote to Stalin – with the prior approval of President Roosevelt – pointing out that, with PQ17, the Germans had at last used their forces in the manner that had always been feared. Churchill pointed out that if only one or two of Britain's battleships were lost or seriously damaged while *Tirpitz* and other big ships, plus *Scharnhorst*, remained in action, the whole command of the Atlantic would be temporarily lost. He added that besides affecting vital food supplies, the war effort would be crippled, and above all, the great convoys of American troops, running at 80,000 a month, would be prevented, and the building up of a really strong Second Front – dear to Stalin's heart – would be rendered impossible. Churchill awaited the Soviet leader's answer. Subsequently, on receiving Stalin's response, Churchill added: 'I need scarcely say I got a rough and surly reply.' Stalin queried why the escorts had turned back, but the cargo boats had continued on their journey without any protection. He could not understand why supplies were being stopped when the land battle situation was so critical, and he doubted that the question of starting a Second Front in Europe was being treated with the seriousness it deserved.

In a particularly Churchillian phrase, the wartime Premier said Britain had given its heart's blood resolutely to the Russians. In October 1942 it was decided to experiment with sailing merchantmen independently from Iceland, sending them as near the ice-edge as possible. Of eleven ships that sailed at intervals of twelve hours, the first three arrived safely but the next two were sunk. The sixth fought through undamaged, but the Master returned to Iceland, fearing further attack. The seventh was diverted to Spitzbergen but struck a reef in appalling weather, was bombed and became a total loss. Of the remaining four, two were sunk but two made it to Murmansk. Only five of the eleven had achieved their purpose. However, this was virtually the end of German successes on the convoys. A further 44 convoys sailed, and despite having to fight their way through, only 12 suffered small losses, which amounted to 25 ships out of a further 1,015 safe arrivals.

Commodore Dowding – torpedoed during the convoy – was to comment about PQ17, with masterly understatement, in his report to the Senior British Naval Officer at Archangel on 13 July: 'Not a successful convoy.'

# Chapter 8

# Outfoxing the Desert Fox

On 23 October 1942 came one of the defining moments of the Second World War – the Eighth Army attack on Rommel's newly named command, the German–Italian Panzer Army, at El Alamein at the gates of Cairo. The outcome would be decisive: either the swastika would fly over the Egyptian capital and the Middle East and its oil would be at the mercy of the German war machine or Hitler's ambitions in North Africa would be over. There could be no third way – further stalemate in North Africa, chasing each other up and down the deserts, had to end. A few weeks earlier, on 13 August, the Eighth Army, which had fallen back to the Egyptian border, was given a new commander – General Bernard Montgomery. 'Monty' took over at a crucial moment, as decrypts from German Army Enigma were now coming to the fore, particularly in a cipher known to Bletchley Park as 'Chaffinch'. A number of ciphers had been codenamed after birds, and some were singing louder and more often than others. Chaffinch was to sing merrily. Ultra was to help make Monty's reputation following the victory at Alamein. From May to July 1942 British and Allied forces were in retreat until forming up at El Alamein, and in May, during Rommel's attack on the Gazala line, there had been confusion over Enigma decrypts. Sigint had given plenty of warning of the attack, but twenty-four hours before the onslaught, problems arose. *The Official History of British Sigint* recalls that owing to inexpert presentation of the Sigint to I(a) – Operational Intelligence Staff at Army Commands – and to I(a)'s inexperience in Sigint appreciation, the evidence was disregarded in the face of conflicting evidence from reconnaissance sources. Disastrous as were the immediate consequences, the effect on the development of military Sigint was wholly salutary.

I(s) [Special Intelligence (Ultra) Staff at Army HQ or Army Group] took the necessary steps to ensure that evidence from

Sigint sources would in future be presented in a form that I(a) could fully understand, and I(a) henceforth accepted Sigint as a vital source of military intelligence.[xxii]

One of the key Sigint special wireless sections was captured at Bagush on 29 June, but the intelligence continued to flow. By the time of Alamein, an effective Sigint organisation had been built up, and for the first time in the campaign Army Sigint had become a unified whole. The enemy's rapid retreat after Alamein brought a considerable reduction in intercepted traffic, and two special units worked in unison, leapfrogging each other in pursuit until, with the occupation of Tripoli on 23 January 1943, active field Sigint in the Western Desert came to an end. Subsequently, the official view was that its organisation and functioning 'were one of the greatest achievements of the Sigint Service during the war'.

There was also a smaller Air Sigint organisation with its headquarters at RAF Suez Road, near Cairo, which included a traffic section responsible for interception and an intelligence section responsible for exploiting the traffic – other than Enigma – intercepted. Among the facilities was a fully mobile field section whose task was to provide a watch at battle headquarters for information of immediate tactical use to both Air and Army commanders on the spot, which were operating with two direction-finding sets and sixteen intercept sets. Of the total amount of intercept resources – sixty-six sets and eleven direction-finding stations – most were at RAF Suez Road.

The Allied landings in French North-West Africa on the night of 7–8 November 1942 known as Operation Torch under the command of General Eisenhower was the first joint Anglo–American operation since the First World War, and the US was part of the Sigint planning. The aim was to clear the Axis Powers from North Africa, improve naval control of the Mediterranean and prepare for an invasion of Southern Europe. The main Sigint base for Torch was in Britain and Ultra traffic was serviced by Special Liaison Units and Special Communications Units, formed especially to handle Enigma decrypts in the field. There was a main unit attached to Allied HQ and three mobile units for the landings at Oran and Casablanca and one to accompany the forces pushing, ultimately, to Tunisia. Naval Ultra was also involved for authorised recipients afloat. At this time, America had no experience of field Sigint and the British view was that the difficulties encountered in collaboration were largely attributable to imperfect British and American understanding of the details of each other's organisation and procedure. Particularly troublesome were the differences in national security standards. To whom might be told how much?

For the British, the demarcation between high- and low-grade intelligence was clear, but Ultra's secrets might be held as low down the military chain of command as an American  RI – radio intercept – platoon. In the balance between security and efficiency, the Americans preferred the latter, the British the former. However, the setting up of a Sigint committee in North Africa with an American chairman helped overcome these differences. British shortcomings following the landings were that they, too, lacked experience of Sigint in the field. There had been virtually no liaison with Eighth Army and much valuable time was wasted breaking codes that had already been broken. According to official reports, training in the UK had been 'desultory' largely because training material was not available, and units had not been able to settle down before embarkation.

Enemy shipping losses providing supplies to Rommel had played a crucial role in the defeat of the Axis forces. Back in August 1941 the amount of Ultra was such as to provide intelligence on prospective sailings, routes to be taken, the volume of shipping and losses. *The Official History of British Sigint* makes clear that the volume of enemy shipping losses due to Ultra 'must be rated high'. So accurate was this intelligence that, according to an official report:

> While it was desirable to sink all Panzer Army Africa's supply ships, it was worth letting a cargo of rations pass unharmed if, for instance, the effort thereby saved could then or later be devoted to sinking a tanker.[xxiii]

The report gives a particular example – during Rommel's offensive of 31 August 1942 – when five tankers were sunk in rapid succession, immobilising his tanks because target selection had, for at least two months, consistently starved the enemy of fuel. The *Official History* records:

> In no theatre of war at any time did Special Intelligence [Ultra] give fuller information at all levels, and, more particularly, nowhere did it more completely reveal the Axis supply situation or permit the Allied policy for the interruption of lines of

communication to be so closely and directly related by deliberate selection to specific targets.[xxiv]

One senior intelligence officer commented that from 1939 to 1942 'Intelligence was the Cinderella of the Staff, and information about the enemy was treated as interesting rather than valuable' – until Ultra came along – adding: 'Ultra and Ultra alone put Intelligence on the map.' Indeed, so comprehensive was Ultra that it became 'dangerously valuable' and seemed the answer to an Intelligence Officer's prayer.

> Instead of being the best, it tended to become the only source. There was a tendency at all times to await the next message and, often, to be fascinated by the authenticity of the information.[xxv]

It was particularly useful for planning in periods between battles when other sources tended to dry up, and also provided an opportunity to study it in relation to context so much better than during a fast-moving battle such as occurred in desert warfare. But the Y or intercept service, which, apart from interception, carried out preliminary analysis of intercepted signals, covered the reading of low-grade codes at the point of interception and studied enemy W/T traffic characteristics, filling many gaps in Ultra. German operators sending messages encrypted on Enigma were telling the truth, but what they transmitted was not necessarily true to the situation as a whole. Moreover, despite the speed with which Ultra was received, it was often out of date, and intercept intelligence provided by the Y Service usually superseded Ultra in battle. As a senior intelligence officer put it: 'Y is the only source of intelligence that a commander has in battle, and no commander who has had his own Section is ever willing to work again without one.' Moreover, given the stringent security regulations surrounding the handling of enemy decrypted messages, often Ultra was used more in a passive form than as an active medium.

The first – and some have argued wrongly named – battle of Alamein, a desert railway halt some sixty miles west of Alexandria, under General Claude Auchinleck, had blocked Rommel's attempt in July 1942 to break through to Cairo near Ruweisat Ridge. The German attempt to break through to Suez was again frustrated at Alam Halfa in September. The general outline of the second, and decisive, battle of El Alamein from 23 October to 4 November 1942 can be briefly explained.

Rommel was short of everything – armour, troops, fuel, adequate air support and other key supplies – and prior to going on sick leave on 23 September (he did not return until 25 October when the battle had begun) – had laid massive defensive anti-tank minefields comprising around half a million mines, and inside these were other minefields sown with anti-personnel mines. This formidable defensive deployment was dubbed 'the Devil's gardens' by the Allies, and was to hold up the Eighth Army's advance. Rommel also interspersed his troops with the weaker Italians and placed his armour in six groups to prepare for any counter-attack. Monty planned a northern attack against the German forces with four infantry divisions of 30 Corps, and to clear minefields on the way to give passage to two armoured divisions of 10 Corps. A deception plan and diversionary attacks in the south with 13 Corps completely surprised the enemy. A barrage of nearly 1,000 artillery pieces opened up the battle, but the German depth in defence proved formidable. However, Rommel's counter-attacks around Kidney Ridge were contained, and constant Allied air and artillery bombardment backed up the infantry assaults. The 9th Australian Division forced a northern salient. Montgomery launched a second attack which cleared the way for the armour. Despite further resistance, the German-Italian forces were in full retreat. The Allies had taken more than 13,000 casualties but captured 30,000 Axis troops. Such is the broad background to what follows – a story of a major triumph for Ultra.

The number of wireless sets available in spring 1942, just before Rommel's final push to Alamein, was seven at Gibraltar, two at Malta, three at Heliopolis, seven at Alexandria, four at Sarafand in Palestine and five at Bagush in the desert. The Bagush sets provided the first mobile section, exclusive on Enigma, with the object of intercepting low-powered transmissions of enemy forward units whose transmissions could not be detected at Malta or Heliopolis. These mobile units provided the best cover for Phoenix, the tactical key of the Afrika Korps, but there was delay in getting the traffic home. However, the entire picture changed rapidly after Alamein. The first intercepts taken by mobile sets in the desert arrived at Bletchley Park via bag to Heliopolis by daily plane (flying weather permitting), then by high-speed W/T link to Bletchley Park, involving delays of up to five days between interception and arrival at Hut 6, an intolerable delay. So it was decided to provide a mobile signals unit using high-speed W/T to operate alongside the intercept sets, which enciphered in Typex – the British cipher machine – the intercepted traffic and sent it on to

Heliopolis. Delays still occurred because Heliopolis had to re-encipher the traffic for onward transmission to Bletchley Park. Later on, the hand speed unit worked direct to England, eliminating the need for a second re-encipherment, reducing the delay. Eventually delays were down to five hours from interception to reaching Bletchley Park.

However, the impression should not be given that the codebreaking battle between Britain and Germany was all one-sided. Far from it – the Germans were not asleep, and Rommel had a particularly good direction-finding and codebreaking unit working for him during the North African campaign. Rommel's intercept and decoding organisation was the 3rd Company, 56th Signals Battalion (3/Nachrichtenabteilung 56) – later 621 Company – commanded by Captain Alfred Seebohm. But this unit had the bad habit of being too close to the fighting, as was to prove fatal later in the campaign. In December 1941 and again in January 1942, the unit lost direction-finding sections when it was overrun. Carelessness by German operators made life easier for Bletchley Park, and poor discipline by the Allied wireless operators helped Rommel. One of Rommel's intelligence officers, Hans Otto-Behrendt, recalls that soon after the start of wireless traffic each morning the structure of the enemy wireless net became clear.

> An especially rich field was the chatter between some British radio operators whose pompousness impelled them to drop valuable hints that they knew more than the others and even to hint at what it was.[xxvi]

According to Behrendt, guarded language and code words were initially rarely employed. He explains that seaborne supplies from Italy to Rommel particularly suffered, and that clearly the British were conducting a close surveillance of German and Italian wireless nets. As an example, Behrendt explains that the British always executed the air attacks at the time of day for which the Italian signals had announced the arrival of cargo-carrying submarines. Thus, on the very evening of the planned arrival of submarine *Zoea*, 10 August 1941, the British delivered an air attack. In fact, says Behrendt, this submarine had been unloaded early by local arrangement and so no harm came of it.

Rommel, according to Behrendt, did not underestimate British monitoring and deciphering skill. He once asked Behrendt how long it took German cryptanalysts to break an Italian wireless signal, to which the reply came that it was about three days. Rommel responded that 'the English manage it in two!' The crucial Battle of Sollum (15–17 June 1941) – British codename 'Battleaxe' – aimed at relieving the besieged garrison at Tobruk gives an insight into how Rommel's listeners discovered vital information. They picked up the codeword 'Peter' on 14 June, which they took as advance warning of an attack. According to Behrendt, the Battle of Sollum 'was a classic in the history of wireless intelligence'. The Germans had deduced the timing of the offensive and wireless monitoring supplied Rommel with the most important British signals. On 17 June came a key British message: 'Send umbrella for Proctor 1600 hours. Send Attaché Case to landing ground. Arrange onward home passage.' It was the signal for a British retreat.

There was also another source of intercepted intelligence available to Rommel – the enciphered messages being sent by Colonel Bonner Frank Fellers, US Military Attaché in Cairo, to Washington. The Italian military intelligence organisation – SIM – had managed to photograph a copy of the 'Black Code' and the code-key tables used by Fellers and kept locked in his safe at the US embassy. So, from autumn 1941, all Fellers' messages were being read by both the Italians and the Abwehr – German military intelligence. In view of the great frankness between the Americans and the British, this information was not only strategically but tactically of the utmost usefulness. According to Behrendt, 'it was stupefying in its openness'.

> This information, enciphered in the Black Code, was deciphered in Germany, translated, re-coded, and was in the hands of the General Staff and Rommel only a few hours after its transmission from Cairo.[xxvii]

It was a report from Fellers that revealed that at the end of June 1942, the Eighth Army had pulled back to the Alamein position. But, on 29 June, this impeccable source ended. Bletchley Park had picked up the leak on Enigma messages and traced the source to Fellers. The Americans changed their code book. Another blow to Rommel was the capture of most of Seebohm's unit on 10 July 1942 near Alamein, Seebohm being captured and subsequently dying of his wounds. His unit had been too far forward and had been overrun by the Australians. This was always the fear of Bletchley Park – that one of its Special Liaison Units, which handled disguised Enigma messages in the field, might be captured. Although the Germans reorganised their wireless section, once they were in full retreat its value was largely diminished.

For the Eighth Army, however, it was a better situation on listening to the enemy and reading its enciphered messages. Four days after he assumed command, Monty had in his hand a decrypt giving details of a planned German offensive set for the next full moon on 26 August. Rommel, however, had put in an important caveat to his superiors: in order to advance, he would need more supplies. It was the failure to obtain these necessary supplies – largely due to Enigma decrypts revealing enemy shipping movements in the Mediterranean – that helped turn the tide at Alamein. In the event, the German advance began during the night of 30–31 August, but thanks to Bletchley Park, and the delay caused by supply shortages – particularly fuel – Rommel lost the element of surprise. Indeed, the attack on the crucial Alam el Halfa ridge failed, not least because of the supply problems, the details of which were picked up by Ultra. In addition, as Enigma revealed, the Luftwaffe had been diverted from land attacks on the Allies to supporting the supply ships. Indeed, the German Air Force Enigma plus the decrypts of the Swedish Hagelin C38M cipher machine used by the Italians had played the major part in giving the Allies the intelligence edge at this time, although information about the convoys had come mainly from German army decrypts via Rommel's main cipher, Chaffinch. The Germans blamed British agents in the Italian ports as the main source of their supply ship losses. The Italian Navy used the C38M – which Bletchley Park had broken – but had been urged by the Germans, who were concerned at Italian cipher security, to use Enigma! In addition, Luftwaffe Enigma decrypts, largely through a key called Primrose by Bletchley Park, were also providing supply information. Bletchley Park named three Chaffinch keys – I, II and III. Two dealt with supplies and the third for special communications, and the codebreakers were assisted by captures of secret cipher documents. Among information revealed was a request for maps of Tobruk and assault equipment. Another communications key – Phoenix – was also producing high grade intelligence as the number of keys proliferated.

The Alamein battle began on 24 October 1942, and the first Enigma decrypt showed that the plan to convince the Germans that the attack would come in the south had succeeded – there had been complete surprise. Indeed, Rommel had to return hurriedly to the desert from Germany, not least because his temporary replacement, General Georg Stumme, had been killed after venturing too close to the front line. On

3 November, Hitler sent Rommel an order to stand and fight, which Bletchley Park decrypted. However, the following day Rommel asked Hitler for permission to withdraw, and had actually begun the pull-back before this was approved by the Führer. But Monty's openness on how he saw the coming struggle being fought had sent alarm bells ringing among defence chiefs and at No 10, with the fear that his outspoken comments might compromise Ultra. These fears were heightened when Bletchley Park informed Monty that Rommel was unwell and had asked to be sent home to recuperate. When this information burst on the world's press in the first week of September, Churchill ordered an inquiry into the leak. However, throughout the pursuit, Montgomery was fully apprised by Enigma as well as by air reconnaissance and by Army Y of the state of Rommel's forces and, more importantly, the Enigma gave him advance notice of Rommel's intentions.

However, the Germans were becoming suspicious of the enormous success the Allies were having in finding and sinking vital supplies to the Panzer Army as well as the public revelations about Rommel's ill health. In September, thirty per cent of Axis shipping heading for North Africa had been sunk, rising to forty per cent in October. Two-thirds of Rommel's petrol supplies had been lost. In four months, the Axis forces had lost more than 200,000 tons of shipping. At this rate, the final battle for Egypt would be lost before it had even begun. An inquiry into cipher security was ordered. It produced the usual result: Enigma was unbreakable.

After the failure of Alam el Halfa, there was some recovery in the supply situation, but it again deteriorated. A decrypt of 6 September revealed that Rommel only had rations for twenty-three days, a fortnight's ammunition and – crucially – only eight days' fuel. Enigma decrypts also revealed the severe cuts in rations for the troops, hardly likely to boost their morale. Moreover, of the supplies Rommel did have, much of it was in the rear, not in forward positions. In addition, the Germans were forced to fly in supplies because of the drastic loss in shipping. Indeed, in the first week of October, no shipping reached Rommel's forces. General Georg Stumme, who had taken over command of the Panzer Army while Rommel was recuperating in Germany, outlined in a decrypted Enigma message the growing superiority of the Eighth Army and his own increasingly dangerous supply position.

To add to his woes, Stumme had water supply problems because of storms in Cyrenaica. And, as if that was not enough, troop replacements were coming in slower than the numbers falling sick. An Enigma message of 20 October revealed that the German–Italian forces had around 104,000 men at the front against the Eighth Army strength of 195,000. Bletchley Park's codebreakers also received confirmation of a new tank destined for the desert – what was to become the famous Tiger Mark VI – but they turned up in North Africa too late to take part in the battle of Alamein. Enigma decrypts were being backed up by other forms of intelligence such as prisoner-of-war reports, ground patrols, and, crucially, RAF reconnaissance flights, which particularly revealed details of German airfields. By contrast, as Luftwaffe decrypts indicated, no German planes had succeeded in flying over the Eighth Army's positions for several days. With the Luftwaffe still busy protecting supply ships, and – on Hitler's orders – organising a massive attack on Malta (the last as it turned out), air support for the Panzer Army had been greatly diminished.

Nevertheless, the going was slow for the Eighth Army. Rommel, never one to be slow to take big decisions, launched his counter-attack on 27 October, but he sustained heavy losses, particularly from air attacks. Rommel's desperate situation was revealed in decrypts sent by him to his superior, Field Marshal Albert Kesselring. As the battle raged, Bletchley Park discovered that a supply ship carrying 4,500 tons of fuel was on its way to North Africa. This vessel and another ship were destroyed by the RAF. Four days later Enigma revealed that Rommel had taken a key strategic decision – to withdraw the 21st Panzer Division from the front line and use it as a mobile force to counter the expected Allied push in the north of the battlefield and replace it with Italian troops. This intelligence was timely, because it was precisely on the night of 1–2 November that the planned Allied breakthrough was to take place in that sector. A major tank battle now ensued, both sides taking considerable losses.

One decrypt from Rommel to his superiors was stark in the extreme: the German commander warned that 'the possibility of the gradual annihilation of the army must be faced'. Further decrypts revealed that Rommel was planning a phased withdrawal from 3 November. Then Bletchley Park received a special Enigma message – from Hitler personally to Rommel, ordering him to fight to 'death or victory'. Rommel saw a chink of light – small as it was – in that the Eighth Army had not at this point renewed its offensive, which he had expected. So he decided to make a stand. But Allied forces were too strong. Again Enigma came in handy, revealing that a request to Hitler from Rommel to withdraw had been agreed by the Führer. Wireless intelligence had also gauged that the Germans were withdrawing. By now decrypts showed that the Panzer Army had barely forty tanks left and fuel stocks were at crisis level. What aided Rommel's retreat was that the RAF did not maintain its bombing of the German forces along the single road down which it had to travel because of supply problems and the need to cover the next Malta convoy and fears that the Luftwaffe was about to receive substantial reinforcements. But it was all too late, and despite fighting a series of rearguard actions, it was retreat all the way for Rommel, until the final surrender in Tunisia in May 1943. Enigma had revealed that only 632 officers and men had escaped – while nearly 250,000 had surrendered, and Rommel was back in Germany to prepare for the Allied invasion of Europe.

Rommel had been denied vital supplies which had helped turn the tide in the desert, largely because Bletchley Park had supplied Montgomery with vital information about the Axis supply ships. In using this intelligence to select priority targets for their anti-shipping attacks, the Allies had cunningly seen Axis ration stocks rising, and it was found that Rommel's food dumps held plentiful supplies. If prisoners-of-war are to be fed, then better they are supplied with their own rations than those of the Allies – a fitting conclusion to the Enigma story of the battle to outfox the Desert Fox.

# Chapter 9

# To the Last Shell

Hitler was not much of a navy man, and he had a particular dislike of the big capital ships after the humiliation of the sinking of the battleship *Bismarck*, the pride of the German Navy, in May 1941. Such was the Führer's hostility to the navy that eventually the naval supremo, Grand Admiral Erich Raeder, submitted his resignation at the height of the war, after having been Germany's top sailor since 1928. It would be left to his successor, the U-boat commander Admiral Karl Doenitz, who succeeded Raeder on 30 January 1943, to carry the Kriegsmarine's torch and, in the dying hours of the Third Reich, be named by Hitler as his successor as Führer as Russian guns pounded his bunker in Berlin in April 1945. Doenitz, however, achieved what many thought the impossible – changing Hitler's mind on an issue – and the capital ships were to be retained, although Hitler did so with undisguised bad grace. But these ships were obviously out on licence. One false move and Hitler would have them – as he had already suggested – as artillery gun batteries to protect coastal regions. It would be an ignominious end for any ship of their size and importance.

The battlecruiser *Scharnhorst* was laid down at Marinewerft, Wilhelmshaven, on 16 May 1935, launched on 3 October 1936 and commissioned on 7 January 1939. She had a displacement of 32,000 tons and a top speed of 32 knots. Her armaments included nine 11-inch guns, twelve 5.9-inch DP guns, fourteen 4.1-inch anti-aircraft guns, sixteen 37mm anti-aircraft guns and ten (increased to twenty) 20mm anti-aircraft guns. In addition, she carried six 21-inch torpedoes and four aircraft and had a complement of 1,800. Bletchley Park was soon on the trail of *Scharnhorst*, but the Admiralty ignored the codebreakers' warnings when the aircraft carrier *Glorious*, homeward bound on 8 June 1940 as part of the evacuation of British forces from Narvik, was sunk by *Scharnhorst* and another battlecruiser, *Gneisenau*.

The German Army and Air Force reigned supreme at this time, but Britannia still ruled the waves, as she had done in the First World War. The Germans desperately needed to break the Royal Navy's stranglehold. By March 1941 *Scharnhorst* and *Gneisenau* had arrived at the French port of Brest, to be followed by the heavy cruiser *Prinz Eugen*, where they remained for nearly a year. What the Admiralty was waiting for was the expected attempt to break out of the vice that kept the German ships at Brest. But which route would they take? The least expected route would be up the English Channel, where British ships and aircraft could follow and attack them. Hitler, using his famous intuition, chose just that route in the teeth of disagreement by the naval commanders. Not for the first time, Hitler was to be proved right and his commanders wrong. *Scharnhorst*, *Gneisenau* and *Prince Eugen* subsequently took part in the famous dash up the English Channel on 11 February 1942, codenamed Operation Cerberus by the Germans. Not only was the move carried out in broad daylight, but it was the first time since 1690, when the French Admiral Tourville had defeated an Anglo-Dutch force off the Isle of Wight, that a large enemy naval force had sailed so close to the English coast.

Hitler desperately wanted these big ships available in Norway, for he had long feared a British invasion there. Ultra decrypts had revealed that the gun crews of *Scharnhorst* and *Gneisenau* were carrying out firing practice in the Baltic aboard the pocket battleship *Scheer*, and the crew of *Prinz Eugen* were training aboard the cruiser *Hipper*. On 18 December and 6 January *Gneisenau* suffered further damage. On Christmas Eve 1942 the Admiralty alerted all Air commands that a breakout from Brest was likely at any time. By 1 February evidence of a possible breakout had grown. Two days later Ultra and other sources showed the Channel defence had been strengthened. On 5 February Ultra revealed that Admiral Ciliax had hoisted his flag in *Scharnhorst*, and that German minesweepers were clearing a new passage through the Bight, indicating an intention to go up-Channel. But breaking into the daily naval Ultra settings at this time was difficult, and the traffic for 10–12 February was not decrypted until 15 February.

Meanwhile, a British plan to counter the breakout was devised, codenamed Operation Fuller. The departure of *Scharnhorst* and *Gneisenau* was delayed by an air raid on the night of 11 February, and when they did sail, shortly before midnight, *Sealion*, a submarine placed close in at Brest to watch for any movement, had just withdrawn to charge her batteries. Luck, so far, was with the German ships. That incredible luck was to continue as two of the three Coastal Command patrols suffered radar failure, and then the third was called home early just as the ships were passing through their patrol areas. Moreover, these gaps in the patrols were never reported to Dover.

It was at 1042 that the RAF spotted the German ships off the mouth of the Somme, but did not break radio silence to report the fact. At the same time, a number of shore radar stations were effectively jammed by the Germans, while the reports of those that were not jammed were disbelieved for too long. It was not until an hour later that Admiral Ramsay, Vice Admiral Dover, was informed that Admiral Ciliax's ships were almost off Calais, but by this time it was too late to launch attacks.

The first information that the German ships were at sea came from coastal radar on 12 February, followed by reports from air patrols. *Scharnhorst* had led the breakout in bad weather late on 11 February accompanied by six destroyers and five minesweepers. It was only later that radar picked up echoes of aircraft and finally that of large surface ships, and this was confirmed by two Spitfire crews, despite air and sea attacks, but the German ships made it up the Channel. However, during the dash north, *Scharnhorst* hit a mine off the Scheldte and was damaged by a second mine, but reached Wilhelmshaven early on 13 February. Meanwhile, the hapless *Gneisenau* was attacked by destroyers and also hit a mine, but she and *Prinz Eugen* reached Brunsbuttel in the Kiel Canal the same day. Then *Gneisenau* was hit yet again, this time by RAF bombs while in dry dock in Kiel, so her refit was abandoned and she took no further part in the war. With anger in Britain at the audacity of the German ships, it was unfortunate that the information about the damage to *Scharnhorst* and *Gneisenau* could not be made public to raise a cheer back home, but to have done so could well have compromised Britain's most secret weapon – that Germany's Enigma cipher machine messages were being read. However, such was the humiliation that Churchill was forced to announce a Board of Inquiry into what went wrong.

It was not until March 1943 that *Scharnhorst* finally made it to Norway from the Baltic. Two unsuccessful attempts were made in January by *Scharnhorst* and *Prinz Eugen* to reach Norway, but Ultra decrypts each time enabled counter-measures to be put into effect, forcing them back to the Baltic port of Gdynia each time. But it was third time lucky for *Scharnhorst* when, on the evening of 6 March, she passed through the Great Belt and finally beat the blockade. Ultra discovered *Scharnhorst* at sea on 10 March, and the following day Bletchley Park found out that she had reached Narvik, where she arrived on the ninth. Ultra decodes from Luftwaffe signals also revealed that another warship, possibly the *Lützow*, could shortly be on the move. The following day messages in an unreadable cipher (called Neptun by the Germans and Barracuda by Bletchley Park) were exchanged between *Lützow*, *Tirpitz* (based at Trondheim) and German naval commands. On 14 March Ultra disclosed that *Tirpitz* had joined *Scharnhorst*, *Lützow* and the cruiser *Nürnberg* in the Narvik area. On 22 March it was learned that *Scharnhorst*, *Tirpitz* and *Lützow* had moved from Narvik to Altafjord, arriving on the twenty-fourth. Ominously, the Arctic was approaching the period of long daylight – ideal conditions for a German attack on the convoys. All convoys outward bound to Russia stopped after JW53 left Loch Ewe, on the west coast of Scotland, on 15 February, fifteen ships reaching Murmansk on the twenty-seventh and seven more arriving at Molotovsk in the White Sea on 2 March. On 1 March, Convoy RA53, westbound from Murmansk, left for home. No more convoys were to tackle the hazardous journey either way that spring and summer during those long daylight hours. The scene was thus set for a showdown between these formidable ships and the British fleet when the convoys resumed later in the year. The value of Bletchley Park's Ultra decrypts was about to prove priceless. If Germany's big surface ships joined the convoy battle, the result could be a massacre.

Wartime events can hinge on small but what later turn out to be significant incidents. This was to be the case with *Scharnhorst* because, but for a decision by a Luftwaffe officer to leave out a crucial part of a message on the sighting of British naval forces, *Scharnhorst* would almost certainly not have been sunk. The Admiralty well knew that inactivity by *Scharnhorst* and the rest of the big surface fleet could not last forever. In March 1943 *Scharnhorst* eventually left the Baltic and joined *Tirpitz* and the 4th Destroyer Flotilla in Altafiord at the beginning of April. However, *Scharnhorst* was not completely idle, and Admiral Sir Bruce Fraser, who had taken over from Sir John Tovey as Commander-in-Chief of the Home Fleet, was given an Ultra message on 9 March that the German battlecruiser was to carry out exercises in Altafjord. On 19 March Bletchley Park picked up a signal from Admiral Commanding Northern Waters to Battle Group to be at three hours' notice. A further message to the Luftwaffe spoke of 'presumed enemy convoy' and urgently called for reconnaissance from the Lofoten Islands. However, a number of signals decrypted by Bletchley Park showed that the Germans were having difficulty mounting air reconnaissance because of the bad weather. The Luftwaffe was also to experience technical faults with their aircraft, as well as being hindered by using some planes that were not fitted with radar. Subsequently, Admiral Northern Waters signalled the Battle Group to stand down to six hours' notice. The danger of the big ships putting to sea, it seemed, had diminished.

On 20 December, Convoy JW55B, comprising nineteen ships, sailed from Loch Ewe, bound for Russia. Two days later, about three hours before the first known German sighting, the convoy was believed to be about sixty miles north–north–east of the Faroes. On 23 December an escort comprising the battleship *Duke of York* (flying Admiral Fraser's flag), the cruiser *Jamaica* and four destroyers left Iceland to cover this convoy. Meanwhile, Convoy RA55A, heading home to Loch Ewe with twenty-two vessels (one subsequently turned back), sailed from Murmansk on 22 December with a covering squadron of Admiral Sir Robert Burnett in the cruiser *Belfast* and the cruisers *Norfolk* and *Sheffield* in company. Admiral Doenitz, in his memoirs, has described how he saw the situation. He said that a convoy, carrying war material for Russia and protected by a cruiser escort which was no match for the German battleship, was sailing through an area within easy reach of the German battle group, and its position, course and speed were known. Because of ice in the vicinity of Bear Island, which prevented evasive action, and the superior speed of the German ships, the convoy could not hope to avoid an attack. Luftwaffe reconnaissance had not discovered any heavy enemy formation, although that did not mean that no such force was at sea. Doenitz stated that even if it were, it must have been a long way from the convoy, and the *Scharnhorst* seemed to have every chance of delivering a rapid and successful attack.

The first sighting of convoy JW55B was by the Luftwaffe on 22 December through a routine patrol on a meteorological mission, and an Ultra message was signalled to Commander in Chief Home Fleet to this effect, warning that a U-boat had been ordered to operate if conditions were favourable. The Battle Group at Altafiord – *Scharnhorst* and five destroyers – was brought to three hours readiness for sea. The following day the convoy was again sighted and more accurately reported as twenty merchant ships and twelve protective vessels and for the rest of the day and throughout 24 December, contact was maintained.

In the first message sent to *Scharnhorst* decrypted at Bletchley Park, it was revealed that no U-boat was in contact with the convoy, but the Germans did not appear to be aware of the homeward-bound RA55A. It would not be long before the U-boats would be brought into play, and on 24 December seven U-boats – the *Eisenbart* wolfpack comprising U277, U367, U354, U601, U716, U957 and U314 – were ordered to take up specified attacking areas. On Christmas Day, Rear Admiral Erich Bey, Flag Officer (Destroyers), transferred his flag from *Tirpitz* to *Scharnhorst*, having replaced Vice Admiral Battle Group Oskar Kummetz, who had reported sick and gone on extended leave. On Christmas Day one of the U-boats found the convoy, and its position, course and speed were quickly transmitted to the rest of the wolfpack, and *Scharnhorst* and the 4th Destroyer Flotilla were put on one hour's readiness, detected in an Ultra message using the more complicated Offizier (doubly-enciphered Officers-only) cipher.

But there were doubts among the German naval commanders as to the wisdom of putting the Battle Group to sea, as there was concern regarding the weather, with gales of between Force Six and Force Nine expected, creating problems for the destroyer escort. In addition, the Luftwaffe had warned that bad weather would make reconnaissance impossible. However, given Hitler's reprieve of the big ships, Doenitz wanted results. Not only was *Scharnhorst* to go out in bad weather with escort problems and no reconnaissance, but the German intelligence on the strength of British naval forces was poor. The *GC&CS Naval History* records that, had the Germans at this point been aware of the nature of the Allied force which, in detached formations of varying strength, lay between *Scharnhorst* and the fulfilment of its task, it is certain that the battlecruiser would not have been risked. That a close escort of destroyers and corvettes was disposed about the convoy, the Germans knew. They appreciated also that a remote screen, including a cruiser as the largest unit – *Belfast*, *Norfolk* and *Sheffield* – lay to northward. The *Naval History* goes on:

> They did not yet know, however, that the British battleship *Duke of York*, with a covering force [cruiser *Jamaica* and four destroyers], had left Iceland an hour before midnight of 23rd December bent upon the destruction of the Battle Group.[xxviii]

As Christmas Day drew to a close, a boat was instructed to proceed to

*Scharnhorst* in Langfiord and await further orders. On 26 December the Battle Group was brought to one hour's notice and in the afternoon it was sent an Offizier signal to be ready for sea at 1630. Then, forty-five minutes later, a patrol vessel was told that *Scharnhorst* would pass outward bound as from 1800, although departure was delayed for another hour. The plan was to attack the convoy the following morning. These messages were broken by naval codebreakers at Bletchley Park in the middle watch of 26 December. An emergency Ultra message was flashed in the early hours of Boxing Day to Commander in Chief Home Fleet that *Scharnhorst* had probably sailed, and followed a decrypt of a message containing the codeword 'Ostfront' – called 'Epilepsy' by Bletchley Park – the cover name for *Scharnhorst* to sail. By now the Germans had re-established contact by air with the eastbound convoy. Another Luftwaffe report later stated on Christmas Day that there was no support group within fifty miles of the convoy, while a further message that night said that the convoy was 'very widely spaced'. By early on Boxing Day the Admiralty calculated that the Russian-bound convoy was sixty miles southeast of Bear Island and the homeward-bound convoy was some 200 miles west-south-west of Bear Island, while U-boats were informed that *Scharnhorst* and five destroyers had left Lopphavet the previous night. Early on Boxing Day the first U-boat report came in of the convoy sighting. This information was sent out by Ultra at 1304 on the twenty-sixth.

At 0730 on 26 December, the German force was closing the convoy and the first location of *Scharnhorst* came from the cruiser *Belfast*. The cruiser *Sheffield* also sighted the German battleship and shortly afterwards the action began. Almost immediately *Scharnhorst* signalled that she had been fired on by what appeared to be a cruiser using radar-controlled firing apparatus. With no very clear idea of his destroyers' position, Admiral Bey ordered them to break off and return to port. However, before the destroyers headed for home *Scharnhorst* had been in action again, with the cruiser *Belfast* locating her. Seventeen minutes later the German battleship was again attacked, and exchanged fire for about twenty minutes. At 1525 *Scharnhorst* reported her position and the intention to return to base via the approach route to Narvik. However, nearly an hour later the main British force, led by *Duke of York*, made radar contact. At 1650, *Scharnhorst* was illuminated with star shell and *Duke of York* opened fire with her main armament. The critical period of the battle had begun. Just after 1700 *Scharnhorst* was engaging both *Duke of York* and *Jamaica*, while taking evading action to the eastward. While the action was in progress, four escort destroyers – detached from the westbound convoy – crept slowly up for a torpedo attack on each quarter. To northward four other escort destroyers manoeuvred to gain bearing for their own torpedo assault. By 1820 the many hits had reduced the speed of *Scharnhorst* and twenty minutes later the range was only 10,000 yards. Torpedoes were discharged at 1,800 yards and *Scharnhorst* was hit three times. *Duke of York* and *Jamaica* re-engaged the battlecruiser and scored immediate hits. Between 1901 and 1928, now under fire also from *Belfast* and *Norfolk*, the *Scharnhorst*'s speed fell to five knots. At 1925 she said she was making for Tanafiord. Five minutes fire was checked in *Duke of York* to enable *Jamaica* and *Belfast* to close *Scharnhorst* for the final rites. In addition, the battlecruiser suffered further hits from torpedoes fired from four destroyers. At 1939 *Jamaica* went in for a further torpedo attack while the *Belfast*, approaching shortly afterwards, illuminated the area with star shell, but by then *Scharnhorst* had sunk.

The part played by Ultra during the battle is also given in *Ultra in Royal Navy Operations*, which states that just after midday on 26 December, the Battle Group 'reported being engaged by several heavy units' while another message reported action with a 'heavy battleship'. At 1819 *Scharnhorst* reported that her opponent 'was firing by R D/F [radio direction-finding] location at over 18,000 metres range'. Further reports were received from her and from another destroyer – Z33 – at 2000. At 2330 Admiral Commanding Northern Waters acknowledged a signal from the Signals Officer of 4th Destroyer Flotilla that all five destroyers were proceeding to port. Then came a forlorn German rescue attempt for the crew of the *Scharnhorst* and only 36 of her crew of 1,943 survived, none of them officers. Early on 27 December, U-boats were ordered to continue the search on a reciprocal course after completing the seventy-mile sweep, but the search was broken off just before 1700 that evening. Inevitably, there were German reactions to the sinking of the *Scharnhorst*. This was embodied in a decree promulgated on 29 December by Doenitz and at Bletchley Park the same day, which began by emphasising the imperative need for the Battle Group's intervention in support of the Army on the eastern front. As *Ultra in Royal Navy Operations* makes clear:

Doenitz went on to say that prospects for attack were favourable, as air reconnaissance had established the presence of comparatively light forces escorting the convoy, and it was assumed that limitations imposed by weather conditions on the use of armament would be advantageous to *Scharnhorst*.[xxix]

The report adds that Doenitz 'also counted on an element of surprise' as two recent convoys had successfully reached northern Russia unmolested. The report goes on – underlining the Grand Admiral's total ignorance that the most secret signals of the Germans were being read – to say that the powerful concentration of heavy British forces was possibly connected with the passage of a second convoy on its homeward journey, hitherto undetected. Doenitz stressed that the weightiest lesson to be drawn from the battle was the fact that British forces were able to establish the *Scharnhorst*'s presence at over thirty miles, and by the aid of direction finding to shadow her and bombard her unseen at a range of 19,500 yards. However, from the German side they had no idea of the damage which they themselves had inflicted, which amounted to a hit aft in *Norfolk*, which put one turret out of action and flooded a magazine, and minor damage to *Sheffield* and *Saumarez*. Fortunately, ships in the convoy were untouched.

The report concluded that the steady flow of Ultra up to the time that contact was made with the enemy enabled the Admiralty's Operational Intelligence Centre to keep the Royal Navy convoy escorts regularly informed of German surface, aircraft and U-boat moves. The interval between the time of origin of a German message and that of the Ultra signal based thereon varied from five to twelve hours. *Ultra in Royal Navy Operations* concludes:

> The value of Special Intelligence [Ultra] in this particular operation can be judged by the fact that it provided the only source of information on *Scharnhorst*'s departure from Altafiord. It also revealed the enemy's ignorance of the odds with which he was called upon to contend.[xxx]

Hitler was in a black mood over the sinking. He referred to the 'criminal error' of the Commanding Officer – Admiral Bey – and expressed his opinion that 'such events occur because of a desire to preserve the ship intact. The ships do not want to fight to the bitter end.' Doenitz, however, defended his naval colleague.

In war very small events can cause major disasters. The sinking of the *Scharnhorst* could have been avoided but for a decision by a senior Luftwaffe officer to change an air reconnaissance message. At 1100 on 26 December *Scharnhorst* received a signal about the sighting of five warships far to the northwest of the North Cape. When the Admiral commanding the German fleet received the message, recalls Doenitz, he assumed these were his own destroyers which had been ordered back to port as a result of the instructions to the *Scharnhorst* to deliver her attack without the destroyers. He added that neither he nor Naval High Command saw any reason to interfere as a result of the aircraft's report with the Group Commander's operational intentions, particularly since at that moment they were not precisely known to them. Doenitz notes that:

> It was only after the loss of the *Scharnhorst* that it was established that the aircraft's report had, in fact, stated: 'Five warships, one apparently a big ship, northwest of the North Cape.'[xxxi]

However, Doenitz states that in passing the signal on to the Admiral Commanding the Fleet and to the *Scharnhorst*, the Air Officer Commanding had struck out the words 'one apparently a big ship', because he wished to pass on only definite information and no conjectures. Doenitz describes the omission of these important words as a 'tragedy'. Had the words 'one apparently a big ship' been included in the signal sent to him, Admiral Bey could with certainty have assumed that the big ship in question was British and he would then probably have acted in accordance with that part of Doenitz' operation order which read: 'Engagement will be broken off at your discretion. In principle you should break off on appearance of strong enemy forces.'

Doenitz goes on to make the point that at the time of the signal – 1100 – *Scharnhorst* could have turned away unobserved and reached Norway before she came into contact with the enemy battle group advancing from the west. He also took the view that nobody knows what interpretation Admiral Bey placed on the crucial signal. Doenitz saw the disaster as the result of unfortunate events which dogged the *Scharnhorst*. With a little more luck, he believed, everything might have turned out differently and with happier results.

He also thought it was possible that Admiral Bey, in the battlecruiser, thought that a more westerly course would bring him too close to the group of five warships which the 1100 signal had reported as advancing towards him. Hence the reason for the course he eventually took. As to the two convoys, the first section of JW 55B comprising ten ships and a tanker reached the Kola Inlet at Murmansk on 29 December, and the second section arrived in the White Sea, 450 miles further east, two days later. No ships in the convoy were lost. The homeward-bound convoy RA 55A arrived at Loch Ewe on New Year's Day 1944, twenty-one vessels reaching port, one having turned back.

The sinking of the *Scharnhorst* was a major triumph for Bletchley Park, given the speed at which vital information was supplied to the Battle Group and the Task Force. In its death throes, a defiant Enigma message was sent from the doomed battlecruiser personally to Hitler. Dated 26 December 1943, it read:

TO: THE FUEHRER

WE SHALL FIGHT TO THE LAST SHELL

This message underlined the extreme difficulty for the German Navy to operate because of the ever-present threat of the Royal Navy, but in addition – although they were not aware of it – they faced a second although invisible and formidable foe in Bletchley Park. It was proving to be a deadly duo in the war at sea.

# *Chapter 10*

# In Napoleon's Footsteps

Stalin was an extremely difficult ally for both Winston Churchill and President Franklin Roosevelt during the Second World War. The Soviet leader was highly suspicious of both Britain and America. Even when the Russians entered the war, Stalin's belligerence and almost paranoid behaviour did not end, as Churchill was to find when the Arctic convoys set sail in a sea of U-boats, plus a vigilant Luftwaffe, to deliver vital supplies to Russia at the height of Nazi military power. During Hitler's build-up to his attack on Russia, Stalin disbelieved British warnings of an impending invasion. Churchill, of course, could not reveal to Stalin that the information he had about an imminent attack came from the Germans themselves through their Enigma cipher machines. The Nazi-Soviet pact signed by Hitler's Foreign Minister Joachim von Ribbentrop and his Soviet counterpart, Vyacheslav Molotov, in Moscow in August 1939 on the eve of the Second World War had come as a profound shock to Britain, which did not receive any advance intelligence about the Pact, either from the British embassy in Moscow or from any other source. The only certainty was that it could not last. A month later, following the invasion of Poland, Russia and Germany signed a trade agreement which would have considerable economic benefits for the Nazis, in particular the provision of vital supplies that would oil its formidable war machine. On 30 November the Russians invaded Finland and forced the Romanians to concede Bessarabia, prompting Hitler to guarantee Romanian independence.

Hitler, triumphant in the west, and making inroads into the Balkans and North Africa, believed his invincible military machine could be at the gates of Moscow in weeks. The Red Army would be no match for him. As such, Hitler prepared for the greatest gamble of his life, at the same time breaking the golden rule of military strategy – never to fight on two fronts at the same time. But in the quest for 'lebensraum' – the Nazi quest for living room for the German people – he was to find to his ultimate cost the Russians were made of sterner stuff than he had envisaged. Hitler had begun his preparations against Russia a year earlier, in July 1940, although he had given indications of his intentions in 1925 when he published *Mein Kampf* (*My Struggle*). By the end of the month Germany's divisions in the East had trebled from five to fifteen, while early in August the Army High Command – the Oberkommando des Heeres (OKH) – had received its first invasion study. At the same time, the Soviet military attaché in Berlin warned Moscow that Germany was preparing to attack. But the diplomatic wires were rife with rumour and counter-rumour. In August, Stalin, anxious to continue to appease Hitler, attacked moves by Britain for what he interpreted as an attempt to cause divisions between him and Germany.

Winston Churchill did not disguise his utter contempt for Stalin's indifference as to the ultimate fate of the west against Hitler's aggression, not least the Soviet leader's failure to bring together Turkey, Romania, Bulgaria and Yugoslavia to form a Balkans front along with Britain to withstand the Nazis. He described as 'amazing ignorance' the situation in which Russia found itself, and Churchill said he doubted whether any mistake in history had equalled that of which Stalin and his henchmen were guilty when they failed to rally the Balkans. He added that 'Stalin and his commissars showed themselves at this moment the most completely outwitted bunglers of the Second World War.'

Churchill believed that Allied resistance in the Balkans, plus the Yugoslav coup against the pro-Axis government, had caused a five-week delay in putting *Barbarossa* into action, which may have saved the Russians from defeat. Churchill has admitted that until March he had not been convinced that Hitler was hell-bent on war with Russia, or how near that conflict was. Moreover, he argued, the German military movements eastward could be readily explained by Hitler's policy in Romania, Bulgaria, Greece, Yugoslavia and Hungary. That Hitler was about to unleash a war against Russia, Churchill said, was 'too good to be true'. Churchill liked to get intelligence reports firsthand and not receive them 'sifted and digested by the various intelligence authorities', as he told his chief of staff, General Hastings Ismay. On *Barbarossa* he was to receive conflicting reports from the various intelligence agencies as well as Bletchley Park decrypts, particularly from Axis sources, on the diplomatic front. He wanted to form his own opinion of the raw intelligence material, which is why the key Enigma decrypts were sent to him each day in their purest form. In particular, Churchill's view on German intentions against Russia changed dramatically following the movement of three Panzer divisions from Bucharest in Romania to Cracow in Poland, picked up by Bletchley Park on railway Enigma. Then, following the bloodless Belgrade anti-Axis coup on 27 March in which the Yugoslav government, which had signed a pact with Hitler under duress, was removed, they had returned to Romania. Hitler reacted furiously, and issued Directive 25 for the invasion of Yugoslavia. Hitler had gradually been coercing the Balkan countries into the Axis fold. On 1 March Bulgaria had joined the Tripartite Pact of Germany, Italy and Japan, to which Hungary and Romania had also earlier signed up, and on the twenty-fifth Yugoslavia had followed suit, but the coup had changed Belgrade's stance. An impatient Hitler attacked both Yugoslavia and Greece on 6 April. On 17 April Yugoslavia surrendered, and on the twenty-fourth the Greeks were overwhelmed. Crete fell the following month. The way was now clear for the invasion of Russia.

As a result of this boomerang movement of the three Panzer divisions, there then followed an extraordinary event in which Churchill asked Sir Stafford Cripps, Britain's ambassador to Moscow, to personally deliver a note from him to Stalin. Dated 3 April, this would be his first direct communication with Stalin for ten months. Churchill's 'short and cryptic' message was based on Enigma intelligence which the Prime Minister described in his note to Stalin as 'information from a trusted agent'. Clearly, if Britain could persuade Stalin to unite with the Greeks and Turks, this might give the Russians more time to prepare to receive the Nazi onslaught on their country. However, Cripps had already conveyed similar views to Andrei Vyshinksy, Russia's deputy foreign minister, and he considered that to give Stalin the Prime Minister's message under the circumstances could prove 'a serious tactical mistake' as he informed Foreign Secretary Anthony Eden. In turn, Eden told Churchill he thought Cripps had a point and that if the ambassador's views given to Vyshinksy were well received, then Churchill's views could be expressed to Vyshinsky by Cripps. Churchill was not at all pleased that Cripps had queried giving his message to Stalin, and insisted it be sent. Unfortunately, the telegrams confirming that Churchill's message had been delivered to Stalin were delayed because of an error, which did not help the Prime

Minister's temper in any way. Post-war, Churchill reflected that he could not judge whether his message would have altered the course of events, but he nevertheless regretted that his instructions were not carried out effectively. He felt that if he had been able to have direct contact with Stalin, he might have prevented him from having so much of his Air Force destroyed on the ground.

On 7 May Stalin took over as chairman of the Council of People's Commissars, replacing Molotov, so making himself head of the Soviet government and taking full responsibility for domestic and foreign affairs. Russia sought to placate Germany by recognising the pro-Nazi government of Rashid Ali in Iraq and expelling the Belgian, Norwegian, Yugoslav and Greek representatives in Moscow. The official Soviet news agency Tass had meanwhile dismissed rumours of a German invasion.

The first inkling of the invasion, which took place on 22 June 1941, had come a little over three weeks earlier, on 31 May, when Germany made demands on the Russians backed by the threat of armed force. Such substantial movements of troops and material eastward in Poland could not go undetected, but the German explanation was that they were not frontline troops, and they had been moved because they could not be kept in France. By October 1940 the number of divisions had more than doubled from fifteen to thirty-three, and the German argument was not entirely accepted by the Russians. The Germans were failing to keep to their trade treaty obligations with Russia, and in a tit-for-tat move, Moscow cancelled all long-term exports to Germany. The same month Army Group East had been set up in Poland and the Army High Command had relocated from France to Zossen. At this time MI6 had been receiving information that the German army intelligence section that covered Russia – OKH Foreign Armies East – had been increasing and that the activities of German military intelligence, the Abwehr, had has also been stepped up. But the general view in Whitehall was that Hitler would not invade Russia until he had finished off Britain. Another British theory was that the eastward move was to protect Germany against a Russian attack while Hitler marched into the Balkans following his invasion of Romania in October. Another reason for the eastward move put out by the Germans was to enable training for the invasion of England, codenamed Sealion, to be carried out away from British bombers and air reconnaissance.

On 18 December 1940 Hitler issued his Barbarossa Directive for the attack on Russia which, crucially, stated that the Russians would have to be defeated quickly even though Britain remained unconquered, but knowledge of this Directive did not get back to London. Despite this tight secrecy in Berlin, the media were in full cry around the world about an impending Nazi invasion of Russia, notably in the *Neue Zürcher Zeitung* and the *Chicago Daily News*. However, Whitehall was still not convinced that Germany planned an attack. But while British intelligence may have been in ignorance of Hitler's plans, American intelligence was apparently better informed. For example, the US Commercial Attaché in Berlin had, apparently, been kept informed of the initial planning between August and December 1940 by a senior member of the Nazi Party, and sometime between early January and mid-February 1941 he had been given full details of Hitler's Barbarossa directive of 18 December and of the Führer conference on the subject of 9 January 1941.

Some accounts reported that Washington received this intelligence on 21 February and gave the information to the Russians on 1 March. But the Americans did not, apparently, inform Britain in general terms until 21 March and then on 17 June – the latter not received until 25 June – when the British Embassy in Washington sent secret documents dating from the previous January and April to London. Meanwhile, forward airfields were being constructed in the east and by April 1941 there were forty-six divisions facing the Russian front. By now reports were reaching London of German forces reaching Poland from France, Russian speakers being recruited into the army and Russian exiles entering the German intelligence units. By December 1940 Bletchley Park had broken the Abwehr hand cipher, a major achievement. German activity was also noted in Finland in the form of setting up bases on the Finnish-Russian frontier, but London interpreted this as a possible move to land in Ireland or Iceland for a possible invasion of Britain or to support the Finns against the Russians.

Hitler's deception plans continued apace. On 10 January 1941 he issued a Directive postponing Sealion and Felix – the planned invasion of England and the seizure of Gibraltar via Spain respectively – and disguising the Barbarossa preparations as part of the build-up to attacking England. There was a serious lack of intelligence about Russia, whose communist system was exceptionally security conscious. However, this lack of insight into Soviet intentions was not peculiar to Britain; Germany, too, had little idea of what was going on in Russia.

Meanwhile, the Americans were keeping Britain and the Russians informed of German intentions, as they were deciphering encrypted messages used by Japanese embassies. Then, on 24 April, Bletchley Park decoded a Luftwaffe message outlining the first eastward movement of a Luftwaffe unit from France to Poland. A Signals regiment was also ordered to Cracow as part of Fliegerkorps V, which had been in France and, in addition, airfield construction was taking place in Poland. Two days later movement of ground forces from the Balkans to the Cracow area resumed after being halted at the end of March. May was to show Bletchley Park an acceleration of Luftwaffe movements eastward to the Cracow region, involving units formerly used in the bombing of Britain – indicating that an invasion of the UK mainland was now on hold – and from Greece. Decrypts also showed that the Luftwaffe was flying over Finland, another indicator of a planned eastwards push. The same month came the first Enigma message via the Luftwaffe of Barbarossa as the codeword for the invasion of Russia. The invasion intelligence was strengthened with a decrypt indicating that a prisoner-of-war cage from 2 Army at Zagreb was to join a division at Tarnow, east of Cracow. Clearly a prisoner-of-war cage would only be required if plans were of an offensive, rather than a defensive nature. Then, on 15 May, one of the biggest shocks of the war occurred – the arrival in Scotland of Hitler's deputy, Rudolf Hess, who denied that any attack on Russia was being contemplated. According to Hess, he had come to Britain to bring about a rapprochement between England and Germany. Hitler had no designs against Britain, he said, but wanted a free hand in Europe. On 17 May, Churchill conveyed to President Roosevelt some of the replies of Hess to his interrogation. The Deputy Führer had spoken of Hitler having a free hand in Europe and he was asked if he included Russia in Europe or in Asia. Hess replied, 'in Asia'. Hess added that Germany had certain demands to make of Russia which would have to be satisfied, but denied rumours that an attack on Russia was being planned.

But this view by Hess was at odds with what Bletchley Park was picking up. Luftwaffe decrypts revealed that German Air and Army units carrying bridging equipment were to join a movement starting for Moldavia on 6 June. This was an early indication of the earliest date at which operations might begin. The first mention of codename Barbarossa had occurred in a Luftwaffe Enigma message on 8 May. Despite this overwhelming evidence, there was confusion in diplomatic and intelligence circles as to German intentions. However, the decision to attack had been made by Hitler even while Soviet Foreign Minister Molotov was in Berlin. Molotov had come with specific demands: that Finland was a Soviet sphere of influence, agreement must be reached on Poland, and Soviet interests in Romania, Bulgaria and the Dardanelles should be acknowledged. Molotov later reiterated these demands in a note to the German government. Colonel-General Heinz Guderian, the famous tank strategist, who became one of the panzer commanders in Russia and was later Chief of the Army General Staff, recalls Hitler telling him of Molotov's visit, and how it shaped the Führer's thinking on Russia. Hitler had concluded from Molotov's visit that war with the Soviet Union was inevitable. He was to repeatedly describe to Guderian the course that the Berlin conference took. Guderian added:

> It is true that he never talked to me about this matter before 1943, but later on he did so several times and always in exactly the same terms. I have no reason to believe that what he said to me was not a repetition of his opinions at the time in question.[xxxii]

When Barbarossa was revealed to Guderian, he says he could scarcely believe it. Here, against all military thinking, and in direct contravention of Hitler's criticism of Germany in the First World War, in which a war on two fronts had been carried out, the mistake was about to be repeated. Guderian added: 'I made no attempt to conceal my disappointment and disgust.' Not least of Guderian's concerns was that military preparations were inadequate for the huge size of the undertaking – even most of the vehicles for the new divisions were French and not capable of meeting the demands of warfare in Eastern Europe. Neither could German production meet the hugely increased requirements. One crucial question Guderian asked himself was whether German armour was superior to that of the Russians. He recalls a curious event when Hitler had ordered that a Russian military mission be allowed to visit the tank schools and factories – nothing was to be hidden, no doubt to impress the Russians what they were up against. But the Russians were deeply suspicious, not being convinced that the latest German tank, the Panzer Mk IV, was the heaviest in the German army. They believed they were not being shown everything. Guderian added that the military commission was so insistent on this point that eventually the German manufacturers and Ordnance Office officials concluded that the Russians must already possess better and heavier tanks than themselves.

It was at the end of July, 1941, that the T34 tank appeared at the front and the riddle of the new Russian model was solved.[xxxiii]

By mid-May, intelligence had estimated German military strength in Poland, East Prussia the Balkans and Finland at 100–120 divisions, as against the actual numbers of 121 divisions. However, in the guessing game on German strategy, other considerations had to be examined. The Germans had successfully invaded Crete, but this had proved a pyrrhic victory, having sustained very heavy casualties. Germany might advance through Turkey and the Middle East, taking Suez via Syria. Hitler had plenty of options. Which would he take?

Countdown to the invasion was underlined when Luftwaffe Enigma showed that a major conference took place on 4 June involving the senior commanders of the major units likely to be involved in an invasion of Russia. During this period one of the most productive areas for Bletchley Park was the use of Enigma by the German railways, which was giving top quality intelligence on movements of men and material eastwards. Further reinforcements had also been revealed in Norway, and there had been a noticeable increase in W/T traffic in Scandinavia and even an attempt at radio deception (called 'Sham'), aimed at hiding the eastward movement of troops and equipment. Meanwhile, another Enigma message revealed that Reichsmarschall Göring, Luftwaffe supremo, had invited all the Air Force commanders involved in the invasion to Karinhall, his home just outside Berlin, for talks. By now Bletchley Park had estimated that around 2,000 aircraft were likely to be involved in the invasion, and that Hitler would be ready by 15 June.

Despite this, there was still a view held among some circles in Whitehall that Hitler would not attack Russia before defeating Britain. Moreover, some were arguing that as far as economic considerations were concerned, he could get all he wanted from Russia by the mere presence of his huge forces on the Soviet border. War, on the other hand, would mean that Russian supplies would cease. At this point the Japanese came back into the picture when Bletchley Park decrypted a report from their ambassador in Berlin to Tokyo following his meeting with Hitler, that an attack on Russia was inevitable. Among decrypts, a 'Chief War Correspondent' would be arriving at the northern

Norwegian airfield of Kirkenes, a further pointer that the Nazi propaganda machine would be well geared for the invasion. Further Enigma decrypts from Kirkenes underlined the advanced state of readiness of the Luftwaffe for an attack. But even a week before the German onslaught, while Russia had been increasing her defences, at the same time the Soviets had been renewing the trade agreement and resuming supplies to Hitler. Even as the Luftwaffe was being given its first targets, the Russians again publicly dismissed rumours that Germany was about to attack her.

Churchill was under no illusions that once Hitler had finished off Russia, he would again turn his attentions to the invasion of Britain. London now believed that Germany would overrun the Russians in three to four weeks, and not longer than six weeks. In the first scenario, there would be a further gap of between four to six weeks before the invasion of England finally took place, and if the latter time-scale, Sealion would be six to eight weeks away from the Germans entering Moscow. However, the day after the attack, the intelligence view was that once Russia was disposed of, England would not be attacked until 1942. With Hitler's invasion less than three hours away, Germany's ambassador to Moscow, Count Werner von der Schulenburg – later a conspirator in the 20 July 1944 plot on Hitler's life and subsequently executed by the Nazis – communicated a message to Ribbentrop from Molotov. Schulenburg had been summoned to Molotov's office at 2130 on 21 June when the Soviet Foreign Minister complained that the German government seemed dissatisfied with the Soviet government and rumours of a war between the two countries persisted. Molotov also made the point that the German authorities had made no comment on the Tass denial of an impending invasion, nor had that news agency's message appeared in the German media. Molotov wanted to know how the current German–Soviet relations had come about. Schulenburg sent his note to the German Foreign Ministry at 0117 on 22 June. Less than three hours later, at 0400, Ribbentrop handed a formal declaration of war to the Soviet Ambassador in Berlin. By then 153 German divisions comprising 3.6 million men, some 3,600 tanks and over 2,700 aircraft were already across the Soviet border following the release by Hitler of the codeword 'Dortmund'. They faced 140 Red Army divisions and 40 brigades of around 2.9 million men with between 10,000 and 15,000 tanks and 8,000 aircraft – many of them obsolete.

The question has often been asked about Hitler's decision to fight on two fronts – contrary to what he had written about this as a cause of Germany's defeat in the First World War in *Mein Kampf*. There had been plans to overthrow Hitler by some generals in 1938, but the abject surrender of the western allies to Hitler at Munich had halted that – the Führer carried all before him; he was invincible. Then, his swift victories in the west had stunned his military critics. Hitler would now have his war against Soviet communism. It was all glory. But Hitler was not to have his quick victory this time. And it was not to end in triumph in Moscow, but in his death in the ruins of the Reich Chancery, with the Soviet Union triumphant. Where Napoleon had trod with such confidence the previous century, and been brought to defeat, so a new tyrant had marched across the vast expanse of Russia and ended in snowbound defeat. But at least Napoleon had entered Moscow – something that Hitler failed to achieve.

# Chapter 11

# An Incomparable Target

With the sinking of the battleship *Bismarck* in May 1941, the pride of the German navy rested on the battlecruiser *Scharnhorst* and the battleship *Tirpitz*, but when the *Scharnhorst* was sunk on Boxing Day 1943, *Tirpitz* became the number-one British target. With a speed of thirty knots, a standard displacement of 42,900 tons and a complement of 2,400 she tied down much of the Royal Navy, and was a constant threat to the Atlantic and Arctic convoys. Bombed from the air by the RAF and Fleet Air Arm on fourteen occasions, as well as coming under attack from mines and both midget and Soviet submarines, she seemed indestructible. The Germans regarded her as unsinkable. Churchill was extremely irritated by the German battleship and wrote sharply to the First Sea Lord in January 1942:

> Is it really necessary to describe the *Tirpitz* as the *Admiral von Tirpitz* in every signal? This must cause a considerable waste of time for signalmen, cipher staff, and typists. Surely *Tirpitz* is good enough for the beast.[xxxiv]

Bletchley Park had been keeping a close eye on *Tirpitz*, and from decrypts obtained during Baltic exercises in late October 1941, it was seen as significant that the exercises had been largely concerned with torpedo firing and very little with gun firing. The first reference to torpedoes in *Tirpitz* came that September after about three months in dock at Kiel. On 12 January 1942 Hitler gave permission for *Tirpitz* to move to Trondheim in Norway, where she arrived four days later.

On 17 January Bletchley Park decrypts revealed that *Tirpitz* was at sea. Key indicators of the intentions of big German surface vessels was the movement of German Air Force units, and on 18 February the Home Fleet was alerted by Bletchley Park that certain Luftwaffe units

The Abwehr (military intelligence) Enigma machine differed from the standard three-rotor machine in that it had four rotors but no plugboard and also contained the numbers 0–9, unlike the standard Enigma keyboard. On the right of the rotors is a counter.

This rebuilt checking machine was used to determine whether stops provided by the bombe were right or wrong. It found the stecker pairings of the menu letters which helped to find the key.

Cottage 3, where Bletchley Park's first wartime Enigma message was broken on 20 January 1940. Codebreakers Alan Turing and Dilly Knox worked here.

The standard three-wheel Enigma machine as used by the German Army and Luftwaffe. However, the wheels shown are alphabetical as used by the Navy – the Army and Air Force used the numbers 1–26.

The various components of an Enigma wheel showing the internal wiring connecting letters of the alphabet. Each wheel had different wiring.

The twelve-wheel Lorenz SZ 40/42 cipher machine as used by the German High Command for sending mainly Army strategic information. Colossus was used to help find the key.

The original codebreaking operations at Bletchley Park took place in the Mansion, occupied by the codebreakers in August 1939.

Sculptor Stephen Kettle's Welsh slate statue of Alan Turing at Bletchley Park. (*www.kudosfinearts.com – Turner Fine Arts Agency*)

Typex was a British cipher machine, some of which were modified like this one to replicate an Enigma machine on which the messages from the recovered cipher were deciphered.

The Uhr was an attachment to Enigma used by the Luftwaffe with forty different stecker wirings. (*Dirk Rijmenants*)

Rare photos of Enigma machines being used in the field by the German Army. Because the machines were portable they could be used under most battle conditions. (*Helge Fykse*)

# W/T RED FORM.

| Ship or Station. | Set | H.R.O. № 2. | Date. | 26.12.43 | Operator's Remarks.* |
|---|---|---|---|---|---|
| HMS "Duke of York" | Opr. | D Rough. | Time Ended§ | Sie blow. | Q.S.A. 5. |
| | To† | | Frequency & System. | | Last transmission from "Scharnhorst" |
| | From† | | | 6475 kc/s. | |

All before the Text

Text, Time of Origin, Signature, etc. Write ACROSS the page, code and cypher on every third line.

1)    de KR ANA   KR. KR ANALLE  A

      (Time ended:- 1823 Z.)


2)    Priority Dos.   1925    21.

      UTKZ      RBSB      YKAE      NZAP
      MSCH      ZBFO      CUVM      RMDP
      YCOF      HADZ      12ME      FXTH

      FLOL      PZLF      GGBO      TGOX
      GRET      DWTJ      IQHL      MXVJ
      WKZU      ASTR      UTKZ      RBSB.   A

      (Time ended:- 1832 Z. Erratic noise. No further heard.)

Last message of the battlecruiser *Scharnhorst* shortly before she sank in the Arctic on Boxing Day 1943. This message was intercepted by the battleship *Duke of York*. (*Colin Waghorn*)

Sir Edward Travis was a First World War cryptographer. He became deputy head of GC&CS in 1925, head of Bletchley Park in 1942 and director of GC&CS in March 1944. He was the first director of GCHQ until his retirement in 1952. (© *National Portrait Gallery, London*)

Alan Turing's outstanding codebreaking work included being head of naval Hut 8 and devising the prototype of the bombe, which broke Enigma messages. (© *National Portrait Gallery, London*)

BOMBE

A WAVE – the US women's naval service – seen operating a four-wheel wartime US bombe. It was designed differently from the British bombe but worked just as efficiently. (*Photograph courtesy National Security Agency*)

Herbert Yardley ran America's inter-war Black Chamber codebreaking organization, subsequently closed down by the US government. (*Photograph courtesy National Security Agency*)

Legendary US codebreaker William Friedman, who also helped design the US Sigaba cipher machine. (*Photograph courtesy National Security Agency*)

Japanese naval cipher machine used between 1942 and 1944 and given the US codename JADE. (*Photograph courtesy National Security Agency*)

An Enigma machine in the command vehicle of General Heinz Guderian in France, June 1940.
(© *Imperial War Museum*)

Test plate used by the punch card system based in C Block at Bletchley Park which used Hollerith machines to aid codebreaking by storing searchable information. (*Crown ©. Reproduced by kind permission of Director, GCHQ*)

A US Army sergeant on duty at Bletchley Park in the German Army/Air Force codebreaking Hut 6, working on one of the many registers. (*Crown ©. Reproduced by kind permission of Director, GCHQ*)

The Duddery at Bletchley Park, where difficult-to-break keys were tested. The Enigma machine in the foreground was used when cipher settings had been solved. (*Crown ©. Reproduced by kind permission of Director, GCHQ*)

The inside rear of a bombe showing (right) its heart – the relay gate whose senses detected a 'stop' which could break a day's key. (*Crown ©. Reproduced by kind permission of Director, GCHQ*)

Front view of a standard three-wheel bombe with 108 drums representing 36 Enigmas. (*Crown* ©. *Reproduced by kind permission of Director, GCHQ*)

A Giant – four bombes linked together. Delivered in June 1944, just after D-Day, they were designed to combat the new pluggable Reflector Dora. (*Crown* ©. *Reproduced by kind permission of Director, GCHQ*)

The Siemens & Halske ten-rotor Geheimschreiber T-52 teleprinter cipher machine, used mainly by the Luftwaffe for strategic messages. (*Crown ©. Reproduced by kind permission of Director, GCHQ*)

The Cipher Office at Bletchley Park. The ladies in the foreground are using the British Typex cipher machine. (*Crown ©. Reproduced by kind permission of Director, GCHQ*)

The Tunny Room at Bletchley Park. These machines were used to reveal messages enciphered on the Lorenz SZ 40/42 cipher machine whose keys were partly broken by Colossus. (*Crown* ©. *Reproduced by kind permission of Director, GCHQ*)

Colossus, the world's first digital programmable computer. The WREN on the right is operating the 'bedstead' around which ran the teleprinter tape containing the Lorenz cipher. (*Crown* ©. *Reproduced by kind permission of Director, GCHQ*)

had been transferred to southwest Norway. This pointed to the movement of German main units to Norway. Ultra was again active on the twentieth when Home Fleet was told that all indications pointed to a very early passage, probably that day, of a unit or units from Germany to Trondheim. As a result, Commander in Chief Home Fleet, flying his flag in the battleship *King George V*, with the carrier *Victorious*, the cruiser *Berwick* and seven destroyers, sailed from Hvalfjord in Iceland early on the morning of 19 February. *Ultra in Royal Navy Operations* explains:

> It was unfortunate that Special Intelligence [Ultra] was baulked of current information on this German Fleet movement on account of the number of messages in Offizier cypher [Officers Only – not currently readable on this particular occasion], but it was clear that Admiral Commanding Battleships was at sea by 0013 on 21st February with a force consisting of at least two cruisers, three destroyers and a number of torpedo boats.[xxxv]

Air attacks carried out on 22 and 23 February were unsuccessful, a severe snowstorm preventing the sighting of enemy ships, but German air reconnaissance against the Home Fleet at the same time was also fruitless. On the night of 22 February the pocket battleship *Admiral Scheer*, the cruiser *Prinz Eugen* and destroyers *Friedrich Ihn*, *Richard Beitzen*, *Paul Jacobi*, *Hermann Schoemann* and *Z25* left Bergen for Trondheim. On 23 February *Prinz Eugen* was hit by a torpedo from the submarine *Trident*.

At this time Britain was concerned with a possible Japanese occupation of Madagascar, which would involve British naval forces, so Churchill asked President Roosevelt for temporary reinforcement in the Atlantic. Churchill was concerned that *Tirpitz* was still a threat almost a year later when he asked the Service chiefs if they had given up all plans of doing anything to *Tirpitz* while she was at Trondheim. He was not happy that the Italians should be so much better in attacking ships in harbour than Britain. He wanted the Service chiefs to take stock of the position and report back to him. On 5 March, an Enigma decrypt revealed German preparations for action against the convoys. Focke Wulf aircraft had been moved from Rennes to Trondheim, and U-boat strength was up to eleven – two in Trondheim, one in Narvik, one bound for Narvik and seven at Kirkenes. The decrypt also revealed the first signs in north Norway of the system of co-operation between

Focke Wulf aircraft and U-boats, which had previously been used on the Gibraltar routes.

There had been one unsuccessful attempt by *Tirpitz* to attack a convoy (PQ12), which left Iceland on 1 March comprising sixteen merchantmen bound for Murmansk, the first use of German surface ships in the Arctic. However, *Tirpitz* had been ordered home if the convoy was not found by nightfall on the ninth. Early that day six Albacores were flown off *Victorious* to search for the battleship, and when she was found, the torpedo planes attacked in two waves. However, the torpedoes appeared to have been dropped at an excessively long range which enabled *Tirpitz* to 'comb the tracks' by turning sharply first to port and then to starboard. No hits were scored and *Tirpitz* retired at high speed to her safe anchorage near Trondheim. Destroyers sailed from Scapa Flow and submarines were on station, but *Tirpitz* came out in thick snow and passed close to the submarine *Trident* without being seen.

The PQ12 convoy revealed confusion at the highest levels of the German navy as to who was in charge of operations in Norway. Admiral Northern Waters had been told on 5 March that air reconnaissance had obtained a sighting in the early afternoon of fifteen large ships, one cruiser, two destroyers and two escort vessels near Jan Mayen Island. This was the first time the Luftwaffe had found a PQ convoy. Admiral Northern Waters made immediate plans for intercepting the convoy, and Ultra revealed that he had complained at what he saw as the leisurely way in which the sighting had been reported to him. Later that day four U-boats (the Werewolfpack) were ordered to form a patrol line 200 miles northeast of Jan Mayen. At the same time, Gruppe Nord – the supreme German naval command for Northern Waters, the Baltic and the North Sea between July 1940 and May 1944 – was asked to approve the use of two more U-boats that were covering the approach to Narvik, to join the Werewolfpack. Permission was given, provided the boats did not operate westward of twenty-six degrees east. The same day *Tirpitz*, with the 5th Destroyer Flotilla, was ordered by Gruppe Nord to leave Trondheim the following day to operate against the convoy between Jan Mayen and Bear Island. During the next few days no U-boat made contact with the convoy until 12 March, when U454 sighted it entering the approaches to the Kola Inlet. An unsuccessful Luftwaffe attack was launched that afternoon, and all the convoy made it safely to port. More galling for the German Naval High

Command, neither *Tirpitz* nor her attendant surface forces sighted the convoy. *Tirpitz* remained inactive at Trondheim, but on 21 March she was joined by the heavy cruiser *Admiral Hipper*, accompanied by three destroyers – *Z24*, *Z26* and *Z30*. *Tirpitz* was immune from most forms of attack while berthed in the Foetten Fjord near Trondheim. She lay surrounded by mountains and was moored close in to the cliffs on one side and surrounded by torpedo nets on all others. On the occasional fine day which made air attack possible, she had only to put up a smokescreen to rectify the climatic defect. Despite this seemingly secure position, she was attacked by Bomber Command during the early hours of 31 March, and on 28 and 29 April 1942. Weather conditions during the first of these attacks were so bad that only one aircraft succeeded in even finding *Tirpitz*, the usual smokescreen was in use and the attack was abortive. During the second and third attacks, most of the aircraft despatched – thirty-two and thirty respectively – found the ship, but again the smokescreen prevented any successes.

The lessons being learned by the allies were that some of the bombs being used in the attacks on *Tirpitz* were largely ineffective. The official account of attacks on *Tirpitz* comments that although the difficulties of carrying out an attack against a capital ship under such conditions were fully appreciated, the 4,000lb blast bombs with instantaneous fuses which seem to have constituted the major part of the bomb loads carried in these early attacks were rather unsuitable.

A hit would have caused only superficial damage to superstructures, while near misses would have detonated on the surface with little fragmentation and practically no effect on such a heavy ship.[xxxvi]

A better choice, it was suggested, would have been the 2,000lb AP bombs dropped in level flight, since twice as many of these bombs could have been carried, and any hits would have had a direct effect on the vessel's fighting efficiency. The small Mk XIX mines containing 100lb of explosive, and fitted with hydrostatic fuses to operate at a depth of thirty feet, had an almost negligible target, and the 500lb and 250lb GP bombs had little chance of producing serious damage against a ship of this size. A much bigger bomb would be needed if *Tirpitz* was to be destroyed from the air. The RAF now had such a big bomb – the 12,000lb Tallboy. Now Bomber Command had a weapon that could finally put paid to *Tirpitz*.

Given all the unsuccessful, or partially successful, attacks on *Tirpitz*, it was to be Barnes Wallis, of the Dambusters' 'bouncing bomb' fame, who was to finally provide the answer that dealt the fatal blow to the battleship. Churchill warned Stalin that because of *Tirpitz* and other enemy surface ships at Trondheim, the passage of every convoy had become a serious fleet operation. Apart from the ineffectual sortie of *Tirpitz* against PQ12, little use had been made of the surface fleet against the convoys. This was because the build-up of heavy unit strength in Norway had fallen considerably short of that originally planned, and the use of main units, without regard to class relationship and proven tactical principles, involved difficulties which could not be ignored.

When *Tirpitz* set out against PQ12, the pocket battleship *Admiral Scheer* was the only other main surface unit in Norway. The heavy cruiser *Prinz Eugen*, which had started out with *Admiral Scheer* on the northward voyage in February, had been torpedoed and forced to undergo a lengthy period of immobility. It had been planned that *Tirpitz* and *Scheer* would operate together against PQ12, but they could not sail in company because, although she had the necessary range, the *Scheer* could not maintain the speed of the battleship.

After the *Tirpitz* fiasco against PQ12 it was decided that to achieve results, heavy units should operate in pairs. But this was impossible with only two ships available, so it was decided that main unit operations should be abandoned until the heavy cruiser *Admiral Hipper* had arrived in Norway. It was also intended that the battlecruiser *Gneisenau* should sail in company, but bomb damage put paid to this idea. This move was completed by 21 March, the day *Admiral Hipper* arrived in Trondheim. But the Germans were further frustrated because the state of training on *Admiral Hipper* was far short of that required for active service. The German Naval High Command decided to re-examine the question of bases for main units in Norway. Originally it had been decided that Trondheim was the best base, being centrally situated in the event of an Allied landing in either south or north Norway. Moreover, Trondheim was not itself thought likely to be an objective for an invasion force. It was also ideally situated to attack the convoys, and offered shorter routes for the naval supply traffic from the Baltic.

However, thoughts began to turn to Altafiord and Narvik as better forward bases – Altafiord especially – during the summer and autumn months when the ice boundary receded to the north. Narvik was also favoured for its closeness to the vulnerable Lofoten Islands, and its favourable situation for short-notice sorties by Arctic main units against the convoys. Bletchley Park quickly picked up the northern movement of the surface ships. On 9 May, *Admiral Scheer* left Trondheim and arrived at Bogen Bay, Narvik the following day. Six days later the pocket battleship *Lützow* left the Baltic, and by 25 May was bound for Narvik from Trondheim. Now the German Navy had *Tirpitz* and *Admiral Hipper* in Trondheim with two destroyers and three torpedo boats, *Admiral Scheer* and *Lützow*, with six destroyers in Narvik, forming Battle Group Kummetz – named after Vice-Admiral Kummetz, flying his flag in *Lützow*, in command of the group. All looked well for the German surface fleet, but yet again a problem arose – fuel stocks were so low that only the pocket battleships could take part in operations. However, the German Navy was now preparing for an all-out assault on a convoy. It was to be the ill-fated PQ17.

By now Bletchley Park had learned that several Focke Wulf aircraft had arrived from Rennes to Trondheim on 28 January 1942, while the number of U-boats had increased to fourteen during the PQ13 convoy period. The *Prinz Eugen* and *Admiral Scheer* had joined *Tirpitz* at Trondheim by 23 February. At least twelve further Focke Wulf aircraft had arrived at Gardermoen and Allborg from Bordeaux, while *Admiral Hipper* had arrived at Trondheim from Hamburg on 21 March to join fleet units already there. *Admiral Hipper* was accompanied by three destroyers, bringing the total to seven destroyers at Trondheim. At the beginning of July, *Tirpitz* moved up to Altafiord for a projected operation against Convoy PQ17, but when these plans were cancelled, she returned to Narvik on 8 July, where she remained until October. *Lützow* returned to the Baltic the same month, and the cruiser *Köln* arrived at Narvik at the beginning of August, during which time *Tirpitz* took part in various exercises in the area. Around September, *Admiral Hipper*, *Admiral Scheer* and *Köln* moved to Altafiord. *Tirpitz*, with *Admiral Scheer*, moved south to Trondheim on the night of 24–25 October, where *Tirpitz* was to remain for three months, while *Admiral Scheer* returned to the Baltic in November. *Tirpitz* underwent trials around Trondheim during January 1943, and Ultra messages on 11 and 12 March indicated that she might shortly move, probably to Narvik, which proved correct. Then *Scharnhorst* moved from the Baltic to Narvik, while between 23 and 25 March *Tirpitz*, *Lützow* (which had returned from the Baltic early in December 1942) and *Scharnhorst* moved to Altafiord. With such a heavy concentration of Germany's big ships posing a major threat to the Arctic operations, it had been decided to suspend the Russian convoys for the six months from March–November 1943.

The Germans now put together plans for a major surface fleet sortie, largely to raise the morale of sailors who were idling away either in port or on exercises. Action was what they needed. The attack would be centred on British bases in Spitzbergen. The plan was that *Tirpitz* and *Scharnhorst* would be the main force, backed by nine destroyers. While *Tirpitz* continued to take part in extensive exercises, there was no operational threat until aircraft reconnaissance from a Spitfire on 7 September showed that both *Tirpitz* and *Scharnhorst* had left Altafiord. The force had actually sailed at midday on the sixth, and failing any Allied report, the Germans were confident that its presence at sea had not been detected. The following day Spitzbergen wireless station reported the presence of an enemy naval force comprising seven destroyers and three cruisers in the Ice Fjord area. The Germans intercepted the signal, and the Battle Group was alerted. Against slight resistance, the German force carried out its assignment. Batteries on Spitzbergen were silenced by the guns of *Tirpitz* and the ship's aircraft were used against pockets of resistance. Quay installations at Barentsberg were destroyed and at Longyearby and Advent Bay, *Scharnhorst* wiped out enemy targets. Coal and oil stocks were burned, stores looted or rendered unusable, and houses razed to the ground. By 0930 the operation was completed and troops were re-embarked in the destroyers, which then rejoined the ships patrolling the entrance. Bletchley Park had found it difficult to forecast and assess this essentially morale-building operation. On the sixth it was known that very extensive Luftwaffe reconnaissance had been laid on that day for an operation, extending throughout the Narvik–Jan Mayen–South Cape (Spitzbergen)–North Cape (Norway) area.

During September 1943 one of the most spectacular raids of the Second World War took place, by midget submarines, known as 'X-craft', on *Tirpitz*, which caused considerable damage, to an extent that the repairs to her would not be completed until March 1944. As a base for surface ships, Altafiord was believed to be virtually impregnable. *Tirpitz* lay moored at Kaafiord, an arm of Altafiord, about fifty miles from the sea, totally protected by torpedo nets. Although the Germans were aware of the existence of British midget submarines, they had no information about their armaments. They did not know, therefore, whether the attack was with torpedoes, mines or limpet charges. To check for limpet mines they pulled a wire strop from stem to stern around the ship under the keel. Preparations were made to get underway, but this was halted as it was not known what other trouble lay out in the fiord. The battleship's bow was moved away from the submarine known to have sunk off the port bow, by tightening and slackening the port and starboard forward mooring cables. However, unknown to the Germans, this caused a clearing of the forward part of the ship from the three charges placed abreast 'B' turret. Therefore, only the single charge aft remained effective. Shortly after, two heavy explosions were heard in quick succession and spray was thrown up over the ship, which shuddered violently. The other two X-Craft were destroyed in turn after this, and an intensive depth-charging of the fiord commenced. As a result of the attack the net defences were strengthened by securing them to the seabed, and floating torpedo batteries were installed for which 'Fat' (*Federapparat*) torpedoes, an area search torpedo weapon able to change course in finding its target, were provided.

From Ultra it was known that the second explosion caused an intake of water into *Tirpitz* and she asked for a power ship capable of electric welding to be sent. Subsequent photographic reconnaissance showed that the sea area around *Tirpitz* was covered with oil to an extent of two miles to seaward. The big question was whether *Tirpitz* would ever be operational again. An Admiralty appreciation on 20 March, based largely on Ultra (particularly reports from *Tirpitz* regarding trials held on 15 and 16 March 1944), assessed that the battleship would be unlikely to go to sea for operations against a well-escorted convoy unless she had no heavy ships or aircraft carriers with which to contend. The damage caused by the X-Craft had been repaired by early March 1944, and *Tirpitz* began a series of trials. The first movements in Altafiord were observed by reconnaissance aircraft, and Commander in Chief Home Fleet was asked to lay on a bombing attack using Fleet Air Arm aircraft, and this attack – Operation Tungsten – took place on 3 April. Two days earlier Ultra had revealed that full speed trials by *Tirpitz* had been postponed for forty-eight hours and that the new sailing time would probably be early on 3 April. Bletchley Park subsequently flashed the news that *Tirpitz* would leave at 0530 that morning. The weather was good and the German ship was caught completely by surprise as she was about to leave her berth. The first strike began just as the second anchor was being weighed. The upperworks of the battleship were strafed before a smokescreen could be put up or the flak batteries could be fully manned. The result was nine hits and a near miss, while the second strike attack found *Tirpitz* surrounded by smoke, suffering five hits and three near misses. However, because of the low height from which the bombs were released, none penetrated the armour deck. In fact, only two bombs reached it. Two other bombs ricocheted off the two-inch thick upper deck, and one lodged halfway through this deck. As all the vital parts of a large capital ship lie below armour, only superficial damage to living spaces and other unessential compartments was caused by the direct hits. This damage, however, was fairly extensive and several large fires resulted. One bomb struck the water a few feet from the ship's side, penetrated the side plating beneath the armour belt and detonated near the main longitudinal protective bulkhead. This bomb flooded bulge compartments nearby and extensive repair work by divers was required. There were heavy casualties.

In about a month *Tirpitz* was again operationally fit, no significant damage to armament or main machinery having been sustained in the attack. About two more months were required to complete the less important repairs. Another planned attack – Operation Planet – was set for 23 April, but was cancelled because of bad weather. Further attempts on 15 and 28 May (Operations Brawn and Claw respectively) were similarly abandoned because of poor weather conditions. By now the Germans were thoroughly alarmed at the prospect of further air attacks on *Tirpitz* and an intercepted wireless message on 14 June underlined this fear, as an immediate demand for sea reconnaissance was requested in order to prevent a second successful attack.

Ultra was again at work, indicating that *Tirpitz* might be on the move again after 16 July. On 17 July, with the Arctic summer at its height, another huge air attack was launched by the Fleet Air Arm (Operation Mascot). Intelligence reports and reconnaissance photographs indicated that the battleship was ready for further action, and attacks by bomber forces from carriers were made against her. The Germans received warning of the attack about half an hour before the aircraft arrived. According to a German report, because *Tirpitz*'s berth was immediately concealed by a smokescreen, the bombing was blind.

On 18 August, Commander in Chief Home Fleet, in the battleship *Duke of York*, CS1 in the carrier *Indefatigable* and a force of carriers and destroyers, left Scapa Flow for Operation Goodwood, another planned attack on the battleship. On 22 August, two waves of carrier-borne aircraft were carried out, but without any success. However, Ultra revealed that three days later *Tirpitz* put in a request for a bomb disposal squad to make safe an unexploded bomb. Two days later the next attack was launched, this time with eighty aircraft. Although the familiar smokescreen had been put up, two of the twenty-three large armour-piercing bombs and ten smaller semi-armour-piercing bombs scored hits. One of these detonated on the armoured roof of 'B' turret, which was only slightly damaged, but the other – a 1,600lb armour-piercing bomb – hit the port side of the upper deck abreast the forward conning tower, and penetrated through the armour deck to the lower platform (inner bottom), where it came to rest. The official German report on the attack admitted that it was the heaviest and most determined so far experienced. The report said that the English showed great skill and dexterity in flying. For the first time they dived with heavy bombs, adding:

> The fact that the armour-piercing bomb of more than 1,540lb did not explode must be considered an exceptional stroke of luck, as the effects of that explosion would have been immeasurable.[xxxvii]

To complete the month, an attack was made on 29 August from the carriers *Indefatigable* and *Formidable*, but no hits were obtained. August 1944 was a turning point for the battleship, as Grand Admiral Karl Doenitz has made clear. After the attack in August by the British with heavy six-ton bombs, one of which severely damaged *Tirpitz*'s bow, he ordered that *Tirpitz* should be used merely as a floating battery for the defence of north Norway. It was no longer possible to keep her in a sea-going condition, and only such personnel would remain aboard as were required to man the guns.

> To ensure that the worst did not happen and *Tirpitz* capsize as the result of one of these air attacks I ordered that she be berthed in as shallow water as possible.[xxxviii]

By now a new and far more deadly bomb was available – the 12,000lb Tallboy. Developed by Barnes Wallis, it was believed that even near misses would have considerable destructive value. The RAF launched its first Tallboy attack – Operation Paravane – on 15 September 1944, employing thirty Lancaster bombers which had flown from Scotland to north Russia, where they were based for the attack. The attacks were made in close formation in groups of about six. With the smoke screen up, only the boom surrounding the battleship and small portions of the ship were visible. Her main armament, directed by the shore radar installations, was used to put up a barrage against the attackers. Of the twenty-one heavy bombs dropped, only one fell sufficiently close to damage the ship. The explosion wrecked a large part of the fore end, particularly that part below the waterline, which resulted in the first 120 feet of the ship flooding to the waterline. This damage could not be repaired without docking her, and it was decided by the German Navy High Command that her seafaring days were over. A German document quoted in the official report on various attacks on *Tirpitz* sums up their reaction to the raid. This explained that it was eventually decided at a conference on 23 September 1944, at which the Commander in Chief and Naval War Staff were present, that it was no longer possible to make the *Tirpitz* ready for sea and action again. In order to preserve the remaining fighting efficiency of the ship, she should be used as a reinforcement to the defences in the Polar area. For this purpose *Tirpitz* was to be moved as soon as possible to the area west of Lyngenfjord, moored in shallow water and brought into operation as a floating battery. A suitable berth had to be selected which would be reasonably secure and would offer favourable operational possibilities for the ship's armament.

Adequate anti-aircraft, smoke-cover and net protection were to be provided. Makeshift repairs were made and *Tirpitz* was moved by tugs. A berth was selected near Tromsö, at Haaköy, and provided with a net enclosure. The ship was protected against underwater attacks and aerial torpedoes by a double net barrage. Shore anti-aircraft guns and smoke screen units were moved from Kaafiord to Tromsö. It was found that there were varying depths of water at the berth, and in particular there was a hollow below the midship section. Too many difficulties would have arisen if the ship were to be moved again, so it was decided to fill in the hollow till the water was two metres deep below the keel, and about 14,000 cubic metres had to be filled in at both sides below the midship section.

Crucially, *Tirpitz* was now within range of RAF heavy bombers operating from British bases. On 29 October, thirty-two Lancaster bombers, each carrying a 12,000lb Tallboy bomb, made yet another sortie in Operation Obviate. No direct hits were scored, but there was a near miss off the port quarter, which damaged the port shaft and rudder and flooded about 100 feet of the after end of the ship on the port side, involving an intake of 800 tons of water into the hull.

The end, when it came, was swift, as the Barnes Wallis Tallboy bombs took only twenty minutes to capsize the mighty *Tirpitz* – the 'unsinkable' ship – in a raid lasting eight minutes, from 0941 to 0949 on 12 November 1944. A force of twenty-nine Lancasters from 5 Group Bomber Command (617 and 9 Squadrons), flying out of Lossiemouth in Scotland, each carrying one 12,000lb Tallboy bomb, took off on one of the most effective air operations of the Second World War in what was to become the final attack on *Tirpitz*. The weather was clear and visibility excellent, there was no smoke screen and no enemy aircraft were encountered, although the battleship had received ample radio warning of the impending attack. The attacks were made at heights varying from 12,500 feet and 16,500 feet, and the ship received considerable structural damage and capsized on her port side. The first indication of the raid came in a German report that at 0800 a single Lancaster was over the Bodoe area, and fifteen minutes later three Lancasters on an easterly course were reported near Mosjoeen. Because of this and the close similarity between prevailing weather conditions and those of the previous raid, the anti-aircraft officer aboard *Tirpitz* suspected that another attack on the battleship was impending. At 0852 an air-raid warning was given following a report that aircraft were within 200 kilometres of *Tirpitz*. By this time, the ship's gun crews were closed up and request for fighter support had been made. At 0938, eight minutes after sunrise, the attack on *Tirpitz* was launched.

*Tirpitz* brought her forward main armament into action at a range of about thirteen miles, but in the meantime there was no sign of the requested air support, although the pilots were at cockpit readiness, but were prevented from taking off because the RAF was flying over the area there was a fear that the Bardufoss air base was the target. Later, nine fighters did penetrate the target area during the attack, but made no contact with the Lancasters. From captured documents it seems that, although the smokescreen units had been moved from Kaafiord to Tromsö, they were not operational on the day of the attack. *Ultra in Royal Navy Operations* explains:

The absence of fighter protection is not easy to explain. Fighter aircraft were apparently available and according to a long and detailed report (part of the Special Intelligence on the attack) promulgated by Admiral Polar Coast, fighter protection was being continually asked for from 0815 onwards.[xxxix]

*Tirpitz* lay off the south coast of Haaköy island, west of Tromsö, with her bows pointing east, within the rectangular boom enclosure. The attacking force was accompanied by a Lancaster of the RAF Film Unit equipped with three cinematograph cameras, and a dramatic reconstruction of the attack with timings for the bombs being dropped was calculated on the basis of the camera operating at a speed of twenty-four frames a second. Only 880 of her complement survived, while twenty-eight officers and 874 men perished. Salvage of the battleship was declared to be hopeless. Doenitz lamented the fact that the Luftwaffe failed to appear in time, and *Tirpitz* was left alone to combat the attack with her anti-aircraft armament.

As ill luck would have it the special, ultra-heavy bombs all came down on the port side of the ship, which was badly damaged; in addition these bombs blew great craters in the bottom of the fiord, making it immediately possible for *Tirpitz* to capsize, which she did.[xl]

The day after the sinking, Doenitz ordered an inquiry by the men responsible for selecting the berth. Preliminary investigation showed that the depth of water under the ship had either been miscalculated in the first place, or altered by the explosion of the heavy bombs. The summary of findings stated that the actual depth of the berth did not conform to the requirements and directions of the Commander in Chief. After the war, Admiral Ciliax, Naval Commander in Chief Norway, blamed the failure of the GAF to provide cover, rather than the choice of the berth, for the sinking.

From the unexpectedly swift capsize most of the men on the lower decks were not able to reach the upper deck. Only individual turret crews were able to escape. While the crews of the after-fire control position were still able to open the heavy armoured door of the forward fire control position, most of the crew on the upper deck saved themselves by swimming, or by the aid of floats on the net barrage or rafts from shore. Those who swam were greatly hampered by oil on the surface of the water. When 'C' turret blew up, some of those in the water were killed by the blast or by splinters. Doenitz realised that after the loss of the *Tirpitz* the surface ships were unable to take any further part in the war at sea. He observed that air power was becoming an ever-increasing menace to heavy warships, a development 'which finally led to the paying off of the British and American battleships in 1957 and 1958'.

A full inquiry was ordered by Doenitz, at the heart of which was the question whether, contrary to orders and reports, *Tirpitz* had not been anchored sufficiently securely. To ensure that the worst did not happen and *Tirpitz* capsize as the result of one of these air attacks, Doenitz had ordered her to be berthed in as shallow water as possible. On receipt of these instructions Rear Admiral Peters, commanding the battle group, proceeded to search for a suitable berth in one of the fiords near Tromsö. Along the irregular and steeply precipitous sides of the Norwegian fiords, however, the desired shallow water was not readily to be found. Admiral Peters tried to fill in the holes with sand. The results of the investigation concluded that the actual depth of the prepared berth did not conform to the requirements and directions of the Commander-in-Chief 'as had been reported to the Commander-in-Chief and to the Führer'.

The clear view of the Admiralty was that *Tirpitz* could have played a much bigger role in the war, pointing out that she only fired her armaments in action once, in the Spitzbergen incident in September 1943. As Roskill comments in his official history of the Royal Navy during the war:

> As no single British ship was able to engage her on equal terms we had always been forced to keep a powerful combination of carriers, battleships, and lesser vessels ready in the offing ...[xli]

Once again, Hitler's continual interference with the professionals in his armed forces proved fatal to his objectives. By his tight control over the movement of his main naval units, he denied his admirals the flexibility they required to be an effective force against the Royal Navy and its allies.

# Chapter 12

# Shark-Infested Waters

On 1 February 1942 disaster hit Bletchley Park. The Germans had, as the codebreakers already knew they would, added an extra wheel to their U-boat Enigma machines in the Atlantic and Mediterranean. Four rotors now put Britain totally in the dark as to the movement of the U-boats. It would be ten months before this new system – called Triton by the Germans and codenamed Shark by Bletchley Park – would finally be broken. Paddy Mahon, who was to head Hut 8, Bletchley Park's naval codebreaking section, described it as a depressing period, as they had clearly lost the most valuable part of the traffic and no form of cryptographic attack was available to them. Harry Hinsley, who worked in Hut 4, which handled the intelligence of naval decrypts, has commented that the delay of nine months in breaking the U-boat four-wheel Enigma was regarded by Bletchley Park at the end of the war as having been 'the most serious cryptanalytic failure' in the record of its work on German naval ciphers.

Bletchley Park had received advance warning of the coming into force of the fourth wheel by the end of 1941, and a signal that December was sent erroneously on the four-wheel setting, the operator making the blunder of then re-transmitting it in the three-wheel version, enabling the wiring of the fourth wheel to be recovered. A fourth wheel meant that existing bombes had to multiply by twenty-six (all the letters of the alphabet) the number of possible positions of the machine for each wheel order. It also made impossible a codebreaking system for enciphered naval messages invented by Alan Turing known as Banburismus, which helped find the middle and right-hand wheels on Enigma machines. According to Mahon:

> The introduction of the fourth wheel did not catch us by surprise. The earliest mention of M4, as this machine was called,

is in a captured document dated January 1941 where instructions are given for adapting it to three-wheel keys.[xlii]

He adds that it was clear that the machine must have been designed in 1940 – or even before the war – and the interest of the document was that it betrayed the characteristic feature of the four-wheel machine: it was an adaption of the three-wheel model and the fourth rotor was to be a reflector wheel, a part of the reflector to be considered apart from the three wheels making up the wheel order of the day. The new wheel was called Bruno and its reflector Beta and both were wired in such a way that if Beta was set at position A on an Enigma machine, they equalled in effect the three-wheel reflector B. This meant that while Beta was set at A, then M4 could be used as a three-wheel machine 'and the change from three to four wheels need cause no complications'. During 1942 there were a number of 'duds' – messages for which the reflector wheel had been wrongly set other than at A – which enabled Hut 8 to find the wiring on both the new wheel and the new reflector. Eventually the four-wheel bombes came on stream, in which its fast wheel turned at around 10,000 revolutions a minute leaving only 1.5/1000 seconds for the complete examination of each machine position. Mahon says that for that split second, every contact on every wheel 'had to be precisely in the right position or the job would probably be missed'.

The blackout period of February–December 1942 came at a crucial stage in the war, and put the U-boats back into the ascendancy, and in November the total amount of Allied shipping lost reached an all-time high for the war to date, 721,700 tons. During the first six months of 1942, only eleven U-boats had been sunk, and in November only two boats were lost. The big concern was that the amount of shipping being sunk was larger than what was under construction, and that beleaguered Britain required minimum annual imports of twenty-seven million tons to maintain rations and industry. There was a double disaster in February 1942, because, as ill luck for the Allies would have it, the German naval codebreakers, the B-Dienst, had broken Naval Cipher No 3, which carried most of the information about the vital north Atlantic convoys. The Royal Navy used a cipher for officers, and an Administrative Code for ratings. The B-Dienst had broken the Administrative Code, used by ratings for less secret communications, by the outbreak of war. In August 1940 this code was replaced by Naval Code No 1, which the German Navy codebreakers were also reading.

That same month, No 1 was replaced by No 2, and in January 1942 was itself replaced by No 4. But the B-Dienst was still reading a good deal of traffic, although they did not achieve the same success with No 4 as with No 1 and No 2.

Then in June 1941, the Admiralty's reserve Naval Cipher Basic Book No 3 was used by the Royal Navy, United States and Canadian navies in the north Atlantic. The B-Dienst was reading this cipher until June 1943, when No 5 came into operation. By November 1943, Atlantic communications were being sent by the Combined Cipher Machine, a joint US-British design, which completely frustrated all the efforts of the B-Dienst to decipher. But the B-Dienst was also having success with the Merchant Navy Code, which came into operation in January 1940. The capture of this code at Bergen in May 1940 greatly assisted the Germans in reading this crucial traffic involving the convoys. When that code was replaced by the Merchant Ships Code, another capture again put the B-Dienst ahead of the deadly game of 'hunt the convoy'. However, the decision in December 1943 to disguise the position of ships, instead of giving longitude and latitude, put an end to the B-Dienst successes on this code.

There were those at Bletchley Park who knew that the only way to break the four-wheel U-boat Enigma was with a four-wheel bombe – the electro-magnetic machines that found the daily Enigma settings. But the decision was taken at the time that it was vital to continue with the construction of the three-wheel bombes. By the summer of 1942 there were some fifty German Army and Air Force keys in operation, keeping Bletchley Park at full stretch. However, by the end of 1941 Bletchley Park had only sixteen three-rotor bombes, of which only twelve were functioning, but by the end of 1942 there were forty-nine in operation. Serious work on Shark did not begin until it came into operation in February 1942 and it was not until the summer of that year that the Americans were able to start contributing to the Shark problem. Three US cryptanalysts arrived at Bletchley Park in June 1942 and the Americans were supplied with a bombe to help them design and manufacture them.  After two visits by Bletchley Park representatives to the United States, co-operation was signified in the Holden Agreement in October 1942, signed by the US Navy Director of Communications Captain Carl Holden and Bletchley Park's director Edward Travis. This Agreement sealed the decision to have full collaboration between the two countries on Shark. Britain also agreed to help the Americans to build bombes and there would be a full exchange of information on German naval ciphers. By the end of 1943, with seventy-five bombes operational, the US Navy equivalent of Bletchley Park's Naval Section, OP-20-G, took over responsibility for breaking Shark. Paddy Mahon has commented that the US contribution of Op-20-G was 'immense', as also were the difficulties which arose, which were 'fairly numerous'. He added that the Americans were second in the field and agreed to play second fiddle and so the people they put into German machine cryptography were not the best cryptographers they had, but rather efficient and intelligent organisers with cryptographic knowledge.

Mahon says that their organisation and machinery was created for the special problem of Shark and was staffed with naval personnel, and there existed no co-operation between the US Services comparable to that which existed at Bletchley Park between Hut 6 (Army-Air codebreaking), Naval Section and Hut 3 (Army-Air Intelligence). Neither did they have the knowledge of, or the dealings with other machine keys, as they did at Bletchley Park. He explains that it was therefore natural, however regrettable, 'that they should tend to be narrow-minded and to regard Shark as the only really important thing in life'. This attitude, however, was rapidly thrown over by Commander Engstrom, Lieutenant Commander Church and the US Navy liaison officers in this Section, and Bletchley Park could be sure at all times of their co-operation in any scheme calculated to increase the return to be had from the bombes.

But progress on Shark was finally forthcoming. According to Hugh Alexander, who also headed Hut 8:

> In November we at last started to read the U-boat traffic, breaking into a Shark day on a WW (weather report). For the next six months we were to break most Shark days on short signals ...[xliii]

Short signals were used for convoy sightings and weather reports and were usually trigrams which could be sent in seconds to avoid direction finding by Allied intercept stations. They were a major source of cribs for Bletchley Park's naval section. For example, a weather report message consisted of readings recorded in a standard order. Such messages were normally sent in response to a signal – sent in the Shark key – from a control station, requesting a weather report at specified times, on receipt of which an acknowledgment would be sent back to the U-boat. The control station would then send the message to a central meteorological station which would re-send it enciphered using the international meteorological code. This was broken by Bletchley Park's meteorological section to give a crib into enciphered weather reports.

The decision to produce bombes in America had been taken many months before and in July 1943 two production models were in action and had their first success early in the month. By late autumn, new American machines were coming into action at the rate of about two a week, the ultimate total being in the region of 125. Cribs were despatched for running with instructions as to wheel orders, priority, etc, and were normally referred to as 'Amirs'. The only reputable cribs available were re-encodements from Dolphin, the Home Waters key, and apart from re-encodements, the only crib was a weather one in the Bay of Biscay, which had a large number of forms and was only rarely worth running. The problem was made much easier by three developments:

1. The appearance on Shark of the new Biscay Weather crib;
2. The increasing skill and wisdom of the Op-20-G cribsters;
3. The steady increase in the number of naval keys and the general introduction of the four-wheel machine.

Biscay Weather rarely broke a day, but at the end of October it produced a lengthy form and continued to use it with minor alterations until after D-Day. According to Mahon it was the longest consistent crib they ever possessed and the number of freak forms it produced was small. In January 1944 German security spotted it and sent a signal to the originator in Shark: 'Biscay Weather appears daily at an almost identical time, much of the text is identical, the length identical, the beginning identical, and it is always repeated on the "Ireland" frequencies.'

Mahon says that the effect of this crib was normally to break Shark currently and so in most cases to remove the problem of Op-20-G running bad cribs because there was nothing else to run. By D-Day, very close and efficient co-operation existed. Priorities of keys were decided at weekly meetings at which the US Navy representative was present. Mahon pays tribute to the Americans:

Op-20-G stuck most loyally to the priorities as laid down, running a vast number of Hut 6 jobs and enabling them to break keys which would have otherwise have remained unbroken.[xliv]

He added that it was a considerable tribute to the good sense of all concerned, and most especially to Op-20-G, who were in a somewhat irksome position, that relations were at all times extremely cordial. Moreover, it was possible to get so much work so efficiently done when the machinery had to be shared by three groups of people. Unfortunately, the first British high-speed bombe did not come on stream until June 1943 and the American version coming two months later. Mahon says that in April 1942, for example, Shark was allocated only about forty-two bombe days out of 600, but the system of using bombes was not the prerogative of any one of the huts at Bletchley Park. For the ten months that Bletchley Park was 'blind' on Shark, only the settings for three days were broken, one of these following the decision of the newly promoted supreme naval commander, Grand Admiral Karl Doenitz, to transmit news of his promotion to the Fleet in the Home key, which had been broken, and in the Shark key, thus enabling the codebreakers into Shark on that day – 14 March 1942. But it was hard going for the codebreakers.

It took six three-wheel bombes seventeen days to break the setting for the day. A three-wheel bombe had to work twenty-six times longer to test the text of a four-wheel signal than to test that of a three-wheel signal. Four-wheel bombes, had they been available, would have been more expeditious. However, Doenitz was not promoted every day, and had to suffice until the capture of Enigma material from U559 made it possible for Bletchley Park to make effective use of the three-wheel bombes against the Shark key from the middle of December 1942.

Two days in February 1942 were also broken, but the big breakthrough had to wait until the end of the year. It was not until the capture of Enigma material from U559, blown to the surface and ultimately sunk near Port Said on 30 October 1942, that the codebreakers were able to obtain a copy of the short signal weather book, which enabled them to read Shark signals. Sadly, the secrets of U559 cost the lives of two brave men aboard the destroyer *Petard*: Lieutenant Anthony Fasson and Able Seaman Colin Grazier. Both were awarded the George Cross (not the Victoria Cross, as their bravery was not in the face of the enemy), and Tommy Brown, a canteen assistant who survived, received the George Medal. It was this trio who reached U559 after the crew had surrendered and abandoned the boat, which had failed to sink, delivering to Bletchley Park its vital Enigma secrets. Without their efforts, says Mahon, 'breaking would have been delayed many months, although the book and indicator tables had already been reconstructed to a considerable extent'. Then, on 10 March 1943, a new short signal weather book was introduced which sent Bletchley Park in a spin, but nine days later this, too, had been mastered. When this third edition of the short weather signal book was introduced, efforts were made to break Shark almost exclusively on B-Bars – Bletchley Park's name for short signals sent by U-boats when sighting convoys – to enable U-boats and surface craft to send a limited number of standard messages without risk of discovery by direction finding through surfacing or transmitting for more than a few seconds. The B-Bar period lasted to the end of June and during this time 87 out of 112 Shark days were broken. On 1 July came bad news that the Kriegsmarine had introduced a new reflector (Caesar) and fourth wheel (Gamma) on Shark. This news came from the decrypt of a message enciphered on Oyster – the doubly-enciphered Officers-only (Offizier) key. Hugh Alexander recalled that this was a serious blow, but not as bad as it would have been earlier when there were fewer bombes and no four-wheelers available. He explained that the real trouble about the change was that it multiplied the possible wheel orders, and therefore bombe time, by four, since any of the four possible reflector/fourth wheel combinations could presumably be used on any day. He commented:

> We had to hope that the enemy would fail in some way to take full advantage of the change; this hope was to be amply fulfilled.[xlv]

There was a sequel to this problem which did not amuse the Hut 8 naval codebreakers. They had managed to find the wirings on Caesar and Gamma, but long afterwards discovered that these same wheels had been captured some time before in North Africa. However, they had not been sent to Bletchley Park on the grounds that they already had plenty of wheels! U559 had also revealed the short signal book used by U-boats for reporting on sightings and battle information. Reading these became possible because the Enigma machine was used with three and not four rotors. However, it was the carelessness of the German Navy in re-enciphering Shark four-rotor signals on three-wheel machines that made life that much easier for Bletchley Park. From August 1943 Shark settings were broken on an almost daily basis, and by September American four-wheel bombes became available in considerable numbers. A very personal explanation of the frustration over the long time it took to break into Shark has been given by Rolf Noskwith, then a young Cambridge graduate:

> I have been asked whether our prolonged inability to break Shark gave us a sense of guilt. While we knew the seriousness of the situation I cannot say that we felt guilty.[xlvi]

Firstly, he said that they genuinely felt that, without more captured material, there was no short-term solution. Secondly, they knew that there was a long-term solution because of plans, in collaboration with the Americans, to build more powerful bombes capable of coping with the four-wheel machines. Finally, they were still regularly breaking Dolphin (the other main key) as well as, from the summer of 1942, a separate key called Porpoise, used for Mediterranean traffic.

On the evening of 13 December 1942, the First Sea Lord, Admiral Cunningham, wrote to Admiral King, US Chief of Naval Operations, urging the need for care in making use of the newly available information. It would be a tragedy, he wrote, if they had to start all over again on what would undoubtedly be a still more difficult problem. By the beginning of November 1943, the codebreakers were, on some days, reading the traffic in time for it to be of operational value. Along with US Navy cryptographers, who made an ever-increasing contribution to the joint effort, they steadily completed its mastery over the Shark settings.

> This mastery was to be total by August 1943, from which time to the end of the war all the traffic for each day was read as a matter of course with little or no delay.[xlvii]

In May 1943, Doenitz withdrew his U-boats from the North Atlantic, and, says Hinsley, the short signals 'ceased to be of service as a regular means of entry into the Shark settings'. Shark had nearly bitten the head off of Bletchley Park at a crucial stage of the war. Ten months going blind on the whereabouts of the deadly U-boats had been a traumatic experience. It led to the eventual taming of this particularly dangerous underwater species.

# Chapter 13

# Storming Fortress Europe

The planning for D-Day was one of the greatest military achievements in the history of warfare and led to the largest invasion of all time. At the heart of this planning was Sigint – Signals Intelligence – backed by the genius of the Bletchley Park codebreakers. This invasion was not going to be a battle fought in haste – both sides had been spending years preparing for it, defence and attack. There was, however, one major advantage for the Allies – only they knew when and where the blow would fall. In the event, the Allies obtained total surprise and many senior German commanders were away from their posts on 6 June, including Rommel, who was on leave in Germany. Rommel had also been absent at the opening of the Battle of Alamein – back home on sick leave. As for Hitler, he was asleep in bed until midday, nobody daring to wake him! Hitler was not sure if the attack would come anywhere from Norway to the Bay of Biscay, but he and the German High Command were fooled about the place of the landings by the Double Cross system of 'turned' German spies captured after they landed in England, who sent controlled messages back to their Abwehr (German military intelligence) handlers. But if the Allies were to have up-to-date information about German plans, then their listening services had to be fully equipped, and it was realised that it would be necessary to provide a very large increase in wireless sets for interception – 500 was the figure given – and that there also had to be a large provision for M/F (Medium Frequency) sets for both fixed and mobile stations. This was achieved by a new large War Office station of 120 sets to assist the intercept station at Chicksands in Bedfordshire with German Air Force cover, which was provided at Forest Moor, near Harrogate in Yorkshire. A special US army intercept station known as Santa Fé was set up at Bexley Heath in Kent for Luftwaffe M/F traffic and a fixed M/F party was formed at Bishop's Waltham in Hampshire. In addition there had been the conversion of the station at Harpenden, in North London, into two mobile M/F parties. Forest Moor began taking traffic in March 1944, and had its full complement of 120 sets operational at the beginning of May. Santa Fé also started operations in March, and Chicksands reached 180 sets by April. Bishop's Waltham had commenced operations in September 1943, and Harpenden began specialising in M/F traffic in early 1943, leaving there for Rustington in Sussex early in 1944, crossing the Channel about four months after D-Day. These mobile units moved in two directions: one on the northern flank and one on the southern, concentrating on M/F and L/F (low frequency) German Army traffic. However, the mobile units sent to France were not well provided. The two units were each to have attached a mobile cipher and high-speed W/T unit for 'scooping' traffic, but to everyone's horror it was found that they had to share one receiving point in the UK – i.e. their respective transmitters would only be able to work to half capacity. Separate terminals were eventually allocated in England, but the stations remained handicapped because, while possessing separate W/T links to Bletchley Park, the answering signals to each had to be sent on a single pair of frequencies.

German Army traffic on the Western Front after D-Day provided Hut 6 – which handled German Army and Luftwaffe Enigma signals – with the most difficult sorting problems it had faced to date. Before D-Day there was very little German Army operational Enigma traffic, but they did hold a series of extensive W/T practice manoeuvres. According to Hut 6 head Stuart Milner-Barry, D-Day could hardly have gone better, although he confesses that while they were producing intelligence worthy of their greatest days, it was fortunate that the level of traffic fell away as quickly as it rose as they probably could not have maintained the peak level for any length of time. Practically all the enormous volume of Air traffic was broken, and Hut 6 lived on the old cribs for a day or two, then on re-encodements until the cribs settled down again, which they did when the Germans had redisposed themselves and recovered from the original disorganisation. For Hut 6, the quantity and quality of intelligence received reached its peak in 1944 – the zenith being about two weeks after D-Day when, for about a week, more than thirty keys were broken each day, and the total number of breaks put it above all previous years. For example, there were many months in 1944 when Hut 6 topped the 1942 record of 550 breaks. There was an immense advance on Army keys, and their importance relative to Luftwaffe keys constantly increased. By the unanimous testimony of generals in the field, the contribution to victory made through Ultra could scarcely be overrated.

This intercepted traffic was carefully studied for D/F, discriminants (three-letter groups, normally placed in the message preamble, indicating the key used) and Order of Battle evidence and it was discovered that key areas corresponded with the areas of the four Western armies and provided valuable information on the type of W/T communication to be expected, the local of headquarters, and in very general outline, key distribution. As to the German Order of Battle, Ralph Bennett, who worked on Hut 3 on German Army and Luftwaffe intelligence, explains that by D-Day Ultra had identified, and in many cases located, well over half the garrison-type divisions which would be the first line of resistance to the landings.

> In addition, all the army and corps commands along the coast had
> been identified at least once, many of them together with
> evidence showing what units or formations each controlled.[xlviii]

Much of the most urgent traffic passed on the high echelon networks, frequencies were fixed and almost all callsigns were equated with their units. But, a good deal of traffic in the same keys passed on lower echelon traffic and was a traffic analyst's nightmare. The most important were the L/F (low frequency) nets which included Divisions, Korps and Armees. There was a steady income of captured keys, but knowing they were compromised, the Germans stopped using many – but not all of them – before they reached Bletchley Park. There were captured Enigma machines, with key settings complete upon them, which arrived frequently at Hut 6. However, not a single message was ever found to decipher with the setting on a captured machine.

No story about D-Day – even one concentrating on codebreaking in particular and Sigint in general – would be complete without reference to the deception plans put in place to outwit the enemy. Hitler's fears were played on by the largest deception plan of the war – Operation Fortitude – which comprised two plans, North and South, and which led the Germans to believe that an invasion army, FUSAG or 1st

United States Army Group, led by US General George Patton, was based in Kent and Essex, poised to attack in July 1944 on the beaches south of Boulogne. This was Fortitude South. Its key element was Operation Quicksilver, to fool the enemy that the Allied force consisted of two armies, 21st Army Group under General Montgomery (the genuine Normandy invasion force) and FUSAG. There were dummy tanks, planes and landing craft and wireless operators simulating heavy traffic of a major military organisation. Fortitude North was the other deception, with its 'headquarters' in Edinburgh Castle. Skye was the radio deception component of Fortitude North. Skye I was Fourth Army headquarters, Skye II the fictional British II Corps (HQ – Stirling), Skye III the genuine American XV Corps stationed in Northern Ireland (but with fictional units added to its Order of Battle) and Skye IV the fictional British VII Corps (HQ – Dundee). Operation Neptune was the naval codename for the actual assault force that would cross the Channel.

It was important to know the German Order of Battle, and the major source of information, after prisoner-of-war interrogations, air reconnaissance and Allied agent and Resistance organisation reports from inside Festung Europa – Fortress Europe – was going to be Sigint. An early Sigint decision was for Special Liaison Units/Special Communications Units – which dealt solely with Ultra in the field – to be sent direct to SHAEF (Supreme Headquarters Allied Expeditionary Force, commanded by General Eisenhower) and 21 Army Group, which was to be in control of the invading armies. Key among the Sigint sources would be the ability to read Germany's top secret messages – a job for Bletchley Park. Plans had been drawn up by military chiefs and the Government Code and Cypher School over a year previous to the D-Day landings. By the spring of 1944 Bletchley Park staff had risen from 3,800 to 5,600, including 150 Wrens in spring 1944 to handle expanded traffic from D-Day. They had also greatly increased the number of tactical Sigint units that would be ready to take the field on D-Day by training 5,000 additional people for Army Y – wireless intercept – units, and bringing about a comparable increase in the number of RAF Y staff. At the same time, the number of Army and Air Force intercept sets rose from 264 in August 1942 to 609 in June 1944.

A major problem for the Allies was that the German Army and Navy had much stricter discipline in their Enigma procedure than the

Luftwaffe, and one of the mainstays of information about Enigma during the war had come from Air Force liaison officers known as Flivos. The mastermind behind German Army Signals was General Erich Fellgiebel, Chief of both the Army's Signal Establishment and of the communications liaison to the Wehrmacht Supreme Command, and later General of the Communications Troops. His laying of landlines to convey military traffic had made Army Enigma messages from Western Europe a rarity, Bletchley Park relying largely on the Flivos, who re-enciphered the unbroken Army keys into the Luftwaffe keys which the codebreakers were reading, thus allowing them to read Army communications.

The Allies had learned the lesson of good advance Sigint preparation from Operation Torch and the disastrous Dieppe Raid, used to test German coastal defences, and conducted largely by Canadian troops in August 1942. Improvements were put into place in the invasion of Sicily and later mainland Italy in July and September 1943 respectively. For Normandy, a Special Intelligence Board was set up to co-ordinate efforts for Overlord – the codename for D-Day – of both the British and US Sigint organisations. As to the volume of traffic, Bletchley Park had estimated in January 1944 that SHAEF would have to handle about 16,000 signal groups a day, but in the event this was 18,000 during the first three weeks after the invasion and only in the first few days was it severely taxed. The codebreakers processed a daily average for Commands of 2,500 Army and Luftwaffe decrypts from some thirty different Enigma keys, plus a smaller number of naval decrypts. On and before D-Day, Bletchley Park was reading the twelve most important of the seventeen naval keys. Indeed, for the first and last time during the war, a security risk was undertaken with the site of the codebreaking organisation – the decision to intercept naval traffic at Bletchley Park direct.

According to the Hut 6 *Official History*, 1944 was its 'finest hour'. But the year began for Hut 6 with a shock which, if the Germans had handled the situation thoroughly, could have put it out of the codebreaking scene altogether, and rendered it virtually useless for D-Day. On 23 December 1943, Hut 6 received the bad news that they were faced – with little more than a week's notice – with a possible cryptographic crisis which could have lost the codebreakers the principal Luftwaffe key, known as Red, which had been broken virtually every day of the war. This was the news that on 1 January 1944 a new reflector for the Enigma machine, called Umkehrwalze (Reflector) Dora, was to come into force. It was christened 'Uncle D' in Hut 6. As the *Official History of Hut 6* recalls:

> But this was a crisis of a new order: a new reflector, if it came into universal use, would (until broken) make all our hundreds of bombes so much waste metal. Till we had solved the D mystery our whole breaking technique was jeopardised.[xlix]

The *Official History* adds that 'Perhaps no single day in Hut 6 history was more memorable in prospect than our D-Day, New Year's Day 1944.' The first break was at 1100 on New Year's Day of Leek, an Eastern Air Force weather key, which had been broken since June 1941. Then, at 1150, came the vital Red key. Hut 6 breathed a sigh of relief – Uncle D was not being used universally. Once again, changes had been brought in piecemeal. The bombes and other breaking devices were fitted with the new reflector, and within a week, at least one Red key was broken running on Uncle D. But, as Hut 6 well knew, the Germans could go over to a 'wholly D' situation at any time. A number of D-breaking machines were devised of which the Duenna – invented by the Americans – proved the best, with a hand method or 'Hand Duenna' being available as a stand-in if required.

As well as cryptography, the Hut 6 Traffic Identification Section (TIS) played a major role, and of considerable help to Hut 6 on traffic identification was the work of Sixta (formerly No 6 Intelligence School). It was not until early in 1944 that the volume increased sufficiently largely due to German anti-invasion exercises, during which they would experiment with different wireless telegraphy (W/T) set-ups, so that both frequencies and serial numbers – fixed for each W/T group, or rows – were liable to change rapidly. Up to D-Day this traffic was sorted by a special process. With D-Day approaching, TIS had to prepare for a huge increase in highly urgent operational traffic and after the invasion caused Hut 6 its most difficult problems since the war began. The traffic intercepted from exercises was studied in the light of direction-finding (D/F), discriminants – three-letter groups, normally placed in the preamble to an Enigma message, indicating the key used in enciphering the message – and Order of Battle evidence. These exercises provided Hut 6 with valuable information on the type of W/T communications to be expected, the locations of headquarters, and in very general outline, key distribution.

Another problem was that towards the end of 1943, there was evidence that the Luftwaffe were considering revising their call-sign and frequency allocation. This would prevent TIS from following the continuity of groups from day to day by means of call-sign prediction. It would also be impossible to establish continuity by frequency measurement. The intercept stations feeding the codebreakers with enciphered Enigma messages would have to start from scratch each day. However, once again the Germans carried out the reallocation with their characteristic insecurity, and the problem became no more than a temporary inconvenience. In the event, frequency changes were only partial – an enormous help to Hut 6 – while other groups changed their frequencies but not call-signs, and others made no changes at all! This, coupled with the fact that the threatened extension of reflector D did not materialise, eased the problems in the run-up to D-Day considerably.

German Army operators were well versed in the need for security, and the history of Army keys was one of spasmodic bursts of traffic followed by long silent periods, so the breaking of Western Army keys was a hand-to-mouth affair, dependent on the closest inspection of current decodes and allowing plenty of scope for ingenuity. Unlike the Luftwaffe, the German Army passed virtually no traffic of significance before D-Day. The first Army break in the West had come back in January 1944, when a routine message from Brussels – a High Command Communiqué – encoded and transmitted, presumably, for practice, and one other day was broken as a result of this discovery, while a major W/T practice in February had led to the first genuine break of an Army key. When D-Day came it brought floods of traffic, and while Bletchley Park had a good idea of what keys to expect, they had almost no idea what the messages would contain.

With the capture of Cherbourg on 25 June, traffic, which had fallen off considerably since the first few days of the landings, dropped to little more than a trickle. There had been a major scare for the Allies when a decrypt from Luftflotte 3 of 8 May 1944 which referred to Allied fighter activity of the previous day, had led the Germans to believe that the invasion would take place in the Le Havre–Cherbourg area. But Field Marshal von Rundstedt took the view that the attack would come from around Boulogne down to Normandy, and these views were echoed in a decrypted signal sent by the Japanese Naval Attaché in Berlin. But Normandy was being reinforced – 21st Panzer

Division was moved to Caen and military strength was increased in the Cotentin peninsula. In addition, the fortifications of the Atlantic Wall were revealed after a visit to them by Baron Oshima Hiroshi, Japanese ambassador to Berlin, whose enciphered messages were intercepted after being transmitted on the Japanese diplomatic cipher machine known to the Americans as 'Purple'.

The German guessing game as to where the Allies would land was gathering pace. On the eve of D-Day the Allies estimated German Army strength as six to seven top quality divisions in reserve in France and the Low Countries and some eleven to fourteen divisions of lower quality. As to the Luftwaffe, the estimate was that there would be about 1,600 aircraft available of which around 650 might be fighters. However, it was argued there was a weakness in Luftwaffe personnel and efficiency, and any attempt to fight a prolonged battle would make it impossible to replace crews and aircraft, which would adversely affect its first-line strength.

Valuable confirmation that Ultra had correctly identified and located all the armour in the west was provided by an announcement by the Inspector General of Panzer Troops, Heinz Guderian, of his itinerary for a western tour on 29 April 'gave a splendid insight into the distribution of the armour a month before the landings'. This vital information had been decrypted via Colossus, the world's first semi-programmable digital computer, of which ten were operational at Bletchley Park by the end of the war, and which was to play a major part in D-Day and its aftermath. This teleprinter traffic used the Lorenz SZ 40/42 to encipher messages, and problems arose on 1 August 1944 when the Lorenz wheel patterns, which Colossus was breaking, changed from monthly to daily settings. The updated Colossus Mk II was installed just before D-Day and this non–Morse traffic, known as Fish at Bletchley Park, was the German High Command traffic and was also used by Hitler. Colossus helped in the Order of Battle intelligence and also to confirm that the Fortitude deception plan was working. The breaking of Lorenz also revealed the huge reinforcements sent to the Cotentin peninsula.

In addition, there was the priceless Enigma information that petrol and oil were in scarce supply, while Bletchley Park's interest in decrypting weather reports suddenly increased. Although nothing much of importance was decrypted at the beginning of the invasion, it was early afternoon before there was any sign that the scale of the landings had been properly appreciated by the defenders. The most immediately useful item was the news that by midday on 6 June the British drive towards Caen had alarmed the Luftwaffe and they were contemplating evacuating Carpiquet airfield west of the city.

As the battle in Western Europe progressed, the bulk and importance of the forward Army keys tended to decrease and emphasis tended to shift to the keys used on the main GHQ network. It became possible to break these high-grade Staff keys fairly regularly, and, from autumn 1944 up to the end of the war, it was from these keys that the main German Army intelligence was derived. Ultra decrypts at this time showed that, despite their growing anxiety about Normandy and their inclination to believe that the invasion would come in June, the Germans remained uncertain as to its place and time. While this was partly due to the Allied deception programme, that programme itself depended on Ultra's information about the enemy's appreciations.

To get around the lack of Army Enigma messages being sent by wireless operator, the heavy bombing of vital communications had forced the Germans to send these messages by Morse operator, providing a huge expansion in these decrypts. Not surprisingly the amount of wireless traffic rose substantially after D-Day and was well above teleprinter capacity for the first month after the landings. Chicksands, an intercept station close to Bletchley Park, was able to send its surplus quickly by dispatch rider, but it was a six-hour motorcycle run from Forest Moor's intercept site, so everything had to be prioritised for teleprinter/dispatch rider communications. Indeed, the period between Dunkirk and D-Day had seen no keys except two, Red (the Luftwaffe operational key) and Snowdrop (the key of Luftgau West), as attention had been focussed on the Mediterranean theatre. This emphasis was reversed on D-Day, and Ocelot, the Flivo key, a re-encodement which had been so productive to Bletchley Park so far in the war, claimed prior attention from 6 June. From the first landings to the drive across the Rhine, the number of German Air keys and the volume of traffic never reached the same proportions as it did on the days immediately after D-Day. Snowdrop's value in the events around D-Day was surprisingly high, but the prophesies that it would not outlive the successful onslaught of the Allies proved substantially correct. However, it was operationally vital, and on 9 June actually passed 820 messages. Bletchley Park's best friend – the Luftwaffe Red key – provided frequent re-encodements into Snowdrop, and although for some time the only profitable line of attack on the keys lay in re-encodements, by the end of June all major Air keys were being broken on cribs.

## TRAFFIC LEVELS OF VARIOUS AIR KEYS 5–11 JUNE 1944

|          | 5th | 6th | 7th | 8th | 9th | 10th | 11th |
|----------|-----|-----|-----|-----|-----|------|------|
| Red      | 324 | 459 | 501 | 546 | 909 | 611  | 462  |
| Snowdrop | 209 | 357 | 611 | 706 | 820 | 678  | 785  |
| Jaguar   | 129 | 180 | 231 | 356 | 584 | 625  | 491  |
| Cricket  | 31  | 168 | 219 | 239 | 328 | 271  | 249  |
| Wasp     | 17  | 23  | 28  | 72  | 49  | 118  | 31   |
| Locust   | 19  | 110 | 221 | 81  | 167 | 218  | 215  |
| Ocelot   | –   | –   | –   | 152 | 179 | 122  | 123  |

Keys and their Luftwaffe units: Red (General Operational), Snowdrop (Luftgau West), Jaguar (Luftflotte 3), Cricket (Jagdkorps II), Wasp (Fliegerkorps IX), Locust (Fliegerkorps II), Ocelot (Flivo).

(Source: TNA,*The Official History of Hut 6*, vol I, p 238.)

The successes on the major keys between 6 June and the end of the month were:

| | |
|--|--|
| Snowdrop: | all days broken (25 days) |
| Wasp: | all days broken except 7th and 11th |
| Lily: | all days broken except 17th and 27th |
| Jaguar: | all days broken except 14th |
| Cricket: | all days broken except 7th |
| Ocelot: | all days broken except 9th |

(Source: TNA, *The Official History of Hut 6*, vol I, p 239.)

The total score was 143 breaks out of a possible 150, and in the last six days of June, of the keys mentioned above, twenty-four breaks were made before 0100 GMT on the following day.

At sea, the Royal Navy had set up special support groups to counter the U-boats, and a major decision was taken to allow a 'first' at Bletchley Park – for Enigma naval messages to be intercepted on its premises. The parachute drops could alert the enemy that an invasion force was on its way, and the initial reports of the paratroopers came just before midnight on 5 June and were relayed to the assault force at 0132 on the sixth. The first news of German naval action came at 0348 and was relayed to the invasion fleet thirty-two minutes later, due entirely to the Bletchley Park direct interception. The average time between interception and sending the message to the Operational Intelligence Centre at the Admiralty in London was half an hour. The naval Enigma keys in use in the west, most of which continued to be read currently, carried considerable traffic in the first few days after the invasion, and the situation reports enciphered in these keys provided valuable intelligence about the German Army and the Luftwaffe throughout the fighting in Normandy.

Rolf Noskwith, who was in the naval intelligence Hut 8, recalls that Dolphin – the German naval Home Waters key – was broken at daybreak on D-Day when a sloppy operator began with his report every day: Wetter Vorhersage Biskaya – Weather Forecast Biscay – a fine crib for the codebreakers to find the Enigma settings for this key on such a vital day. That this massive invasion proved so successful is a tribute to the extensive Allied pre-planning and the role of Sigint. It had tested Bletchley Park and the intercept stations to their limits and they had not been found wanting. The decryption of both Enigma and Lorenz messages had provided the Allies with unprecedented and priceless intelligence about the enemy. The invasion fleet of five assault forces transported by around 6,500 ships including 4,250 landing craft in some seventy-five convoys, each five miles long, had been the subject of last-minute concern. Eisenhower had postponed the original attack – scheduled for 5 June – because of poor weather, and it required a good deal of W/T activity in cancelling this aborted invasion, as some ships had actually sailed. However, the Germans failed to interpret this as pre-invasion traffic, probably because two of their intercept stations had been destroyed. D-Day was, nevertheless, a close-run thing, but its success was to be the final nail in the coffin of the Thousand-Year Reich.

# Chapter 14

# The Terror Weapons

A note dropped through a private door in Oslo barely two weeks after the Second World War led to one of the most remarkable documents of the war – the Oslo Report. The note was sent to Captain (later Rear Admiral) Hector Boyes, Britain's naval attaché in Norway. Its message was brief: if Britain wanted inside knowledge on Hitler's secret scientific and technical plans, the BBC should alter the opening words of its German broadcasts.

The BBC wording was altered and the attaché received a seven-page document containing such remarkable material that the three government ministries responsible for the armed services – the War Office, Admiralty and Air Ministry – turned it down. Enemy propaganda was the general view of its contents. The three Services did not even bother to keep their copies. But one man who received it when it arrived in London was Professor RV Jones, the Air Ministry Assistant Director of Intelligence (Science). He kept his copy.

According to the Oslo Report, among different technical developments in which Germany was engaged was a remote-controlled, engine-less glider, code number FZ21 – Ferngesteuerte Zielflugzeug (remote-controlled target-aircraft) – and a pilotless aircraft, code number FZ10. The document added: 'The testing range is at Peenemünde, at the mouth of the Peene, near Wolgast, near Greifswald.' This was the first time that Peenemünde had been brought to the attention of Britain's scientific and intelligence communities. And it would be more than four years before British experts found that this was the V1 or 'doodlebug' that was to rain down on London. Also known as the Fieseler Fi 103, it used a simple pulse jet engine, and an autopilot to regulate height and speed. It was two Enigma decrypts of September 1943 that finally convinced Professor Jones that the enemy was constructing two special weapons, later known as the V1 and the

V2. Of such importance were these developments viewed in London that a special committee – codenamed Operation Crossbow – was set up to investigate it.

The Germans had been working on these special weapons long before the war. Experiments had been conducted as far back as 1932 at the Army experimental range at Kummersdorf West, about seventeen miles south of Berlin. The first launch tests in the Baltic, on the small island of Greifswald Oie, north of the island of Usedom, in the Peenemünde area, were in December 1937. It rose to sixty miles vertically and went at a maximum speed of 3,600 mph and hit its target at between 2,200 and 2,500 mph. A number of rockets were designed (codenamed A1 – A5), with A4 becoming the V2 – the 'A' standing for 'Aggregat', meaning 'unit' or 'series'. The 'V' originally stood for Versuchsmuster (experimental type), but eventually became 'Vergeltungswaffe' or 'reprisal weapon'. Trial launches commenced at Peenemünde in June 1942. Hitler had made a speech on secret weapons in September 1939, and went hot and cold on the project, sometimes sceptical, and finally enthusiastic. He eventually saw the V-weapons as a means of reversing the tide of war, hopefully enabling him to snatch victory from the jaws of impending defeat. In 1942 the project was revived and became known as FZG76 (Flakzielgerät or anti-aircraft target apparatus), which subsequently took the name V1. In January 1943, an RAF PRU – Photo Reconnaissance Unit – in a flight over Peenemünde confirmed that extensive construction was taking place. At the same time intelligence was coming in of a German capability of hitting Britain with the V1 from sites in France. Eventually a major launch site was discovered by PRU at Watten, near St Omer in the Pas de Calais, at Wissant and Bruneval, near Fécamp.

It was carelessness by Luftwaffe signals operators, using their operational Brown cipher, which gave away the V1 plots from the Baltic which provided height, speed, range and reliability of the V1 so accurately that Professor Jones was able to predict with absolute precision that forty per cent would reach the London area. Brown, which, after the invasion of Russia had declined in importance, began to come back into its own in 1944 with its bearing on V-weapon activities. The main transmitting stations were on the Baltic coast and were often inaudible to the English intercept stations. However, Wick in Scotland, which was fitted with a suitable rhombic aerial, could intercept the main frequency and further cover was provided by another

Scottish outstation at Montrose. A German Army Netz – a W/T network system – dealing with V2 experiments and passing Corncrake – Bletchley Park's codename for this traffic – was also difficult to cover, and although it was double banked at the War Office Y Group station at Beaumanor in Leicestershire and Chicksands in Bedfordshire, required between nine and twelve wireless sets, and the problem of intercepting clean texts on this group was never solved. But Baltic Brown had assumed such importance by the middle of 1944, that experimental, but unsuccessful interception, was made at every available intercept station. Eventually the problem was overcome by sending a group of Chicksands operators to Malmö in neutral Sweden where, as part of the British Consul staff, they successfully intercepted the main group and a previously only suspected medium frequency group.

It was known that the most experienced German radar operators were in the 14th and 15th Companies of the Air Signals Experimental Regiment, and Hut 3 and the Y stations kept a special watch on any movement by these units. It helped that the Germans, when they test-fired the V-weapons, sent the reports between outstations and the base at Peenemünde in a home-made code so simple it could be read on sight. In October 1943 it was discovered that the radar detachments of one regiment – the LN Versuchsregiment – were plotting the trial flights of a new missile in a simple substitution code on the same frequencies as Brown Enigma. Then two W/T networks were discovered operating exclusively on secret weapons. The first was a radar-plotting network service based at Peenemünde, discovered because a special piece of radar equipment known as a Würzburg D had been sent to the LN Versuchsregiment at Peenemünde.

The second were the radar plotting stations themselves. This second network was a link between Peenemünde, the practice ground in Poland and an administrative HQ. After Peenemünde was bombed, a training station to practise firing the rockets was set up at an SS camp, Heidelager, at Blizna in Poland. This location was found once the names of the principal Commands involved in rocket production were known. When the rockets went operational a new group of W/T stations were found, codenamed Vera. This traffic accompanied the firing of rockets and summarised it at the end of the day. Moreover, much of the early and detailed information on the V-weapons were found through decrypts from Japanese diplomatic – mainly naval attaché – traffic.

Prisoner-of-war interrogations and MI6 reports were also adding to the picture. Churchill became involved and, as a result, a special investigation was ordered, of which the chairman was Duncan Sandys, Joint Parliamentary Secretary to the Ministry of Supply, and which went under the codename Bodyline. In November 1943 it was renamed Crossbow, with responsibility being transferred from the Sandys Committee to the Air Ministry. On the night of 17–18 August 1943, an RAF raid on Peenemünde, called Operation Hydra, caused severe damage, aided by a diversionary raid on Berlin, codename Operation Whitebait. Professor Jones, commenting on the information on which this raid had been carried out, said: 'there had been almost no contribution from Ultra'. But he made clear the importance of Ultra when he added:

> I always looked at such actions from this standpoint because, vital though Enigma was, it could at any time have been cut off, and if we had become too dependant on it, we should have been at an enormous disadvantage.[l]

A different view of that day – seen at ground level – comes from artillery specialist General Walter Dornberger, then Director of the Peenemünde establishment, who had been involved in rocket experiments since 1932. He recalled that he had received a warning from the Air Ministry a few days before that we were likely to be raided. At least one copy of all production schemes, drawings and files had been lodged elsewhere and dispersal of the different departments was under way. In addition, all possible air raid precautions had been taken.

> The raid must have been a terrific one. Our carefully laid scheme, covering all eventualities and several times rehearsed, had failed completely.[li]

However, Enigma did provide Professor Jones with vital information when a decrypt revealed a Luftwaffe instruction to personnel at research and experimental stations addressed to establishments in what appeared to be an order of precedence, starting with Rechlin, the roughly German equivalent of the Royal Aircraft Establishment at Farnborough. Peenemünde was second on the list, ahead of several other establishments already known to British Intelligence. Jones said this Enigma information enabled him to provide independent evidence of the importance of Peenemünde. The 8th USAAF also carried out raids against the site in July and August 1944. Another decrypt also proved useful when, in September 1944, a message was intercepted which asked for Flak ground protection for 'Flak Zielgerät 76' and referred to the capture of an enemy agent, adding that the Allies were aware that the weapon would shortly be operational and planned to attack sites before this happened.

Following these attacks on Peenemünde, the Germans subsequently moved much of the work to an underground Volkswagen factory near Nordhausen in the Harz Mountains, to Traunsee, near Salzburg in Austria, and to Blizna, near Debica, in Poland. Other subsequent large sites included Watten, Wizernes, Siracourt and Lottinghem in northern France and Sottevast and Martinvast in the Cherbourg region of Normandy. Another northern French site was at Mimoyecques, but it was the V3 being produced here, known as the Hochdruckpumpe or HDP (high pressure pump), which was a supergun. Further information was obtained by the codebreakers when decrypts of the reports to Tokyo by the Japanese Ambassador in Berlin at the end of September referred to long-range weapons.

Bletchley Park, as part of their role in looking out for these weapons, had been keeping track of the 14th and 15th Companies of the Luftwaffe Signals Experiment Regiment, which had come to the attention of the codebreakers early in the war because of their involvement in the development of navigational beams which guided bombers to their target during the Battle of Britain. Professor Jones had surmised that the Germans would track the experimental flights using radar, and that these two companies would probably be involved. He told Professor Frederick Norman at Bletchley Park's Hut 3 – which handled German Army and Air traffic – of his thoughts, and asked him to see that Bletchley Park and the intercept service followed these two companies as closely as possible. Above all, he wanted to know whether one or the other of them moved up to the Baltic coast and showed signs of deploying itself from Peenemünde eastwards. 14th Company did, indeed, turn up in the Baltic, and by the end of November it had been established from the decrypts from this Company that the speed of the missile was between 216mph and 300mph, and once 420mph, that the rate of its fall was 2,000 metres in forty seconds, indicating that the missile had wings, and the maximum range might be 120 miles.

A key Luftwaffe decrypt, read in December 1943, sent to the Signals Experimental Regiment was the first Sigint reference to A4 – the German name for the V2. Intelligence sources interpreted this decrypt as meaning that a high altitude rocket was being developed on the Baltic. By this time intelligence was clear that both a pilotless aircraft and a long-range rocket were being developed, enabling counter-measures to be considered, with the V1 the most likely early problem, some eighty-seven ski sites for their launch having been identified by PR flights. Many of these sites were subsequently bombed, beginning in December 1943, and by June 1944 it was thought only twenty-five sites were capable of operational activity. It was known that the flying bombs were being fired by Flak Regiment 155 (W) – the 'W' stood for its Commanding Officer, Colonel Wachtel – and that the Germans were building more sites. Meanwhile, Enigma decrypts continued to provide more information. An SS cipher revealed that V1 trials were being carried out at 'Heidelager' – codename for an SS camp at Blizna in Poland – with additional information coming from the Polish underground, who were picking up fragments from the flights after the weapons had landed and retrieving parts and taking photographs. Indeed, the Polish underground would race the Germans to a crash scene, hoping to pick up fragments before them. Eventually, after interminable delays, the first V1 rockets were fired at England in the early hours of 13 June 1944 – a week after the D–Day landings – but only ten in all, of which only four reached England, five having crashed immediately. Three days later 244 had been fired, of which 144 reached land in England, seventy-three hitting London. The V1 had a maximum range of 125 miles, flew at 420 mph and reached heights of 4,000 feet.

The inspection of a V1, which had landed in Sweden after a test flight, debris from early attacks on London and finally the overrunning of launch sites near Cherbourg after D–Day had given the Allies considerable information about this new weapon. By the time the main V1 offensive ended on 5 September 1944, eighty-three per cent had been destroyed by gunfire as they flew over southern England. Indeed, on 28 August, defences destroyed ninety out of ninety-seven flying bombs, only four reaching London. As the Allies advanced, many V1 sites were evacuated and new depots set up in places such as Nucourt, St Leu and Rilly-la-Montagne, all in northern France, which were discovered through Bletchley Park decrypts. But the Germans had changed to a new method – launching V1 missiles from aircraft. Enigma decrypts in July 1944 referred to the Luftwaffe Third Bomber Wing, III/KG (Kampf Geschwader) 3 (later I/KG53), and it was not until the end of the month that the real purpose of this group of Heinkel 111s was realised. The air offensive of V1s on England ended on 13 January 1945, after 4,261 had been destroyed by fighters, anti-aircraft attack and barrage balloons. But, from October 1944 until the end of March 1945, V1 attacks were carried out against Antwerp, Liège and Brussels. Indeed, there were more attacks on Antwerp than London.

The Japanese Naval Attaché's enciphered messages had revealed more information about the V2 and then Bletchley Park had a major breakthrough when a special Enigma key, known as Corncrake, was first intercepted in June 1944 and revealed messages being sent between Peenemünde and Blizna. These decrypts were the first to reveal to the Allies the name of Wernher von Braun who, post-war, was to be a major figure in the American space programme. There were three special cipher keys for the V-weapons: Corncrake, Ibis and Jeboa, which operated between March 1944 and the end of the war. Jeboa was a Luftwaffe key and handled V1 attacks, the other two were Army keys and dealt with the V2, Corncrake handling experimental and preparatory information, while Ibis covered the actual operations. Although these were special V-weapon keys, other keys also provided information on these weapons, such as the Luftwaffe key Brown, which had provided information on the beams directing bombers to their targets during the Battle of Britain as well as other keys.

Corncrake only lasted from the middle of May 1944 until the end of July. It was discovered after a long message was brought into Hut 6's Army Research – which at the time also housed the Army cryptographers – for a routine examination, as was standard procedure for new and obscure groups. The initial break of 13 May is described in the *Official History of Hut 6*:

> The contents of Corncrake created an intelligence sensation in Hut 3 [Army-Air Intelligence]: the exact significance of much of it was obscure but clearly referred to scientific artillery experiments of importance ... Strong representations were made from the highest quarters in the Park in favour of a determined drive to break more days and the work was at once set under foot.[lii]

Corncrake's W/T system comprised three stations – Heidelager (which acted as Control), Peenemünde and Koeslin – and practically all the traffic was to and from Heidelager. Corncrake suddenly ended with the evacuation of Heidelager on 23 July 1944, and no traffic was passed after this date. On Ibis, with one exception, all the breaks occurred in the six weeks from 12 February to 24 March 1945. In fact, Ibis traffic was passed in small quantities back in October 1944 – the rocket attacks had commenced the previous month – and it was not until November that its separate identity was revealed. Ibis passed traffic not only on Enigma, but quite large quantities in other ciphers, and the Enigma messages could be identified by the non-Enigma traffic which, it was discovered, was concerned with the launch of rockets, as the messages coincided with the times of V2 launches. The V2 launch batteries in Holland were in a habit of sending evening messages to their Group Control containing a list of the rocket launches. Bletchley Park dubbed these messages 'Rocket Bradshaws', all providing times of rocket departures from Holland. The times of arrival in England – four minutes later – were not given. Ibis traffic, which reached its peak at the beginning of February 1945 with eighty messages a day, fell to a trickle in March and vanished altogether in the last week of that month. The American Enigma-breaking bombes had done sterling work on Ibis, and it was perhaps fitting that the last V-key to be broken was on VE-Day, 8 May 1945.

Jerboa, the V1 key, gave Bletchley Park twenty days of breaks in a period of less than three weeks from 13 August to 2 September 1944. This key came to the attention of the codebreakers in July 1944 and was known from its three-letter traffic, known as Klavier, which was connected with the launching of flying bombs. In early September 1944, Jerboa disappeared in consequence of the Allied advance through Belgium and France. In December 1944 and later February–March 1945, there was a resurrection of Jerboa, which reached its peak in the week ending 24 February, with a daily average of fifty-one messages. The following week this fell to fifteen and finally disappeared for ever. In July 1944, Professor Jones had concluded that figures contained in Enigma messages were production numbers and that there were around 1,000 rockets available. By now the view of the Crossbow committee was that the V2, manufactured by Mittelwerk, comprised liquid fuel rocket engines, supersonic aerodynamics, gyroscopic guidance and rudders in jet control. In all, 5,200 V2s were built, and they could be fired from a simple site or mobile platforms, and did not require a complex launching mechanism. Such was the concern at the highest levels of government of a combined V1–V2 attack, that contingency measures included the evacuation of two million people and of factories and hospitals from London as well as providing protected buildings for government officials who would have to remain in the capital. On 14 July, a decrypt had revealed a message from Blizna to Peenemünde, referring to the supply of fifty one-ton 'Elephants', which turned out to be the codename for warheads. However, Britain's boffins were still struggling with the weight of the V2 and its exact components, with the weight being assessed at between eleven and fourteen tons, fuelled by a mixture of liquid oxygen and alcohol and some compound including alcohol and with a range of between 120 and 200 miles, depending on the size of the warhead, calculated at between one and two tons. It was also believed to take between about four and six minutes to travel either 150 or 200 miles. Then a hint that the V2 offensive was imminent was discovered in a decrypt from the Japanese Ambassador in Vienna in August, quoting German Foreign Minister Joachim von Ribbentrop as the source. Moreover, there were considerable problems locating the V2 sites, causing considerable anxiety among the top brass. In the hunt for information on the V2, an Enigma message gave a vital clue when it revealed that someone from Blizna was interested in a crater 160 miles away, a distance that was beyond the range of the flying bomb. As Professor Jones recalled, 'This single fact made us think that we were once again on the trail of the rocket.'

On 8 September 1944 the first V2 attack on London took place, fired from Holland and landing at 1843 in Chiswick, followed another sixteen seconds later by one falling at Epping. The Last V2 was to fall on England at 1645 on 27 March 1945 at Orpington, Kent. At Peenemünde, the first successful launch of a V2 – after two failures – was on 3 October 1942. Although an awesome weapon of destruction, for the boffins who had been working on the project, many for ten years, it was a moment to savour. According to General Dornberger, for the first time a machine of human construction, a 5.5 ton missile, covered a distance of 120 miles with a lateral deflection of only 2.5 miles from the target. They had become the first to have given a rocket built on the principles of aircraft construction a speed of 3,300 mph by means of the jet drive peculiar to rocket.

We have thus proved that it is quite possible to build missiles or aircraft to fly at supersonic speed, given the right form and suitable propulsion. Our self-steering rocket has reached heights never touched by any man-made machine.[liii]

There was little defence against these attacks except the bombing of V2 operational sites. In addition, the Double X system – turned German agents sending back false information to their Abwehr (military intelligence) handlers under the control of MI5 – were misleading the Germans about the accuracy of the rockets, persuading them to fire the missiles short of their targets. Bletchley Park was also playing its part, as much of the intelligence was obtained from Corncrake which, temporarily suspended at the end of July when Blizna was evacuated, resumed on 16 August. It first threw light on the V2 organisation on 19 and 21 September, when Bletchley Park decrypted signals between 14 and 16 September. This revealed site visits by SS General Hans Kammler, a civil engineer who took over from Dornberger and became Special Commissioner of the V-weapons programme in August 1944 when it came under SS control. Kammler had designed the extermination camps, including gas chambers and crematoria. He had also been involved in various other secret weapon projects. He is believed to have committed suicide in May 1945, although his body was never found. The decrypts also revealed that V2 trials had been transferred to a new site at Tuchel, north of Bromberg (Bydgoszcz) in Poland. Low grade cipher traffic about the V2 was also read by Allied intercept units in Belgium.

The intelligence gathered on the V-weapons was a classic use of every means of obtaining top secret information. Not least was the heroism of the underground resistance forces, especially in France and Poland, many of whom were captured, tortured and gave their lives to obtain vital information, the use of 'turned' agents to send back disinformation to their German handlers, photo reconnaissance flights and codebreaking. The V1 created havoc and 10,000 were fired at England, 2,419 reaching London, 3,857 were shot down before reaching their target, thirty landed on Southampton and Portsmouth, and one on Manchester, killing a total of 6,184 people and injuring 17,981. The grim statistics of the V2 rocket tell their own story. An estimated 2,511 civilians were killed in London with 5,869 seriously injured, and 213 were killed and 598 injured elsewhere. The V2 statistics from 8 September 1944 to 27 March 1945 are that 1,054 fell on England (about five a day), 517 (less than three a day) hit London and more than 2,700 Londoners were killed. As to the value of the V-keys, *The Official History of Hut 6*, looking to the post-war world, commented that the ultimate significance of the V-keys 'lay in their long-term connection with the probable future of developments of science as applied to war'. The German boffins had come close to finding a decisive weapon, but as General Dornberger commented, only one thing can be said with absolute certainty, that the use of the V2 could be aptly summed up in two words: 'too late'. He complained that lack of foresight in high places and failure to understand the technical background were to blame. Nevertheless, what had been created was new and unique and could never be erased from the annals of technology. He remarked:

> We tackled one of mankind's greatest tasks regardless of circumstances and found a first practical solution; we opened the gate and pointed the way to the future.[liv]

That comment, written at the end of the war, has proved to be accurate. Modern warfare is all about scientific and technological weaponry. Today's armies – and the civil space programmes – can trace their origin to Nazi Germany and the terror weapons.

# Chapter 15

# Fishing for Tunny

The Bletchley Park story has largely centred around the breaking of the Enigma cipher machine, but arguably the greatest codebreaking achievement of the Second World War – also achieved at Bletchley Park – was the breaking of a cipher machine much more complex than Enigma: the Lorenz SZ 40/42 (SZ = *Schlüssel Zusatz* = Cipher Attachment), the numbers referring to the years 1940 and 1942 in which the machine was first used and later adapted. Whereas Enigma had been known about since the 1920s – Dilly Knox, the veteran Bletchley Park codebreaker, is believed to have bought one as early as 1925, but before the stecker (plugboard) was added – this new machine was completely unknown to Britain's codebreakers in 1939. It turned out to contain the most secret strategic information, and was the system used personally by Hitler and by the German High Command. Its discovery came about by accident, and later a mistake by a German operator on 30 August 1941 enabled Brigadier John Tiltman, Bletchley Park's chief cryptographer, to decipher the message, leading to the construction of the world's first digital, programmable computer, and when the Wrens who were to operate this huge machine first saw its size they immediately gave it a name – Colossus. The Wrens who were to work on Colossus did not require any fixed qualifications although a pass in mathematics in School Certificate or 'good social recommendations' was normally considered essential. However, nine per cent had been to university, although none had studied mathematics there. The Wrens were given up to a fortnight's training in the teleprinter alphabet, the workings of the Tunny machine – which was a 'clone' of the Lorenz machine – and, in some cases, computing. There then followed a conducted tour of the section and a written test. Wrens, unlike men, were organised in fixed watches and given fixed jobs in which they could become technically proficient. The reconstruction of how Lorenz worked, following the Tiltman break, was carried out by a research team led by Cambridge chemistry graduate Bill Tutte. Not least of the achievements in breaking Lorenz is that nobody at Bletchley Park even saw the machine until the war had ended. The wartime adage 'Careless Talk Costs Lives' can be changed to 'Careless Operating Costs Security' as far as the Lorenz (and, indeed, Enigma) cipher machine goes.

The Lorenz system – called Tunny at Bletchley Park after the first link – sent enciphered messages by landline or radio signal using teleprinters and this traffic was given the codename 'Fish' at Bletchley Park. It was organised differently from Enigma – which was based on networks – and used one-to-one links, each link being given a fish name, so that, for instance, Berlin–Paris became Jellyfish and Berlin–Rome was called Bream. The first knowledge of the system occurred by accident when the Metropolitan Police intercept station at Denmark Hill in north London, while listening out for any remaining German agents still operating in Britain, heard an unusual sound. It was not a Morse signal, and was not otherwise decipherable, and it turned out to be the radio signal of a teleprinter message. Bletchley Park immediately recognised it as such, took the view that it was enciphered, that it had probably been encrypted using a machine and could even hazard a guess at the system of encipherment being used. This is because the international perforated tape code system used by teleprinters worldwide had been devised by Frenchman Emile Baudot in 1874, and comprised a series of five punched holes and blanks (or 1s and 0s in modern binary language).

The first message on the Tunny link – the name Tunny was given to this traffic in summer 1942 – to be studied cryptographically was sent out shortly after the German invasion of Russia, and passed between Vienna and Athens. Some earlier traffic, apparently practice transmissions, had been intercepted in May and had been transmitted in a five-unit code, so it was suspected that a teleprinter was being used. This was confirmed by a preliminary examination of later traffic, which showed that an alphabet of thirty-two characters was being employed. This comprised the twenty-six letters of the alphabet plus six extra symbols which were instructions to the receiving teleprinter: go to letters, go to figures, line feed, space, carriage return and null (not used). Each message began with a clear preamble in which there appeared, firstly, the serial number (repeated several times), then a set of twelve letters in the form of a name (Anton, Bertha, etc) which was clearly a twelve-letter indicator. The symbol '9' was used as a separator in this preamble, and a group of five 9s separated the clear preamble from the cipher text. Immediately after the cipher text was a sequence of 8s.

The Lorenz machine was attached to a teleprinter, enciphering the message automatically, and deciphering it automatically at the receiving end, because if the two ends of the link each had their machines set up exactly the same, then they were reciprocal. The codebreakers had to find two separate enciphering methods used by the Lorenz machine: the wheel settings and the wheel patterns. The wheel settings were initially sent as letters of the alphabet in the form of names spelt out in full to avoid errors, e.g. ADOLF, HEINRICH etc, for each of the twelve wheels – called the indicator – informing the recipient on how to set up his wheels at the receiving end. The wheel patterns were a set of random letters, in the teleprinter code punched as binary digits 1 and 0, representing a punched hole or a blank on the tape, which could be set up on the twelve Lorenz wheels – the key stream – which enciphered and deciphered the message. These random letters could be arranged by 'lugs' or 'cams' on the wheels – 501 in total – designed so that if a lug was pushed up it was a 'one' and if it remained flat against the wheel it was a 'nought'. Alan Turing, the brilliant Cambridge mathematician who pioneered the development of the bombe, the electro-mechanical machine used to find Enigma settings, and who played such a crucial role in breaking naval messages, was called in to try and solve the wheel pattern problem. He succeeded, and his method was dubbed 'Turingery'.

In December 1942 a special section to develop machine methods of finding the Lorenz secrets was set up at Bletchley Park under Professor Max Newman – known as the Newmanry – and another section under Major Ralph Tester – the Testery – to find settings by hand. In April 1943 the first machines arrived – a Robinson (which predated Colossus and was named after cartoonist Heath Robinson who drew amazing-looking machines) and a Tunny – and the section began with one cryptographer, two engineers and sixteen Wrens. By May 1945, there were 26 cryptographers, 28 engineers and 273 Wrens with ten Colossi, three Robinsons, three Tunny machines and twenty smaller electrical devices. The section moved into F Block at Bletchley Park in November 1943 and expanded into H Block in September 1944.

The encipherment method being used – as correctly guessed by the codebreakers – was that invented in 1919 by American Gilbert Vernam of the AT&T Company, which mixed the plaintext Baudot system with the random sequence of teleprinter code, but using tape, not a machine. The Germans went a major step further – as also anticipated at Bletchley Park – by enciphering on a machine. It worked by the Modulo 2 method, in which addition and subtraction are the same, thus, using the binary system: 1 + 0 = 1, but 1 + 1 = 0. By adding the plaintext teleprinter letter to the random letter it is possible to obtain the cipher letter:

| | | |
|---|---|---|
| Plaintext Letter | A | 1 1 0 0 0 |
| (plus) Random Letter | C | 0 1 1 1 0 |
| (becomes) Enciphered Letter | F | 1 0 1 1 0 |

At the other end, the system would work in reverse by feeding in the enciphered letter F to be added to the same random letter C, which would bring it back to the original plaintext letter A:

| | | |
|---|---|---|
| Enciphered Letter | F | 1 0 1 1 0 |
| (plus) Random Letter | C | 0 1 1 1 0 |
| (becomes) Plaintext Letter | A | 1 1 0 0 0 |

The wheel pattern settings were changed monthly until July 1944, when they were changed daily. The wheel settings were changed for each message. There were two sets of five wheels and two motor wheels. The five set known as the 'X' wheels moved each time a letter was typed on the teleprinter keyboard. The other five – the 'S' wheels – moved intermittently and were rotated by the two motor wheels. The total number of pin positions was 501 and were distributed on each wheel as under:

| | | |
|---|---|---|
| X1 41 | S1 43 | M1 61 |
| X2 31 | S2 47 | M2 37 |
| X3 29 | S3 51 | |
| X4 26 | S4 53 | |
| X5 23 | S5 59 | |

The key change periods for the wheels were important to the codebreakers and during the war they were changed as follows:

| Date | X-pin patterns | S-pin patterns | M-pin patterns | X, S & M wheel setting |
|---|---|---|---|---|
| Start of use | Monthly | 3 months | Daily | Each message |
| May 1942 | Monthly | 3 months | Daily | Each message |
| October 1942 | Monthly | Monthly | Daily | Each message |
| July 1944 | Daily | Daily | Daily | Each message |

At the beginning, the wheel setting indicator system consisted of twelve names, but in October 1942 was changed to a twelve-character QEP codebook, which contained around a hundred or so different wheel settings, so that, for instance, a message sent in clear might say QEP46, and the operator would go to page forty-six in his codebook and use that twelve-letter indicator for that particular message.

A special intercept station was set up in May 1942 at a farmhouse at Knockholt, near Sevenoaks in Kent, to deal solely with Fish traffic and eventually had a staff of 815, of whom 84 were women in the Auxiliary Territorial Service (ATS), the female section of the British Army. It contained thirty receiving sets at the height of the war and two receiving sets were required for each message in a 'belt and braces' system to ensure (hopefully) that if part of a message was missed on one wireless set, it would be picked up on the other. The radio signal passed through an undulator, which transferred the sound on to a tape known as a 'slip' which comprised the enciphered letters of the message. This slip was read by the ATS ladies, known as 'slip readers', who transferred the information on to the standard international perforated teleprinter tape. After each message was taken down twice, the 'doubling' continued on to two undulators and then on to two teleprinter tapes. Then the two ATS ladies would match their tapes, and if there were more than six errors in a thousand characters – and some of these messages could be 15,000 characters long – they had to start again! This tape was then sent to Bletchley Park. While Colossus found the settings, Tunny enabled the message to be read by inserting the ciphertext tape to a teleprinter attached to it.

According to Jack Copeland, Director of The Turing Archive for the History of Computing, Knockholt intercepted about 12,000 Tunny transmissions from November–December 1942. In 1943 they peaked at more than 34,000 from October–December, then fell to less than 7,000 in the same period of 1944. The number of message tapes sent from Knockholt to Bletchley Park rose sharply during the war, from 73 in April–June 1943 to 10,555 during the last four months of the war. Copeland adds that Knockholt intercepted more messages than Bletchley could possibly decrypt, and the selection of messages for despatch was governed by cryptanalytical and intelligence priorities.

> In all, 27,631 Tunny messages were sent from Knockholt to the Bletchley codebreakers, of which 13,508 were deciphered successfully – a total of 63,431,000 letters of decode.[lv]

But in the early days after discovering this traffic, the codebreakers had no idea what was in the messages – all they had was the enciphered tape. Then there came the vital breakthrough on 30 August 1941 with a transmission of some 4,000 characters from Athens to Vienna using the indicator HQIBPEXEZMUG, usually known as the 'ZMUG' message. At the Vienna end, the message was garbled due to poor atmospherics, and a request was sent back to send it again. In Athens, the operator, in re-sending the message, made two crucial errors – he told his colleague to reset the twelve wheels to the same position as for the previous message, then sent the same ZMUG indicator again, then transmitted a slightly shorter message. This provided Bletchley Park with 'depth' – the encipherment of two or more messages using the same setting. When a depth was broken into it was found that the messages were essentially the same, but the spacing, mis-spellings and corrections were different. Evidently the same message had been typed out twice – by hand. As a result, the two versions at the same number of letters from the beginning would be at slightly different places in the true text of the message. This divergence increased slowly, until at the 3,976th letter, where the shorter message came to an end, it had increased to more than 100 letters. This depth was much easier to read than earlier depths, for at any stage the next letter of clear language in the less advanced message could be predicted from the clear language derived for the other. The messages were, in fact, decoded over the entire length of the shorter message, so that the ambiguity in the key was resolved. From this depth, a length of subtractor key of 3,976 letters was reconstructed – with a few letters doubtful. During the remainder of 1941, Cambridge chemistry graduate Bill Tutte and the Research section successfully analysed this keystream of random teleprinter characters, and so discovered the nature of the machine which had produced it. The Germans had probably noticed this breach of security, for the traffic almost stopped.

Tiltman realised that the plaintext and key could be found using 'Mod 2', and that by adding the two ciphertext messages together he could remove the key, leaving another tape which comprised the sum of the two plaintext messages. Using 'cribs' – Bletchley Park parlance for guesses at the original German plaintext – he was able to extricate the original text from both messages, because although the German was not the same in the two signals, they were very similar. Then, by adding the plaintext to the ciphertext it gave him the keystream. The messages all began with a serial number preceded by the word SPRUCHNUMMER – message number. On the famous ZMUG indicator message of 30 August 1941, when the two messages were sent in depth, in the second message the operator shortened the word to SPRUCHNR, thus changing the line-up of the two messages. Where two letters in two messages are the same, they cancel each other out with the teleprinter symbol / or 'forward slash', e.g:

|  | 1 | 2 | 3 | 4 | 5 | 6 | 7 | 8 |  |  |  |
|---|---|---|---|---|---|---|---|---|---|---|---|
| Message No. 1: | S | P | R | U | C | H | N | U | M | M | E | R |
| Message No. 2: | S | P | R | U | C | H | N | R |  |  |  |  |
| Add together = | / | / | / | / | / | / | / | F |  |  |  |  |

The different letters in the two messages at position eight – U changed to R – results as follows using Mod 2:

|  | R | 0 | 1 | 0 | 1 | 0 |
|---|---|---|---|---|---|---|
|  | U | 1 | 1 | 1 | 0 | 0 |
| Add together = | F | 1 | 0 | 1 | 1 | 0 |

By these steps Tiltman found the first eight characters of the key. However, if the two messages had been identical, then the entire second message would have comprised the symbol /. It was now necessary to try and work out how the machine worked, and this is where Bill Tutte and the research team came in. After some months they finally worked out its construction – a major feat of Second World War cryptography.

The next step was to find a means of designing a machine to decipher the message once the settings had been found by hand, which was carried out by the Telecommunications Research Establishment at Malvern, Worcestershire and built by the Post Office Engineering Research Establishment at Dollis Hill, London. It was called Tunny, the same name given to the original Athens–Vienna link. In May 1943, the Robinsons were developed to speed up the process. The Robinsons were also developed at the Telecommunications Research Establishment and the first one was delivered in May 1943 while Tommy Flowers was building Colossus. It worked on the principle that no machine could develop a truly random sequence of letters. It compared a ciphertext tape with a wheel pattern tape to look for statistical evidence to indicate the wheel settings and was designed to keep the two tapes running in synchronisation at one thousand characters a second, but the sprocket wheels which kept the tapes on the machine would rip the tape, so a more reliable method had to be found, and the Colossus idea of Tommy Flowers was the answer. Heath Robinson was built mainly from relays and had only around a couple of dozen valves, and it was the use of these relays that slowed Heath Robinson down.

There were several types of 'Robinson' but it was clear that something even better was required. This problem was put to Tommy Flowers, one of the Dollis Hill postal engineers, and he proposed the revolutionary idea of an electronic machine using valves.

It was in the 1930s that Flowers had pioneered the large-scale use of electronic valves to control the making and breaking of telephone connections. At the time, telephone switchboard equipment was based on the relay – a small automatic switch – but electronic valves were much faster and more reliable. Valves were originally used for purposes such as amplifying radio signals and their use as a very fast switch, producing pulses of current, was the eventual route to high-speed computation. After the war, Flowers was involved with the first all-electronic telephone exchange in Europe at Highgate Wood. The Mark I Colossus, as it was known, was constructed during 1943 with 1,500 valves and was assembled at Bletchley Park in January 1944. Only one Mark I machine was built (later converted to a Mk II), as Flowers and his team moved almost immediately to building the improved Mk II, with 2,400 valves (by comparison, the first Robinson had fewer than 100 valves), which was ready on 1 June 1944 – just in time for D-Day.

Ten Colossi were built, and each machine used a pulley system running on what was known as the 'bedstead', round which the ciphertext tape was driven by friction at about 40 feet or 5,000 teleprinter tape sprocket holes per second. It then passed through a gate, where it was scanned by photo-electric cells. Each Colossus had two bedsteads – while one was in use another tape could be put on the other ready to be run immediately when the first tape had completed its task. An on–off switch by each bedstead controlled both its driving motor and its lamp, and there was a switch on the selection panel whereby each bedstead could be selected – but not both at once. The maximum length of tape was either 11,000 teleprinter characters, or on five of the Colossi, up to 20,000 characters, but they did not work well with a tape of less than 2,000 characters.

Colossus relied on statistical analysis rather than conventional codebreaking. There were two sets of five wheels (five X or chi wheels and five S or psi wheels), each driven by a motor wheel. The chi wheels moved one stop each time a key on the teleprinter keyboard was depressed, and the psi wheels only moved when the first wheel was a 1 or punched hole, which in turn moved the second motor wheel. This was known as the 'extended psi' and, as a result, the chances of the cipher repeating itself were a vast 1.6 x 1019. It comprised valves arranged as logic circuits controlled from a switch panel to analyse ciphertext and find wheel settings. A tape with 1,300 characters would be nine feet long. Circuits were synchronised by a clock signal generated by the punched tape and used shift registers and systemic arrays, enabling five simultaneous tests (for each of the five punched holes or blanks of each teleprinter letter or figure), each involving up to 100 Boolean (an algebraic notation system used to represent logical propositions by means of the binary digits 0 and 1) calculations on each of the five channels of the punched tape, although only one or two channels were normally examined in any run. Colossus could find both the wheel settings and the pin patterns (known as wheel breaking). It also used vacuum or thermionic valves, which emitted electrons from substances heated to very high temperatures. These valves were used as switches to turn electric circuits on and off, and worked thousands of times faster than metal contact mechanical switches – relays – which had been used to make processors up to that time. They were like those used in radio sets, except that in radios valves do not operate as switches. In order to speed up the operation, processors used the new technology for all the processing and not just part – as with Heath Robinson – and many of the parts were made at a Post Office factory in Birmingham.

Colossus also used thyratrons (a type of gas-filled tube used as a high energy electrical switch and controlled rectifier, and the forerunner of transistors) and photo cells to optically read a paper tape, and then applied a programmable logic function to every character, counting how often this function returned 'true'. The thyratron rings or EKG – electronic keytext generators – were analogues of the Lorenz wheels. The EKG produced strings of zeros and ones electronically rather than by reading a keytext tape, as was the case with the earlier Heath Robinsons. EKG was an early programmable Read Only Memory and consisted of twelve shift registers which produced pulses with the same patterns as the Lorenz wheels. To find the pin patterns, a system known as 'rectangling' was devised by Bill Tutte. Colossus was the first practical application of a large-scale program-controlled computer. Determined mainly by the setting of external switches and plugboards, it was looking for sequences that were not random. If the wheel patterns were known these were plugged up at the back of the machine on a pinboard. There were double holes all down the pinboard for 'one' or 'nought' impulses to set the wheel patterns, looking for a score above the random for each wheel. Once the enciphered message had been stripped of the effect of the first set of five wheels (the 'X' or chi wheels), then the part-deciphered message went to the Testery, named after its head, Major Ralph Tester, where the second set of wheels (the 'S' or psi wheels) were worked out by hand.

Among the vital information revealed by Colossus was that Hitler and the German High Command still believed that the main attack for the invasion of Europe would come via the Pas-de-Calais, and anywhere else would be a feint. Colossus was a huge improvement on the Robinsons and could find both the wheel settings and the key stream patterns, using 5.5kw of power. Of the ten Colossi built, eight were dismantled immediately after the war, the other two going to GCHQ – as GC and CS was now known – where they, too, were dismantled at Cheltenham in 1959–1960. During the course of the war, the ten Colossi broke sixty-three million characters of cipher – equivalent to roughly twelve bibles. Colossus would print out the wheel positions and patterns on a typewriter and this information would then be plugged up on a Tunny machine, the ciphertext tape which had originated at

Knockholt would then be attached to a teleprinter connected by a cable to Tunny, and the message could then be decrypted.

Another cipher machine using the teleprinter system was also discovered – the Siemens T52 – known at Bletchley Park as Sturgeon. But this was mainly used by the Luftwaffe, and there was plenty of German Air Force traffic on Enigma, so the decision was taken to concentrate on Lorenz, as it carried mainly Army messages. Operationally, the Fish traffic proved invaluable, complementing that of Enigma. For instance, in April 1943 Colossus revealed the German strategical thinking as they were about to launch the Kursk offensive on the Russian Front, and subsequently provided vital information about the critical situation for the invaders after the Russian counter-offensive. This decrypt was derived from Bletchley Park's reading of the Squid link between Army Group South and Army Command, and was the earliest example of the great addition to operational intelligence of the highest importance about the eastern front that these decrypts were to make for the rest of the war.

By 1944 there were some twenty-six Fish links with two main stations, Straussberg near Berlin for western traffic and Königsberg for eastern stations. A major contributor to the Fish traffic was Sixta – the Bletchley Park traffic analysis group known as log readers – who charted the various links. Shaun Wylie, who had been a codebreaker in Hut 8 dealing with naval Enigma, was transferred to the Fish section in autumn 1943. He explained that by early 1944 they had broken the patterns and decipher transmissions on any link/month that had one long transmission or a readable depth. He pays tribute to Sixta, who had discovered that some messages on perforated tape were sent on more than one link. For this to be fruitful, he explained, three things had to go right: a pair of such transmissions had to be spotted, one of them had to be deciphered, and the plain text had to be matched against the correct stretch in the other and the resulting key broken.

Wylie added that Sixta had useful clues to spotting a pair – each message had a serial number, which could be enciphered. When deciphered by the recipient, he often sent, as a receipt, the last two digits of the serial numbers of each message transmitted. When Sixta found among the receipts of different links the same pair of digits at similar times, there was a chance that they included the same message. Since links generally passed more than a hundred messages daily, there were many coincidences that did not arise from re-transmission. Sixta became familiar with pairs of links liable to be sending the same message, and could often make use of priority signals and other indications. But Fish traffic was not – unlike a number of Enigma keys – read currently. The average delay was three days in 1943 and 1945 and as much as seven days in 1944, but with the increase in Colossus machines, more transmissions were decrypted between October 1944 and May 1945 than between November 1942 and September 1944. Colossus made invaluable contributions to D-Day. The Berlin–Paris (Jellyfish) link had first been intercepted in January 1944 and broken in March, and although not numerous they included valuable detailed returns for individual divisions in the Commander in Chief's Command as well as strategic appreciations. The first was an appreciation obtained on 6 April. Similar appreciations had previously been decrypted on the Fish link between Berlin and Italy (Bream), and this source continued to provide general appreciations and order of battle intelligence.

One remarkable D-Day story is told by Tommy Flowers himself. He claimed that on 5 June Eisenhower was in conference with his staff when a courier arrived from Bletchley Park and handed him a note which contained Hitler's order to Rommel, decoded with the aid of Colossus, that the invasion of Normandy was imminent, but was a feint to draw troops away from the channel ports, against which the real invasion would be launched later. Therefore, Eisenhower knew that he could start the invasion of Normandy assured of five days without determined opposition. Whatever the truth of this story, certainly without Colossus D-Day planning would have been much more difficult. Since the German occupation of Western Europe, most Army Enigma traffic had been transmitted by landline, out of earshot of the interceptors. Colossus was, therefore, a vital means of intelligence at this crucial time.

Certainly Colossus was a wonder to behold when in action. As the end-of-war top secret report on the machine put it:

> It is regretted that it is not possible to give an adequate idea of the fascination of a Colossus at work: its sheer bulk and apparent complexity; the fantastic speed of thin paper tape round the glittering pulleys; the childish pleasure of not-not, span, print main headings and other gadgets; the wizardry of purely mechanical decoding letter by letter (one novice thought she was

being hoaxed); the uncanny action of the typewriter in printing the correct scores without and beyond human aid; the stepping of display; periods of eager expectation culminating in the sudden appearance of the longed-for score; and the strange rhythms characterizing every type of run: the stately break-in, the erratic short run, the regularity of wheel-breaking, the stolid rectangle interrupted by wild leaps of the carriage-return, the frantic chatter of a motor run, even the ludicrous frenzy of hosts of bogus scores.[lvi]

### KNOCKHOLT AND BLETCHLEY PARK FISH STATISTICS

| | Transmissions received at Knockholt | Tapes received | Tapes set on Chi's | Decodes | Decode in thousands of letters | Keys broken |
|---|---|---|---|---|---|---|
| **1942** | | | | | | |
| Nov–Dec | 12,180 | — | — | 872 | 4,467 | 4+ |
| **1943** | | | | | | |
| Jan–Mar | 16,615 | — | — | 991 | 3,386 | 10+ |
| Apr–Jun | 23,970 | 73 | 2 | 965 | 3,063 | 15+ |
| Jul–Sept | 21,550 | 272 | 17 | 745 | 3,047 | 19+ |
| Oct–Dec | 34,740 | 955 | 199 | 733 | 3,145 | 18+ |
| **1944** | | | | | | |
| Jan–Mar | 28,000 | 1,670 | 1,205 | 680 | 3,189 | 13 |
| Apr–Jun | 6,215 | 4,160 | 1,446 | 1,044 | 4,695 | 19 |
| Jul–Sep | 5,210 | 4,450 | 1,638 | 1,139 | 6,860 | 80++ |
| Oct–Dec | 6,922 | 5,496 | 2,182 | 1,861 | 9,607 | 166++ |
| **1945** | | | | | | |
| Jan–May | 812,325 | 10,555 | 4,332 ** | 4,478 | 21,972 | 374++ |
| **TOTAL** | 167,727 | 27,631 | 11,021 | 13,508 | 63,431 | 718++ |

** Of these, 1,040 were set mechanically on all 12 wheels
+ These were all broken by means of depths
++ Over half of these were broken by rectangles

(Source: TNA, *General Report on Tunny*, p 394.)

The added importance of Colossus was in the future development of computers as a pioneer programmable electronic digital computer. The fact that this machine had been pioneered in Britain had to remain a secret for more than thirty years, but has now rightly taken its pride of place in the history of computing.

There is now a working rebuild of a Colossus Mark II and a Tunny machine at Bletchley Park, now part of the National Museum of Computing in H Block, one of the wartime sites for Colossus. It stands on the site where Colossus number nine stood during the war, and it took the team led by Tony Sale fourteen years to reconstruct. Eventually, under the US Freedom of Information Act, the US personnel who had worked on Colossus had their end-of-war top secret report to their government declassified, and finally the British secret document *General Report on Tunny* was made publicly available. Bletchley Park also has a Lorenz machine on public display – it belonged to Field Marshal Albert Kesselring. Full information on Colossus is available on Tony Sale's web site at www.codesandciphers.org.uk.

# Chapter 16

# As If By Magic

On 31 October 1929 US Secretary of State Henry Stimson closed down America's codebreaking organisation MI8 or Cipher Bureau (also known as the Black Chamber) and later wrote in his memoirs that 'Gentlemen do not read each other's mail.' He had withdrawn the State Department portion of the funding for the Black Chamber and the other contributor – the US Army – refused to bear the entire cost. However, Stimson's views on cryptography had changed by the time he became Secretary for War during the Second World War. In 1931, the Black Chamber founder and head, Herbert Yardley, short of money, published a sensational book entitled *The American Black Chamber* and blew the whistle on the top secret operations which had led American codebreakers to read Japanese enciphered signals during the Washington Naval Conference of 1921–1922. Yardley had been able to furnish the US government with the Japanese negotiating position for the talks, which ended in agreement on the ratio of capital ships between Japan, Britain and the United States as 3:5:5. Following publication, the Japanese completely changed their cipher system.

The Black Chamber took its name from a succession of similar codebreaking organisations which went back to medieval times – to Henry IV of France in 1590 – and was set up in June 1917 under the cover of a New York commercial code company, selling codes on the open market, but its real task was to read the codes, particularly diplomatic, of foreign governments. Yardley wrote another book, *Japanese Diplomatic Codes 1921–1922*, but it was seized by the authorities and was not published until it was declassified in 1979. But Yardley had upset the authorities by his authorships and during the Second World War he worked for the Canadians and the Chinese, but was never again employed by the US government.

However, almost as soon as the Black Chamber was shut down, a new organisation – controlled by the Army – sprang up: the Signal Intelligence Service (SIS), later the Army Security Agency. It began work in April 1930 under William Friedman, who started up the organisation by recruiting three mathematicians, Frank Rowlett, Abraham Sinkov and Solomon Kullback. Friedman was one of the great names in cryptography. He even designed the impregnable US cipher machine known as Sigaba, in co-operation with Frank Rowlett and, later, the navy's Commander Laurence Safford of the naval codebreaking organisation, Op-20-G. Working on a similar basis to Enigma, it included fifteen rotors rather than Enigma's three and, unlike the German machine, had no reflector. Sigaba had two rows of five rotors, the action of two of the rows controlling the stepping of the third. Sigaba was later adapted to work in conjunction with Typex, Britain's wartime cipher machine, and was used from November 1943 as the CCM – Combined Cipher Machine. Even Friedman's wife Elizebeth (an odd spelling of the name) played her part in the US secret war, as she was given the task of setting up the cryptographical organisation for a newly formed top secret organisation – General William Donovan's OSS (Office of Strategic Services, the forerunner of the CIA). Friedman had decided to go down the mathematical route of codebreaking, a change from the traditional language-based approach, which was a system using the technique of conducting a 'frequency analysis' of the most used words and letters in a particular language. This mathematical approach to cryptanalysis had also been adopted by the Poles in their successful attack against Enigma. But the SIS did not restrict its wartime operations to the Axis countries, for in 1943 they began intercepting Soviet messages sent largely from New York, to which was given the codename Venona. The first break into Venona came on 20 December 1946, revealing the extent of Soviet espionage at Los Alamos, where the atomic bomb was built.

Following the Yardley revelations, in 1931 the Japanese strengthened their security by building a cipher machine known as 91-shiki injiki or Type 91 print machine, the 91 standing for the year 2591, the Japanese Imperial Calendar equivalent of 1931. This machine was also used for diplomatic messages by the Japanese Foreign Ministry, where it was known as Angooki Taipu-A or Type A cipher machine, which was given the codename Red by the SIS. The Japanese navy used the 91-shiki injiki kana-letter model. A significant weakness of the machine was that it enciphered the six vowels of the alphabet – AEIOUY: the letter Y was treated as a vowel – and consonants separately. The Type A machine had an encipherment mechanism which comprised two half-rotors on a fixed shaft, each with twenty-six electrical contacts wired round the circumference of one of its sides and a forty-seven-pin gear wheel which moved the half-rotors either one or two positions at every stroke of the typewriter keys. The operator connected the two typewriters to the machine through the plugboard using a daily changing setting. Each message was preceded by a five-figure group indicating the start positions for both the rotor and the gear wheel, as well as the pins which were to be removed from the gear wheel. The plaintext was typed into the input typewriter which sent an electrical impulse through the keyboard socket to which it was wired, then through an endplate and into the circuitry of the two half-rotors. This reflected it out via the endplate to the output typewriter, which typed the enciphered letter. The decipherment was thus determined largely by the plugboard settings and the fixed wirings of the half-rotors, and only varied by the movement of the gear wheel. This normally moved the rotor forward by one contact for every letter inputted, but where a pin had been removed, it jumped a contact.

The first to break this machine were the British pair Hugh Foss and Oliver Strachey of the Government Code & Cypher School (GC&CS) in 1934, while a replica of the Japanese model known as the J machine was constructed by the Metropolitan Police intercept unit led by Harold Kenworthy, which covered diplomatic and commercial traffic, to break Japanese diplomatic ciphers in August 1935, working on behalf of GC&CS. The American cryptanalyst Frank Rowlett led an SIS team which broke Red in 1935, and Agnes Driscoll broke the naval attaché version, which was virtually the same model. But even earlier success against Japanese ciphers was that of GC&CS's John Tiltman with the naval attaché cipher in 1933.

In 1937, the Japanese brought in a new machine, the 97-shiki injiki or Type 97 print machine, and the diplomatic model was called the Angooki Taipu-B or Type B cipher machine, codenamed Purple by the Americans. Unfortunately for the Japanese, they made the same mistake as the Germans with Enigma, bringing in changes piecemeal, and both Red and Purple machines operated at the same time and were used to send identical messages, enabling the breaking of Purple. The new system was an improvement on Red, as it was using a stepping-switch system of encipherment. However, the Japanese made a fundamental error with Purple, because it had adopted the separate six-vowel and twenty-consonant encipherment system used in Red, and became known to the Americans as the 'Sixes-Twenties' system, although Red was later modified to allow any six letters to be encrypted.

It was discovered by US naval codebreakers, who were separate from their Army counterparts and known as Op-20-G (Office of Chief of Naval Operations or OPNAV, 20th Division of the Office of Naval Communications, G Section/Communications Security). Set up on 1 July 1922, they were involved in breaking diplomatic as well as naval ciphers. There was a major row when navy agents broke into a Japanese consulate office in New York in 1922 and photographed code books. The SIS were furious, as it could have compromised the whole of the operation against diplomatic ciphers should the Japanese have discovered the break-in and changed their systems. In order to disguise this traffic as having been obtained by reading Japanese ciphers, the Americans codenamed the Purple traffic as Magic.

One of the navy cryptanalysts, Francis Raven, discovered that the Japanese had divided the month into three ten-day periods, and within each period they used the keys of the first day with small predictable changes. The big breakthrough in the attack on Purple was the building of an analogue of the Japanese machine by Leo Rosen of the SIS in 1939. In fact, it was on 20 March 1939 that the first indication of a change of machine became evident when three diplomatic messages from Warsaw to Tokyo did not fully conform to the normal traffic pattern. The Americans were aware from Red decrypts that a Japanese cryptographic expert was visiting embassies to install the new system and that one of the last he had visited was Warsaw. It was because of the nature of the 'sixes and twenties' that the Americans decided they would have to design an analogue of the Japanese machine. Rowlett explained that their design for such a device included a keyboard of twenty-six keys, a solenoid-operated typewriter, a twenty-six position plugboard, and a cryptographic mechanism which would duplicate the substitution process they had recovered.

> Everything we needed was already available to us except for the cryptographic mechanism, which would have to be specially designed and built.[lvii]

The breakthrough into Purple was provided by a brilliant piece of work by Genevieve Grotjan who, said Rowlett, was 'one of our most skilled cryptanalysts' and made 'the discovery of the first case of positive evidence that we were on the proper course to a full recovery of the Purple machine'. The main difference between the Red machine and Purple was that the latter did not use rotors but worked through a series of telephone stepping switches. A single main switch controlled the encryption of six letters (NOT the vowels), but changed daily. The other switches were organised in banks of three and controlled the remaining twenty letters. The switches were designed to simulate the action of the rotors on a standard cipher machine such as Enigma, moving to change the method of encryption as each letter is typed in. The single main switch stepped one level every time a letter was keyed in, while the other three banks moved at different speeds. The first bank was 'fast', stepping once for the first twenty-four key strokes. When the twenty-fifth was typed in, the first bank stayed where it was and the second 'medium' bank of switches stepped once. The second bank also only moved twenty-four times before the third or 'slow' bank came into operation. At the end of the next full rotation of the first bank of switches – the 625th operation of the machine – both the fast and medium banks remained where they were while the slow bank stepped once. The stepping switches were fixed into the machine, drastically cutting the number of encipherment options. There was a tangled web of wiring connecting the banks of stepping switches, and if the wiring could be worked out, then the traffic could be broken. The cipher clerk used a specific letter sequence listed in a book of one thousand daily changing sequences to plug the connections from the input and output typewriters into the plugboard. He then selected a five-figure random indicator group from a list of 120, each of which had different settings that should be applied to the banks of stepping switches and to the main switch which controlled the encryption of the 'sixes'. This five-figure indicator group was enciphered using an additive and sent immediately before the enciphered text. To encipher the message, the operator first encoded it using a basic commercially available substitution cipher known as the Phillips code. He then typed the enciphered text into one of the typewriters, generating an electric current which ran through the internal wiring and typed out the enciphered text on the second keyboard.

All Purple machines around the world were destroyed by the Japanese after the surrender, but the Americans obtained part of a Purple machine from the Japanese Embassy in Berlin at the end of the war. It was messages sent on Purple by Baron Oshima Hiroshi, Japanese ambassador to Berlin during the war, that provided such vital information for the Allies, in particular the Atlantic Wall fortifications prepared to combat the Allied invasion of Europe, following a tour of these defences by Oshima. The Japanese were supremely confident that their cipher machines could not be broken – an error also made by the Germans with regard to Enigma. In addition, the Japanese believed their language would also prove an insurmountable decryption mountain for western cryptanalysts.

Japanese is written in a combination of three scripts: hiragana and katakana, collectively known as kana, and kanji, the Chinese ideograms, in the form of brush strokes, adopted by the Japanese in ancient times. Kanji represents ideas or objects, hiragana expresses the grammatical relationships between them and katakana is largely used for words of foreign origin. The sounds of words depicted by kanji can be represented using kana. But this could lead to ambiguity, as Japanese has many different words which, while having a distinctive written form, sound the same, i.e. 'principle' and 'principal'. Romaji allows kana syllables to be spelt out in Roman letters. Japanese Morse contained all the kana syllables plus the romaji letters and was totally different from the standard international Morse system. Though Japanese is usually written in a combination of three scripts, Japanese sentences can be written in either hiragana or katakana only. It was Morse messages sent by radio operators in kana, which comprised about seventy syllables, which were intercepted by the Allied listening stations, each kana syllable and the ten numbers having a Morse sign.

Often the Japanese used a 'bisection' – a system of dividing the plaintext into two portions irregularly and placing the second portion first. At the end of 1937 the Japanese military used both codes and ciphers. A message was encoded into blocks of figures using a codebook which gave numerical equivalents for all the main Japanese characters, phrases and kana syllables. They used an additive system with pre-determined groups of figures taken from a cipher table or book, added to the code groups using Modulo 10 – the Fibonacci system – in which 7 + 8 = 5 and not 15, there being no carry-over. As with Enigma messages, so Japanese enciphered messages provided 'cribs' – guesses as to what a few words of the original Japanese plaintext might contain. For example, messages often began with the long-winded expression: 'I have the honour to report to your Excellency that ...' Other weaknesses in the system which helped the codebreakers were that Y was always followed by A, and pairs of vowels were frequent, most commonly OO, UU, AI and AE. YUU and YOO appeared often, preceded by a consonant: RYOO, RYUU, KYOO and KYUU for example. Because the Americans did not operate an integrated Service codebreaking system such as GC&CS, the US Army and Navy had an odd system of providing the State Department with deciphered Japanese diplomatic messages, in which the Navy provided the State Department with translations on odd days and the Army on even days!

At the time, translations provided by SIS carried two dates: that on which the message was intercepted and that on which the translation was made, both of which could be different. A compromise was reached whereby the 'odd–even' system would operate on the basis of the date which the Japanese officially applied to the message when it was originated. With Red, the cryptanalysts were 'promptly solving each new diplomatic code system as it was introduced'. However, it was realised that the Japanese would in time realise that the security of their codes and ciphers needed to be improved and that they might even overhaul their entire cryptographic security arrangements.

Setting up a Japanese section at Bletchley Park first entailed finding sufficient Japanese language specialists – and they were in very short supply. While there were plenty of German-speaking recruits available for Bletchley Park, those who were conversant in Japanese speech and – most particularly – writing, were few in number. When inquiries were made of SOAS (the School of Oriental and African Studies) by Bletchley Park chief military cryptanalyst John Tiltman, about teaching the language, SOAS replied that it took five years, but they might squeeze it into two. Tiltman, never one to be put off, decided it would have to be done in six months – he had learned it in that time. To this end, a remarkable teacher came on the scene, retired naval captain Oswald Tuck, then in his sixties, who began with his first students in February 1942 at Bedford with dictionaries which he supplied himself. According to Alan Stripp, who went on one of the Bedford courses, Tuck had directed some of the most successful crash courses in educational history at one of the most crucial moments in recent British history. A final comment came from Australia, firmly under MacArthur's control, only a fortnight from Hiroshima. According to Stripp, they asked for as many Bedford students as possible:

Could you indicate a possible figure and I shall initiate an official request. Your Bedford-trained translators most highly esteemed and would like as many as we may have; we can never have enough.[lviii]

The Purple machine was put to good use at Bletchley Park after the Americans generously brought two models with them when they visited Britain's wartime codebreaking centre in January 1941, while still neutral. What seemed inexplicable was that while Bletchley Park had two Purple machines, Pearl Harbour in Hawaii had none! Towards the end of the year Bletchley Park also received two Red machines. But the Japanese had grown suspicious about the security of their codes and ciphers, and in May 1941 the Japanese Ambassador in Washington, Kishsaburo Nomura, had been warned by Tokyo that they had strong reason to believe that his messages were being read by the Americans. Amazingly, the Japanese inquiry concluded that neither the Red nor Purple messages were compromised! So, to American relief, both cipher machine systems continued to be used by the Japanese Foreign Office and embassies. By November 1941 the war clouds were looming larger than ever, and on 19 November, Purple revealed instructions to Japanese embassies to await a special signal meaning relations with the US, Russia or Britain had broken down which would be disguised as weather reports. The message to be sent regarding a breakdown with the US would read *higashi no kaze, ame*: EAST WIND RAIN, with Russia it would state *kita no kaze, kumori*: NORTH WIND CLOUDY and for Britain, *nishi no kaze, hare*: WEST WIND CLEAR. Then another message instructed embassies to destroy their codes and ciphers and their machines. There was, at the post-war Congressional inquiry, disagreement as to whether a Winds message was ever received and deciphered. William Friedman did not believe such a message had been received, but Captain Laurence Safford of the US naval codebreaking organisation took a contrary view. However, both men genuinely believed that a Winds Executed order had been issued and that their pleas for action 'were lost in the fog of incompetence and bad luck which seems to have enveloped the service authorities in Washington throughout the weeks leading up to Pearl Harbour'.

However, the message was picked up in Hong Kong about 2300 hours on Sunday 7 December – Saturday at Honolulu – by British interceptors at the Far East Combined Bureau (FECB), which reported having heard the coded Winds message. Intercept stations at Hong Kong and Corregidor had been alerted by Singapore, and a special watch was mounted at FECB to look out for the Winds message. However, owing to poor weather conditions at Singapore, it was Hong Kong that first heard the message and reported it 'about 2300 on Sunday 7th December 1941'. This was Saturday at Honolulu.

On 1 December the Japanese had changed naval callsigns on ships and three days later altered its fleet code. On the political and diplomatic front, US Secretary of State Cordell Hull had sent a warning message to the Japanese to withdraw from China and Indo-China – almost certain to be rejected – and Washington was awaiting a reply: the odds on the reply meaning war was overwhelming. On 6 December the US naval codebreakers received a Purple message that the reply to Cordell Hull would come shortly in a fourteen-part message. The fourteenth part, the message revealed, would contain the date and time at which the message was to be handed to the Secretary of State. The first thirteen parts of the message came in soon after and were uncompromising in their answer to Cordell Hull's demands. But the fourteenth part came later, in the early hours of Sunday, 7 December. Remarkably, it was deciphered by the US codebreakers before the Japanese embassy officials in Washington! It declared that Japan was breaking off diplomatic relations with the US, and was to be delivered to Cordell Hull at 1300 – dawn in Pearl Harbour. But Washington did not expect an attack at Pearl Harbour, and as a general war warning had been sent out several days earlier, they did not send another message. So, it was by a series of errors that Pearl Harbour was taking its Sunday morning leisurely, but that morning eighteen ships – including seven battleships – were destroyed or badly damaged, 164 aircraft were destroyed and 2,341 servicemen were killed. Little wonder that President Roosevelt described it as a 'day of infamy'.

But the success of the US codebreakers was to prove its value again and again, not least at the vital Battle of Midway in June 1942, which became the turning point for the Allies in the Pacific war. Midway was overwhelmingly a cryptanalytical success. The Japanese had issued an order for an invasion of key points in the Aleutian Islands and at Midway. This order should have been encrypted in a new cipher which had been due to come into operation on 1 April, but delay first put this date back to 1 May and finally to 1 June. Then a message was deciphered referring to a target codename AF. Where was AF? The

Americans thought AF might refer to Midway and tried a ruse, sending a message in plaintext reporting the breakdown of the water distillation plant on the tiny but strategically vital island. Two days later a Japanese message reported a water shortage on 'AF'. So the Americans knew the point of attack. But when? Two days later came the answer – 3 June. On 1 June the new cipher came into operation and the Americans were blind. But for the delay in bringing in the new cipher, the outcome at Midway could well have been different.

There were to be a series of shock aftermaths to this triumph of the US codebreakers at Midway, which led to a major Japanese naval defeat, and left the US with naval supremacy in the region. Firstly, the *Chicago Tribune* published a story with the headline: NAVY HAD WORD OF JAP PLAN TO STRIKE AT SEA.

An internal naval investigation into this leak was called off to protect secrecy and the Japanese apparently did not notice the story. Then, having breathed a sigh of relief, there was another panic when a member of Congress made a speech attacking the newspaper article, claiming that the US navy had broken Japanese codes. Again, nothing happened. And if these incidents were not worrying enough, there was to be a further shock. Governor Thomas Dewey of New York, the 1944 Republican Presidential candidate running against incumbent President, Franklin Roosevelt, was threatening to raise the Pearl Harbour controversy publicly, but was persuaded, in the national interest, to let the matter drop after a top secret briefing. This was a clear case of putting country before party.

Perhaps the biggest risk taken by the US authorities themselves with the Purple secret was when they decided to go after Admiral Yamomoto Isoruku, the commander of the Combined Fleet and architect of the attack on Pearl Harbour. Having intercepted a message about his timetable for visits to frontline forces, his plane was intercepted off Bourgainville in the Solomon Islands and shot down – but again the Japanese did not consider that their ciphers had been compromised. In the European war, too, the reading of crucial Purple messages sent to Tokyo from Berlin by both the Japanese ambassador and military attaché proved vital to the D-Day planning.

Following the Japanese expansion throughout south-east Asia, General Douglas MacArthur set up his headquarters in Australia, where his Sigint organisation known as Central Bureau was first in Melbourne and then in September 1942 moved to Brisbane, where

MacArthur had already moved his HQ, and which included British and Australian personnel as well as Americans. Directed by Colonel Spencer Akin, the head of SIS, Central Bureau was reorganised much like Bletchley Park – at both places, each Hut had a specialised task and operated on strict, functional compartmentalisation.

One of the most important ciphers to be broken was the Water Transport messages, known by the Japanese as the 2468 series. Because there are so many islands in the region, Japan had to supply men and material by water, so information from this source was vital. Japan's Shipping Transport Command co-ordinated the movement of military units by sea and used army codes to encipher its messages. It was the intuition of US army sergeant Joseph Richard that led to the breakthrough in April 1943. By 1 August, 1944, US army intercept operators had recorded nearly 750,000 water transport messages, of which about ten per cent contained significant intelligence that merited a complete translation of the signal. Among these, 25,500 were shipping related, with 3,750 convoy related.

Regarding a decrypted Japanese Eighth Area Army signal of 1 February 1944, and the value of 2468, at least twelve Japanese freighters were sunk by Allied air or naval action while en route to resupply Wewak in north-east New Guinea between February 29 and March 24, 1944. According to *MacArthur's Ultra*:

> Eighth Area Army's message sealed the fates of the five convoys and shows how critical Ultra derived from the Army Water Transport Code was in anti-convoy operations.[lix]

While the codebreaking operation was outstanding, there were also some key breakthroughs in the capture of vital enciphering material left behind by the retreating Japanese. Near Sio, New Guinea, in January 1944, the Australians discovered a complete cryptographic library, found by accident as a sapper was sweeping the area for mines. In April 1944 at Hollandia, Dutch East Indies, one careless Japanese wireless operator left 147 worksheets with key and indicator tables, which were captured by the Americans. This information was fed into the IBM machines at Central Bureau and Arlington Hall, the Army codebreaking centre at Arlington, Virginia, enabling cryptanalysts to read messages enciphered in the new key. However, fearing their key compromised, the Japanese quickly discontinued it.

Again, in February 1945, the Japanese General Administrative system codebook was changed, and while the cryptographers were rebuilding this book, a near complete cryptographic library, including the new codebook, was captured. This enabled the Allies to read all the main Japanese Army messages immediately for several weeks and without major difficulty until the end of the war.

Bletchley Park had also been deeply involved in Japanese codebreaking, not least through the Far East Combined Bureau, a cover name for Britain's Asian codebreaking organisation, which had been moved for security reasons from Hong Kong to Singapore, then to Colombo and finally to Kilindini outside Mombasa in Kenya. The rapid onslaught of Japanese forces sweeping through south-east Asia had seen one British bastion after another fall: Hong Kong, Malaya and Singapore. It left British Sigint in total disarray and took time for it to recover. One notable success for FECB while in Colombo was the reading of the Japanese Naval General Cipher when, on 20 March 1942, it gave warning of an impending attack by carriers and heavy cruisers against Ceylon (now Sri Lanka) on 2 April, enabling warships in Colombo harbour to be moved in time. But, while priority in Britain had been given to breaking German ciphers, activity against Japanese encrypted messages went back many years.

Among those who became expert at breaking Japanese codes and ciphers were John Tiltman, who later became wartime chief cryptographer at Bletchley Park, Eric Nave, a Royal Australian Navy officer seconded to work with the British, and Hugh Foss, another British codebreaker. Nave was reading all of the early Japanese naval codes in the late 1920s, while Foss led British codebreakers in the first cryptographers to break a Japanese diplomatic machine cipher in 1934. Another triumph was that of Tiltman, who first broke JN25, a naval cipher, a few weeks after it was introduced in the summer of 1939.

On Bletchley Park's handling of Japanese decrypts, *The Official History of British Sigint* points out that interception of Japanese military communications in the UK was not regularly undertaken until October 1943, but at Bletchley Park a Japanese Military Section had evolved out of the Research Section into independent existence by June 1942. The *Official History* adds:

> Its early tasks, except for the exploitation of military attaché traffic, for which the material came mainly from Foreign Office

stations and America, were concerned with the study of Japanese communication and cypher methods, based chiefly on material received by air mail from India.[ix]

Between them, the British and American cryptanalysts broke many key Japanese ciphers. Here is a sample:

| | |
|---|---|
| JN14 | Four-digit naval code, usually reciphered. Movement of coastal vessels and major fleets. |
| JN16/JN49 | Flag Officers. |
| JN23 | Five-digit reciphered naval code devoted to the construction, launching and completion of warships. |
| JN25 | Major fleet five-digit reciphered naval code. |
| JN36/JN37 | Naval meteorological ciphers. |
| JN40 | Merchant shipping code of 4-syllable kana groups, used to report on Allied submarines or aircraft. |
| 3366 | Army–Air Force general key. |
| 6633 | Variant of 3366. Four-digit reciphered code, mainly for squadrons and above, with information about the Burma area. |
| BULBUL | Army–Air Force three-digit reciphered code. |
| CORAL | Naval attaché machine cipher. |
| JMA | Japanese Military Attaché code. |
| JIG | Medium grade consular reciphered code. |
| KA KA KA | Army field code, chiefly at battalion level in New Guinea. |
| PURPLE | Machine cipher used for high grade diplomatic traffic. |

There was also an unnamed naval code broken which was based on the King James Authorised Version of the Bible in English!

But the dropping of the atomic bomb on Hiroshima and Nagasaki in August 1945 was the end of the Japanese dream of an Asian empire, and the Emperor Hirohito sent a message to his troops – in clear – which the interceptors picked up, ordering them to lay down their arms. The Second World War had ended.

*Chapter 17*

# Wars Have Ears

T he essential ingredient of successful codebreaking is: first
intercept an enciphered message. Without this raw material all
the brains involved in codebreaking and all the sophisticated
machinery is of no use. This interception was carried out on the British
side by a special Intelligence organisation known as the 'Y Service',
which took its name from the first letter of each of the words 'Wireless
Intelligence' – 'WI' or 'Y'. But Signals Intelligence – Sigint – also
comprised other 'black arts'. Among some of the most important of
these during the war were:

**Radio Fingerprinting (RFP)** – an enlarged or elongated film record
of Morse transmissions by which the types of transmission used and
the peculiarities of the individual sets of any type can be distinguished,
serving to identify stations;
**TINA** – a method of distinguishing between W/T operators by the
study of the characteristics or peculiarities of the Morse of each
individual operator;
**Traffic Analysis (TA)** – the study of the external characteristics of
enemy W/T traffic for the purpose of making deductions useful to
cryptanalysis and/or Intelligence;
**'Noise'** – VHF non-communication transmissions used for navigation,
radar, etc;
**Direction Finding (D/F)** – taking of a bearing or bearings upon a
W/T transmission. A bearing or location obtained by these means.

The advent of wireless telegraphy revolutionised warfare, but on the
downside it meant that radio signals could be picked up by the enemy
as well as by friendly forces – hence the need for encryption. In Britain,
Sigint began at the Admiralty's Room 40 during the First World War,

finishing with a staff of around 100. While the initial emphasis had been on codebreaking, TA and D/F as well as recording and research techniques, had been undertaken. This had started with the British Expeditionary Force in France and led to Wireless Observation Groups being set up in Egypt, Greece and Mesopotamia. After the Armistice in 1918 it was decided to amalgamate the Army and Navy cryptography organisations into a single unit and in 1919 the Government Code and Cypher School (GC&CS) was formed and its first head was Admiral Hugh Sinclair, who also became head of the Secret Intelligence Service – SIS or MI6. In 1923, GC&CS was transferred to Foreign Office control. A W/T Co-ordination Committee was formed in 1924 and a Y sub-committee was set up in 1928 under GC&CS control, representing the Services, Metropolitan Police and the General Post Office (GPO), which then had responsibility for wireless telegraphy. The three Services wanted to retain their own Sigint operations and agreed with GC&CS Director Alastair Denniston that GC&CS should remain a cryptographic bureau and not become a Sigint centre, segregating intelligence and TA from cryptanalysis. This led to a failure to stress search and TA as aids to interception.

On the day war broke out – 3 September 1939 – the Directorate of Military Intelligence (DMI) was established separately from the Directorate of Military Operations (DMO). MI8 became responsible for Y duties including illicit wire intercept – later the Radio Security Service (RSS) – for which the War Office had been responsible since 1928. The Air Ministry controlled RAF Y services through AI4 and there was no change in Navy organisation. No German high-grade traffic was read at the beginning of the war and little low-grade, but WTI (Wireless Telegraphy Intelligence) was very productive. At the beginning of the war, Enigma traffic was intercepted at the War Office station at Chatham and in France, aided in 1940 by the Foreign Office stations at Sandridge and Denmark Hill. During the Battle of France, due to limited resources, it was only possible to intercept the most important key – the Luftwaffe 'Red' cipher – and leave the rest. In 1941 wireless sets were obtained at War Office stations Y2 (Harpenden), Y3 (London), Aldershot and RAF Chicksands and SYG (later WOYG – War Office Y Group, which moved to Beaumanor, in Leicestershire, in September 1941). In January 1941, Chatham's Army unit was moved to Chicksands for safety reasons, but remained independent. The decision was taken to make WOYG and Chicksands the two main stations, concentrating on German Army and Air Force traffic respectively.

In March 1940 the Y Committee was reconstituted with more members being added. Cheadle RAF Y station had developed 'footprint' techniques – a peculiarity in signal procedure or phraseology characteristic of air-ground transmissions of a certain unit which enabled the unit's transmission to be recognised. This enabled identification of most Luftwaffe bomber units and activities. It had also solved callsign and frequency systems, while the coming of VHF communications, Radio Telephony (R/T) and 'noises' called for a new frontline organisation.

The Navy and RAF had set up fourteen mobile stations around the south and east coasts of England by the end of 1940, with a 'nodal' point at Kingsdown on the Kent coast between Dover and Deal called HDUs – Home Defence Units – covering enemy fighter and bomber R/T and navigational aids including 'noises'. The discovery of Luftwaffe navigational aids led to the formation of 80 Wing (Bomber Command) for Radio Counter-Measures (RCM), 109 Squadron for airborne intercept investigations and 'Headache' section at Fighter Command to control flights, and fuse all results, ground and airborne. In 1940 began the closely integrated Service co-operation that lasted throughout the war. In November 1940 the CBME (Combined Bureau Middle East) was formed, at first for cryptanalytic work only. At the end of 1940, Bletchley Park was still purely cryptanalytical, but early in 1941 the argument raged again over control of Sigint. The War Office argued for a single, unified Y Service, but the Navy and RAF wanted to maintain separate organisations. This separation of Y and cryptography did not work in practice, especially with Enigma, where cryptographic requirements had to govern interception. No 6 Intelligence School (6IS) – later called Sixta – was set up to cover various Army WTI or TA parties, matching 4IS, at Bletchley Park, which handled Army cryptographic work. Bletchley Park set up an Intelligence Exchange in July 1941 to receive the product of various sections, and the Admiralty, through its OIC (Operational Intelligence Centre) which handled Ultra traffic from Bletchley Park, appointed a liaison officer.

In planning for D-Day, it was soon realised that there would need to be a considerable increase in wireless sets – around 500 in the UK – as well as a large increase in M/F (Medium Frequency) sets in both fixed and mobile stations.

Because of its importance, military commanders wanted Ultra available in the field. However, sending such highly sensitive information out worldwide was a huge security risk, so a Communications Section was set up at Bletchley Park in September 1941 in the form of Special Communications Units/Special Liaison Units (SCU/SLU) to carry Hut 3 intelligence to the Mediterranean and later other overseas Commands. They came under MI6 Section VIII, and the first SCU was set up in Cairo in June 1941, but attempts to organise Y exchanges with the Russians from mid-1941 to early 1943 were unsuccessful. According to former Section VIII member Geoffrey Pidgeon, when a mobile SLU was attached to a Command, such as in North Africa, Sicily, Italy and, later, in the liberation of Europe, the unit consisted of two parts. The SLU cipher crew in one vehicle would be coupled with an SCU wireless van that actually handled the traffic. The cipher element was manned by RAF personnel and the SCU (wireless telegraphy) element by Royal Corps of Signals staff supplied exclusively from Whaddon or Little Horwood, near Bletchley.

The first SCUs were set up in March 1941, when Colonel (later Brigadier) Richard Gambier-Parry took over the RSS on behalf of MI6 Section VIII. SCU1 was based at Whaddon Hall, and became Section VIII's HQ. SCU1's role was primarily to transmit Ultra from Bletchley Park to overseas commands. The RSS became SCU 3 and operated from Hanslope Park, also near Bletchley. In all there were fourteen SCUs formed. These units were handling only Ultra traffic, and, as such, their work in the various theatres of war, attached to the most senior commanders, was extremely sensitive. Geoffrey Pidgeon said that such a unit had to be totally autonomous, protected by complex secrecy, supplied with the finest communications equipment possible and, above all, with highly qualified staff to operate it.

> Most importantly, it had to be beyond the reach of any officer, regardless of rank and status, other than the authorised recipient of the intelligence.[lxi]

When Winston Churchill attended the Tehran conference (28 November–1 December 1943) to meet President Roosevelt and Marshal Stalin, he took an SLU unit with him. Churchill's SLU wireless operator was Edgar Harrison, and it was his task to transmit the Prime Minister's most secret messages. Like many at Bletchley Park, the SLU members suffered over rank, and therefore pay. The officers were never high in rank and the technicians were all sergeants. This was to avoid speculation at HQs as to who they were. Secrecy also made it difficult to award decorations on an appropriate scale. Security was paramount. All foreign friends were vetted. Mobile SLU premises had the outside door locked and were fitted with Yale locks. When a door was opened an SLU member stood guard. Secondary doors were permanently locked. Windows were treated with semi-opaque paint or fitted with curtains. Many windows had bars across them. No maps were displayed on walls, and anyone leaving had to examine their shoes to ensure no Typex cipher machine tape was adhering to their soles. All messages were destroyed after twenty-four hours. Only an SLU member could deliver an Ultra message to a Commander or a designated member of his staff, and had to be recovered by him as soon as the message was read and understood. No Ultra signal could be transmitted or repeated. SLU officers had to watch out for carelessness, particularly among senior officers. Air Marshal Coningham, for example, had a habit of stuffing his Ultra papers in the top of his flying boots. On one occasion an SLU unit received advance warning of an enemy raid on Constantine and took their tin hats with them when they went on duty. When the air raid duly arrived, others looked at them with the deepest suspicion.

Even Churchill was not excluded from this security. When visiting the Italian front line, he was kept waiting for Ultra signals because the officer concerned, Wing Commander Crawshaw, thought it too dangerous to take the decrypts up the line. Churchill's annoyance turned to understanding and Crawshaw was subsequently invited to dinner with the PM. So successful were the SLUs that the Americans copied the system, and formed an organisation known as Special Branch Officers. Advance SLUs were on the Normandy landings and a direct teleprinter circuit was set up between Hut 3 and both Supreme Headquarters Allied Expeditionary Force (SHAEF) and 21st Army Group in France and Germany when these HQs moved across the Channel.

Chicksands Priory in Bedfordshire became the main RAF high-grade intercept station (German and Italian) in the UK, enabling exploitation of German beacons in the latter part of the war to give about one hour's advance warning ahead of radar indications in about eighty per cent of raids. Kingsdown covered VHF W/T and R/T communications and navigational aids including 'noises'. A Noise Investigation Committee was set up with its climax on D-Day, providing extensive pre-emptive action against enemy radar and navigational aids. For the RAF, SALU section – covering all aspects of Air Intelligence, high and low-grade – was formed to tie-up Enigma and Y and a special fighter sub-section was organised for the longer-term study of R/T traffic from Kingsdown. Naval Section at Bletchley Park did not segregate high and low-grade ciphers, and there was a single point of Sigint information – the OIC. When the German U-boat fleet went over to a four-wheel Enigma machine in February 1942, blacking-out the codebreakers, WTI and D/F became the principal sources of information. Naval Section became unified in June 1941. According to *The Official History of British Sigint*, for the naval intercept organisation, almost total intercept was achieved for the Atlantic, ninety-five per cent for other western areas, it was fairly high in the Mediterranean, but a substantial portion of North Norwegian and Black Sea traffic was missed.

> Ship-borne interception also developed, and on D-Day about 50 ships were fitted with VHF. Naval special intelligence [Ultra] was of direct operational use, much more than that for the Army and Air Force.[lxii]

Overseas, as soon as German armed forces entered Italy and the Afrika Korps arrived in North Africa, an expansion in interception was needed in these areas of conflict. Interception was already being carried out at Sarafand in Palestine, Heliopolos – a Cairo district – Malta and Gibraltar. For overseas interception, it was a case of following the enemy. Concentration points shifted from Gibraltar to Malta, from Alexandria to Algiers and from Africa to Italy. Mobile stations kept moving, always attempting to keep the enemy within M/F range, and there was a constant problem of adequate communications. The invasion of Russia in June 1941 led to an increased urgency for overseas sets, because German action in southern Russia was better intercepted in the Middle East. North Africa and the desert campaign was a case in point. In late spring 1942, just before Rommel's final push to El Alamein, there were seven sets at Gibraltar, two at Malta, three at Heliopolis, seven at Alexandria, four at Sarafand and five at Bagush in the Egyptian desert. As *The History of Hut 6* recorded:

> These Bagush sets mark an important development – the provision of the first mobile section, exclusively on Enigma, detailed to intercept low-powered transmissions of enemy

forward units inaudible at Malta or Heliopolis.[lxiii]

Later, these mobile stations became an integral and very important part of Enigma interception, and in these early days provided the best cover for Phoenix, the Afrika Korps tactical key – the drawback was the delay in getting the traffic back to Bletchley Park. After El Alamein the picture improved dramatically, and during summer 1943 plans were being drawn up to deal with the eventual need for interception in Italy, to include one fixed station and two mobiles. In the Middle East and Mediterranean, CBME covered Sigint, but did not include the Navy. In this region the Army developed special field Sigint organisations – Intelligence Signals or I(S) staff at GHQ level to advise on and direct interception, Special Wireless Groups (SWG), with I Section at GHQ to cover enemy strategic links and Special Wireless Sections Type B to cover enemy tactical links. In October 1941, the RAF appointed an Assistant Senior Intelligence Staff Officer (ASISO) to co-ordinate all Air effort in the Middle East. The following month, all RAF units came under the control of RAF Station, Suez Road, Cairo. Sigint in India was virtually autonomous until 1942, while pre-war and to mid-1941, Indian Sigint was mainly concerned with Russia, but in July 1941 a big expansion was planned, involving an inter-Service organisation. In its region, the FECB (Far East Combined Bureau) kept an eye on Japan. In 1940–1941 an international Sigint liaison was set up involving Britain, New Zealand, Australia, Holland and the US. The setting up of a Central Bureau for Sigint in Australia was also a major step forward. A joint fund was established, and orders for equipment were placed in America. Preparations were made for increase of staff and, most important, for the training of intercept operators and the interpretative staffs of the field units, of which Australia stood in such urgent need. In July 1942, General MacArthur moved his headquarters to Brisbane, the bureau transferred there in September, and became known as the Central Bureau Brisbane.

Sigint co-operation with the Americans was crucial, and led to a world-wide series of UK–US listening stations working for the common good, leading to a large expansion of interception and codebreaking activities. Anglo-US Sigint liaison was crucial. The first joint UK–US discussions began in autumn 1940, with the first American party arriving at Bletchley Park in February 1941. At first, Britain was reluctant to talk about Enigma, but eventually there was a full disclosure, and in August 1941, Alastair Denniston, head of

Bletchley Park, visited the US to discuss exchanges, including the first integrated staff. Direct liaison between FECB and the US in Manila began in February 1941.

In February 1942 it was agreed that high-grade cryptanalysis and research should be concentrated in the UK and Washington, while low-grade cryptography, decoding and exploitation should be left to overseas inter-Service bureaux. Special W/T communications were provided to carry Y traffic cryptanalysis, and those personnel who undertook such secret work were to be listed as being in a 'reserve occupation'. An increase of 7,300 personnel – 3,870 Army, 1,680 RAF, 1,600 Royal Navy and 150 Foreign Office – plus more than 900 intercept receivers, 275 D/F sets and 170 cryptographic equipment pieces were also agreed.

In January 1942, Bletchley Park organisation and administration was reformed and divided into two sections – Service and Civil. RSS continued to be responsible for intercept and TA, but the latter was increasingly dependent on access to decrypts, which was restricted until the formation of Radio Intelligence Section (RIS) in May 1943 to provide feedback. The Y Committee was revised to become the Y Board and was much more active. Bletchley Park was now a global Sigint centre and the old rivalry between cryptanalysis and Y was breaking down. Co-ordination of TA was achieved by the arrival of 6IS in May 1942 and the subsequent creation of Sixta in October 1943 to absorb Hut 3 and Hut 6 TA elements, but the battle for control of interception between Sixta and Hut 3 lasted until the end of the war. D/F was also growing in importance to guide interception, leading to the growth of a D/F network and the formation of a D/F co-ordinating committee in March 1943. However, overseas Commands for the Army continued the intelligence/signals split at all levels. The arrival of US forces in Europe in mid-1942 saw an American officer appointed to the Y Committee. By the end of January 1943 intercept services had increased from the previous January from 1,100 sets (4,000 operators) to 1,930 sets (7,000 operators). On Japanese Sigint, there was an extra 1,260 staff (850 for cryptanalysis) and 2,035 (plus around 400 extra sets) for interception. Nevertheless, Sigint did not always get used properly, particularly early on in North Africa, where Army Sigint gave ample warning of Rommel's attack on the Gazala line in May 1942. However, it was apparently inexpertly presented, ill-appreciated and disregarded in the face of conflicting evidence from reconnaissance.

Operation Torch – the November 1942 landings in North-West Africa: Morocco, Algeria and Tunisia – was territory nominally in the hands of the Vichy French government, was an attempt to attack German forces in the rear, and was the first time that Anglo–US co-operation had been required. However, 'there were different UK–US concepts of security' and, while Naval and Air Sigint worked satisfactorily, 'Army field effort was poor'. In the Mediterranean in April 1943, there were three main H/F (High Frequency) intercept stations at Algiers, Benghazi and Sarafand in Palestine. A new RAF organisation covered the Middle East, North Africa and Malta in a single Command. In the European sector, Enigma (German Army/Air Force), greater interception was not matched by an increase in decrypts after autumn 1942. For instance:

|  | Interception Sets | Decrypts |
|---|---|---|
| May 1942 | 210 | 25,000 |
| October 1942 | 299 | 42,000 |
| May 1943 | 349 | 33,000 |
| October 1943 | 403 | 48,000 |

Sigint, and research based on it, contributed to strategic intelligence in three main areas: enemy capacity, intentions, and progress in the scientific and technical fields. When Britain was at its weakest, Sigint was just getting into its stride, and evidence on German invasion plans in autumn 1940 was hazy and imprecise. Sigint was late on the German arrival in North Africa, but gave several weeks warning of the invasions of Crete and Russia.

From then on, it never failed to give evidence of a major enemy strategic intention, even though evidence was sometimes disregarded, as at Gazala in North Africa in May 1942, and the Ardennes in Western Europe in December 1944.[lxiv]

One of the most important and secretive intercept groups of the war was not staffed by people from the Services or the Foreign Office, but was largely composed of amateur radio enthusiasts skilled in Morse code – the Radio Security Service (RSS). At the beginning of the war a small department was set up by the Security Service (MI5) to detect enemy radio transmissions from agents believed to be operating within the UK. The RSS became part of MI5 and eventually Section C of MI8, with the GPO providing men and material for their needs and the maintenance and operation of the intercept stations until the GPO staff were eventually put into uniform in the Royal Signals, before finally being taken over by MI6 as its Section VIII, which dealt with communications. Its first head was Colonel Worlledge. An amateur radio enthusiast, Lord Sandhurst, was appointed to develop the organisation. He contacted Arthur Watts, President of the Radio Society of Great Britain (RSGB), the governing body for radio amateurs. The interview took place in a cell at Wormwood Scrubs, as a number of cells had been taken over for what became the first headquarters of the RSS, with a direct teleprinter link to Bletchley Park. Watts recommended harnessing the entire RSGB Council, and the RSS was in business, at first called the Illicit Wireless Intercept Organisation, and its members were called VIs – Voluntary Interceptors. To disguise their role, many VIs were dressed in Royal Observer Corps uniform and largely worked from home. At the outbreak of war radio amateurs had been ordered to hand in their transmitters but were allowed to retain their receivers, many of which were homemade. With these receivers, radio 'hams' spent many hours in peacetime listening out for other enthusiasts worldwide, and so were particularly adept at picking up faint Morse signals transmitted over long distances, an essential requisite for listening to enemy messages. Some of them had powers to enter premises where they thought illicit wireless activity was going on. At its peak, the RSS had an establishment of 2,094, comprising 98 officers, 1,317 operators, 83 engineers, 471 administrative personnel and 125 civilian clerks, plus the 1,200 amateur radio Voluntary Interceptors. During the war 268,000 RSS decrypts were issued by Bletchley Park, with a peak of 282 a day in May 1944. Of these the Abwehr provided 97,000 in hand cipher and 140,000 enciphered on the Enigma machine. The Nazi Security Service – the Sicherheitsdienst (SD) – produced 13,000 decrypts.

The need for a specialist organisation to intercept illicit transmissions from the UK was recognised as early as 1928. As wireless would be a major factor in any future war it was recommended that the War Office should use voluntary and unpaid 'enthusiastic amateurs of unimpeachable discretion' to develop such an organisation. In 1933 the idea of an organisation that eventually became the RSS began to take hold. In 1939, many 'hams' were called up into the RAF Civilian Wireless Reserve – later the RAF Volunteer Reserve – the Territorial Army Signals Unit and the Royal Navy Volunteer (Wireless) Reserve. The information the VIs fed to Bletchley Park provided much of the raw material required to break into enemy codes and ciphers. In addition, radio amateurs, many of whom possessed considerable technical skills, played a key role in technological developments such as counter-measures against enemy air attacks, in the defeat of the magnetic mine, developing ultra-high frequencies and as instructors at the top-secret radio and radar schools.

The VIs were recruited into nine regions with a Royal Signals Captain as Regional Controller. Initially, messages logged by VIs were sent to Wormwood Scrubs, but the volume became so great that the RSS HQ was moved to Arkley View, a large country house in the village of Arkley, just outside Barnet in North London. VIs were given a reference number, some blank log sheets, postage stamps and envelopes addressed to 'Box 25, Barnet, Hertfordshire'. VIs placed their completed logs inside a stamped addressed envelope which was then inserted into another envelope addressed to Box 25. At Arkley, the RSS had its own D/F and intercept facilities, and became known as Special Communications Unit 3 (SCU3). They were often given particular frequency bands to search for signals using a certain type of procedure, and sometimes were asked to listen out for particular call-signs and to take down any messages which appeared in coded groups of five letters – the standard method of sending secret information by Morse. Frequencies most used were between 3 MHz and 12 MHz, with the concentration from 4 MHz to 9 MHz. Much of this band was occupied by German broadcast stations, their armed Services and the press. But with some five to six million cycles of band, in which a Morse signal only required a one-thousand cycle space, in theory there could be 3,000 stations – excluding that used by broadcasters – which could be operating simultaneously, hence the need for a nationwide team of VIs. At the beginning of 1941 the RSS received improved technical resources. Some of the equipment came from the US and new intercept stations were set up. In August 1941, the RSS moved to Hanslope Park, just north of Bletchley Park. Hanslope officially opened in May 1942 and was so important that it was visited by VIPs such as Field Marshal Montgomery and General Eisenhower. Post-war it became the

Diplomatic Wireless Service.

When it became clear that there was no enemy spying activity within the UK, the RSS was given the task of monitoring signals abroad, and particularly messages of the Abwehr. The largest Abwehr signals came from Group 2 – Berlin (the RSS codename for Berlin was Bertie). In March 1940, the RSS intercepted wireless traffic between Hamburg and the German spy ship *Theseus*, which was carrying out observations inside Norwegian territorial waters. But the ship was left alone because of the cryptanalytical value of her transmissions. These messages were intercepted by the RSS after a tip-off from a double agent and decrypted at Bletchley Park, and were the first examples of intelligence from Abwehr ciphers.

In spring 1940, the RSS intercepted traffic that revealed the forthcoming blitzkrieg on 10 May 1940 against France, Belgium and Luxembourg. Indeed, it was the RSS itself which broke the ciphers, which led to reprimands all round, as codebreaking was Bletchley Park's job. In June 1940, it was decided that, in order to release wireless operators who were desperately needed to intercept Luftwaffe Enigma traffic, the RSS would cease to intercept the Abwehr link, and the objections of RSS were overruled but they later obtained permission to resume the interception. When Bletchley Park finally broke the cipher used by the Abwehr's main wireless network, it turned out to be the hand cipher used by German military intelligence and its agents abroad. Captured enemy agents were either executed or 'turned' and made to send messages back to their German handlers as if they were still free.

This 'turning' of agents became known as the Twenty Committee, and as Twenty in Roman numerals is XX, so the organisation became known as the Double Cross system, whose chairman was the Oxford historian Sir John Masterman of MI5. Again, amateur radio hams were involved, as many of the turned agents were handled by them. Part of their role was to ensure that Morse signals sent back to Germany contained only the content of the messages which had been dictated to them by MI5. Bletchley Park played a crucial role in the Double Cross success through the breaking of Abwehr Enigma ciphers by Dilly Knox through Intelligence Services Knox (ISK) and the Abwehr hand ciphers broken by Intelligence Services Oliver Strachey (ISOS). Christopher Andrew wrote in his officially authorised history of MI5 that ISOS decrypts led directly to the capture of five of the twenty-three German agents despatched to the UK during 1941, identified two more and provided valuable guidance in devising the disinformation with which the double agents deceived the Abwehr.

> Ultra provided crucial evidence that the Germans were successfully deceived by much of the disinformation fed to them by their turned agents.[lxv]

One RSS success story turned out to be so good they found themselves with a problem. The story was told by Hugh Trevor-Roper (later Lord Dacre), who worked with the RSS. In a BBC broadcast called *The Secret Listeners* in 1979, he explained that they knew all about Cicero, the German codename for the spy in Turkey who was valet to the British Ambassador in Ankara, who was passing secrets to the enemy. It was later made into a film, *Five Fingers*, with James Mason playing the lead role of Cicero. Trevor-Roper said that they could not warn the ambassador by telegram, for these were being read by Cicero. So someone was sent to Ankara to brief the ambassador direct. Sadly for Cicero, who fled to South America, he was arrested there shortly after the war for passing counterfeit money – the Germans had paid him in forged currency!

Winston Churchill came into the RSS picture in 1940 when the capacity of the Services to intercept Luftwaffe Enigma traffic lagged behind Bletchley Park's decrypting capacity because of a shortage of wireless operators. On Churchill's instructions, Lord Hankey, secretary to the Committee for Imperial Defence, overruled protests from the RSS operators and transferred them from MI5 to MI6 in May 1941 under Brigadier Richard Gambier-Parry, another radio ham, to form the communications unit of MI6 known as Section VIII. Another radio amateur, Lieutenant Colonel Kenneth Morton Evans, later became his deputy. In June 1941, MI5 complained that it was denied an equal voice in the control of the RSS and was forbidden to have direct contact with Bletchley Park, but these problems were later resolved, and the shared interest of MI5 and MI6 in the RSS produced little disagreement after the middle of 1942. The MI5/MI6 Wireless Committee had been set up in 1941, and in December 1942 it was agreed that it should be replaced by two new committees, one to decide major questions affecting RSS policy and the other a committee at working level. The former, the Radio Security Committee, was established in March 1943, responsible for co-ordinating the interest of MI5 and MI6 in the RSS and for supervising radio security. The overall organisation became known as the Radio Security Intelligence Conference. Within this framework the administrative and technical development of the RSS encountered few difficulties. The RSS maintained intercept units in the Middle East and, to cover traffic in Latin America, in the United States under the auspices of the top secret British Security Co-ordination (BSC). Almost half of the resources were engaged on the interception of known German intelligence and security service traffic. The remainder were divided between general search staff, responsible for recording unidentified traffic, and the Discrimination Section, which used its elaborate records to distinguish between suspicious and innocent intercepts.

> In all its activities the RSS achieved a high and continuingly increasing degree of efficiency.[lxvi]

In January 1942, an RSS officer was posted to the top secret British Security Co-Ordination to promote exchange of intelligence on illicit wireless traffic with the US and Canada. One other interesting part of the RSS work was with double agents. One of the most successful of these agents was a Spaniard, Juan Pujol Garcia, codenamed 'Garbo' by the British and 'Arabel' by the Germans. He played a major part in convincing the Germans that the Allied invasion of Europe would take place at the Pas de Calais, with Normandy as a feint. His Abwehr handlers in Madrid decided to change Garbo's method of transmitting radio messages and the transmissions were lost by the RSS interceptors. Fortunately it proved impossible for Garbo and his control to follow the plan without breaking into each other's transmissions.

> It was a tribute to the efficiency of the RSS's intercept network that after a few weeks it again reported *Garbo*'s transmitter as a suspect station.[lxvii]

Given the importance of the intercept stations, it is worth giving the background to some of those in the UK, although it was a worldwide organisation stretching through the Middle East and through the Far East:

**Beaumanor and Bishop's Waltham:** Beaumanor was the War Office Y Group situated latterly near Loughborough in Leicestershire and manned by military and civilian personnel. At its peak it had 130 sets, mostly covering H/F and M/F German Army groups and GAF Auto, an automatic transmitting set. This specialisation, plus traffic analysis and log reading – an intercept operator's record of enemy wireless activity – meant Hut 6 could rely on WOYG to exploit all developments in intercepting German Army traffic. Bishop's Waltham, near Winchester, came under Beaumanor's control and had seventeen sets on M/F and L/F Army groups, and was so successful that it was able to follow the German Army from Cherbourg to the furthest boundaries of Belgium.

**Chicksands** – an RAF station near Shefford in Bedfordshire, it had 190 sets, including 50 search sets, dealing mainly with Luftwaffe, but sometimes Mediterranean and Balkan Army and certain SS frequencies. Detailed records were kept of the priority commitment of other stations, and when a group was heard of which no record existed, it was safe to infer that it was new. Capel was an offshoot of Chicksands covering L/F GAF networks, western railway traffic and occasionally special Army commitments.

**Forest Moor** – located on Ilkley Moor, near Harrogate, it was the newest of the large stations, and its 120 sets were manned by Army personnel. Results in Norwegian and Western traffic were particularly good. Double-banking of some Italian and Balkan frequencies for cryptographic purposes was also undertaken, and SS networks were also covered. There was a small long reading section that scanned the logs for important and immediate information.

**Harpenden** – an Army stations near St Albans, its thirty sets concentrated on Western Front Army and Air Force. It had a log reading and TA section who studied L/F and M/F western traffic. Later it was reformed into mobile parties, eventually operating from France.

**Denmark Hill** – a Metropolitan Police station under Foreign Office direction. Due to the experience of its operators very little assistance was required. It was from this station that the first information about what became the Lorenz Fish links was discovered.

**Whitchurch** – a Foreign Office station in Shropshire manned by Post Office personnel. There were seven sets covering GAF Auto and SS frequencies.

**Santa Fé** – US Army station at Bexley in Kent, with twenty sets covering Western Air traffic and certain SS frequencies. The unit was most co-operative and the good results obtained were a measure of reward for the keenness displayed, even during the disturbances caused by the V1 and V2 onslaughts.

**Wick and Montrose** – RAF stations using five sets. Due to their isolated position they were able to effectively cover GAF traffic in Norway and Baltic Brown – the special Luftwaffe navigational key.

**Flowerdown and Scarborough** – the two main naval intercept stations. Flowerdown in Hampshire was the principal Italian station and also intercepted naval traffic on German, Spanish, Russian, Portuguese, Swedish and Japanese frequencies. It also conducted Japanese Morse training and covered merchant shipping frequencies for all countries. Scarborough in Yorkshire covered mainly German traffic and was responsible for standardising the measurement of all German frequencies. At the end of the war it had 128 sets listening out and was staffed by 680 civil, naval and WRNS personnel. It was also a direction finding station.

If the codebreaking organisation of the Second World War can be summed up in one word, it would be 'teamwork'. The worldwide Sigint organisation which evolved during the Second World War meant a new assessment of the value of codebreaking and interception. That battle continues today with GCHQ at Cheltenham and the National Security Agency in the United States.

# Bibliography

Alexander, CH O'D, *Cryptographic History of Work on the German Naval Enigma* (National Archives, HW 25/1)

Andrew, CM, *The Defence of the Realm: The Authorized History of MI5* (Allen Lane, 2009)

Beesly, P, *Very Special Intelligence* (Greenhill, 2000)

Behrendt H-O, *Rommel's Intelligence in the Desert Campaign: 1941–1943* (William Kimber, 1985)

Bennett, R, *Ultra and Mediterranean Strategy 1941–1945* (Hamish Hamilton, 1989)

——, *Ultra in the West: The Normandy Campaign of 1944–45* (Hutchinson, 1980)

Birch, F, *Official History of British Sigint 1914–1945* (Military Press, vol I, part I, 2004, vol I, part 2 and vol 2, 2007, also The National Archives, HW 11)

Blair, C, *Hitler's U-Boat War: The Hunters 1939–1942* (Cassell, 1996)

Churchill, W, *The Second World War*, 6 vols (Cassell, 1966)

Clark, R, *The Man Who Broke Purple* (Weidenfeld and Nicholson, 1977)

Clayton, A, *The Enemy is Listening: The Story of the Y Service* (Hutchinson, 1980)

Copeland, BJ and Others, *Colossus* (OUP, 2006)

Doenitz, K, *Memoirs* (Cassell, 2000)

Dornberger, W, *V2* (Hurst and Blackett, 1954)

Drea, EJ, *MacArthur's Ultra* (University Press of Kansas, 1992)

Freyberg, P, *Bernard Freyberg VC: Soldier of Two Nations* (Hodder & Stoughton, 1991)

GC&CS, *History of Bletchley Park Huts and Blocks 1939–1945* (Bletchley Park Trust Report No 18, 2009)

——, *Naval History Vol XXIII: Northern Waters* (GCHQ Archives)

Guderian, H, *Panzer Leader* (Penguin, 2000)

Hinsley, FH, *British Intelligence in the Second World War*, 4 vols (HMSO, 1979–1990)

Jones, RV, *Most Secret War: British Scientific Intelligence 1939–1945* (Coronet, 1979)

Mahon, P, *Naval Enigma: The History of Hut 8* (Military Press, 2009, also National Archives, HW 25/2)

Mallmann Showell, JP, *Enigma U-Boats – Breaking the Code: The True Story* (Naval Institute Press, 2000)

Michie, D, Good, J and Timms, G, *General Report on Tunny* (National Archives, HW 25/44 and 25/45)

National Archives, The, *The Official History of Hut 6* (HW 43/72),
——, *Official Naval History, Battle Summary: Arctic Convoys 1941–1945 No 22* (ADM 234/369)
——, *Tirpitz: An Account of the Various Attacks Carried Out by the British Armed Forces and their Effect on the German Battleship* (ADM 234/349)
——, *Ultra in Royal Navy Operations* (ADM 223/88)

Pidgeon, G, *The Secret Wireless War: The Story of MI6 Communications 1939–1945* (UPSO, 2003)

Roskill, SW, *The War At Sea 1939–1945*, vol I (HMSO, 1954) and vol III, part II, (Imperial War Museum, 1961)

Rowlett, F, *The Story of Magic* (Aegean Park Press, 1998)

Smith, M and Erskine, R (eds), *Action This Day* (Bantam Press, 2001)

Various, *Marian Rejewski 1905–1980: Living With The Enigma Secret* (Bydgoszcz City Council, 2005)

Winterbotham FW, *The Ultra Secret: The Inside Story of Operation Ultra, Bletchley Park and Enigma* (Weidenfeld & Nicholson, 1999)

# Endnotes

i    After the war, Bertrand wrote a book, *Enigma ou la plus grande énigme de la guerre, 1939-1945*, published in 1973. It was never translated into English and was written in reaction to a chapter in a book by Michel Garder entitled *La Guerre Secrète des Services Spéciaux Français, 1935-1945*. This chapter did not mention Enigma, but dealt with the spy Hans Thilo-Schmidt. It was Churchill's SIS liaison officer with Bletchley Park, Group Captain Frederick Winterbotham, whose book *The Ultra Secret*, published in 1974, lifted the lid off the Enigma and Bletchley Park story. However, the earliest book to reveal that Enigma had been broken was by Polish historian Wladyslaw Kozaczuk, entitled *The Battle of Secrets: The Intelligence Services of Poland and the German Reich, 1918–1939*, published in Warsaw in 1967 in Polish. The English version was published in 1984.

ii    Various, *Marian Rejewski*, p 102.

iii    Hinsley, *British Intelligence*, vol 3, part 2, p 959.

iv    Ibid., vol 2, footnote p 163.

v    Beesly, *Very Special Intelligence*, p 53.

vi    Roskill SW, *The War At Sea*, vol III, part II, p 179.

vii    Jones, *Most Secret War*, p 200.

viii    Hinsley, *British Intelligence*, vol 1, p 528.

ix    Clayton, *The Enemy is Listening*, p 85.

x    Jones, *Most Secret War*, p 200.

xi    Blair, *Hitler's U-Boat War*, p 143.

xii    Mallmann Showell, *Enigma U-Boats*, p 106.

xiii    Beesly, *Very Special Intelligence*, p 72.

xiv    Churchill, *The Second World War*, vol 3, p 218.

xv    Bennett, *Ultra and Mediterranean Strategy*, p 51.

xvi    Freyberg, *Bernard Freyberg VC*, p 268.

xvii    Roskill S, *The War At Sea*, vol II, p 134.

xviii    TNA, *Official Naval History*.

xix    Roskill, *The War At Sea*, vol II, p 140.

xx    GC&CS, *Naval History*.

xxi    Roskill, *The War At Sea*, vol II, p 145.

xxii    Birch, *The Official History of British Sigint*, vol 2, p 160.

xxiii    Ibid., p 237.

xxiv    Ibid., p 238.

xxv    Ibid., p 240.

xxvi    Behrendt, *Rommel's Intelligence*, p 50.

xxvii    Ibid., p 146.

xxviii    GC&CS, *Naval History,* p 123.

xxix    TNA, *Ultra in Royal Navy Operations*, p 108.

xxx    Ibid., p 109.

xxxi    Doenitz, *Memoirs*, p 381.

xxxii    Guderian, *Panzer Leader*, p 141.

| xxxiii | Ibid., p 143. |
| xxxiv | Churchill, *The Second World War,* vol 4, p 676. |
| xxxv | TNA, *Ultra in Royal Navy Operations,* p 112. |
| xxxvi | TNA, *Tirpitz,* vol I, report and appendices, p 9. |
| xxxvii | Ibid., p 11. |
| xxxviii | Doenitz, *Memoirs,* p 386. |
| xxxix | TNA, *Ultra in Royal Navy Operations,* p 124. |
| xl | Doenitz, *Memoirs* , p 386. |
| xli | Roskill, *The War At Sea,* vol III, part II, p 170. |
| xlii | Mahon, *Naval Enigma,* p 59. |
| xliii | Alexander, *Cryptographic History,* p 62. |
| xliv | Mahon, *Naval Enigma,* p 87. |
| xlv | Alexander, *Cryptographic History,* p 61. |
| xlvi | Smith and Erskine (eds), *Action This Day,* p 203. |
| xlvii | Hinsley, *British Intelligence,* vol 2, p 552. |
| xlviii | Bennett, *Ultra in the West,* p 53. |
| xlix | TNA, *The Official History of Hut 6,* p 122. |
| l | Jones, *Most Secret War,* p 443. |
| li | Dornberger, *V2,* p 159. |
| lii | TNA, *The Official History of Hut 6,* vol II, p 18. |
| liii | Dornberger, *V2,* pp 28–29. |
| liv | Ibid., pp 255–256. |
| lv | Copeland and Others, *Colossus,* p 86. |
| lvi | Mitchie, Good and Timms, *General Report on Tunny,* p 327. |
| lvii | Rowlett, *The Story of Magic,* p 147. |
| lviii | Clark, *The Man Who Broke Purple,* p 137. |
| lix | Drea, *MacArthur's Ultra,* p 106. |
| lx | Birch, *The Official History of British Sigint,* vol 1, part 2, pp 259–260. |
| lxi | Pidgeon, *The Secret Wireless War,* p 71. |
| lxii | Birch, *The Official History of British Sigint,* vol I, part I, p ix. |
| lxiii | TNA, *The Official History of Hut 6,* p 48. |
| lxiv | Birch, *The Official History of British Sigint,* vol I, part I, p xiii. |
| lxv | Andrew, *The Defence of the Realm,* p 253. |
| lxvi | Hinsley, *British Intelligence,* vol 4, p 181. |
| lxvii | Ibid., p 224. |

# Index